SETTLED VERSUS RIGHT

In this timely book, Randy J. Kozel develops a theory of precedent designed to enhance the stability and impersonality of constitutional law. Kozel contends that the prevailing approach to precedent in American law is undermined by principled disagreements among judges over the proper means and ends of constitutional interpretation. The structure and composition of the modern doctrine all but guarantee that conclusions about the durability of precedent will track individual views about whether decisions are right or wrong, and whether mistakes are harmful or benign. This is a serious challenge, but it also reveals a path toward maintaining legal continuity even as judges come and go. Kozel's account of precedent should be read by anyone interested in the nature of the judicial role and the trajectory of constitutional law.

Randy J. Kozel is a Professor of Law at Notre Dame Law School, where he also serves as Director of the Notre Dame Program on Constitutional Structure. Professor Kozel received his J. D., *magna cum laude*, from Harvard Law School. He served as a law clerk for Justice Anthony M. Kennedy at the US Supreme Court and for Judge Alex Kozinski at the US Court of Appeals for the Ninth Circuit. He also practiced as a litigator with a large law firm and as an in-house attorney at a multinational corporation.

Settled Versus Right

A THEORY OF PRECEDENT

RANDY J. KOZEL

CAMBRIDGE
UNIVERSITY PRESS

University Printing House, Cambridge CB2 8BS, United Kingdom

One Liberty Plaza, 20th Floor, New York, NY 10006, USA

477 Williamstown Road, Port Melbourne, VIC 3207, Australia

4843/24, 2nd Floor, Ansari Road, Daryaganj, Delhi – 110002, India

79 Anson Road, #06-04/06, Singapore 079906

Cambridge University Press is part of the University of Cambridge.

It furthers the University's mission by disseminating knowledge in the pursuit of education, learning, and research at the highest international levels of excellence.

www.cambridge.org
Information on this title: www.cambridge.org/9781107127531
DOI: 10.1017/9781316412237

© Randy J. Kozel 2017

This publication is in copyright. Subject to statutory exception and to the provisions of relevant collective licensing agreements, no reproduction of any part may take place without the written permission of Cambridge University Press.

First published 2017

Printed in the United States of America by Sheridan Books, Inc.

A catalogue record for this publication is available from the British Library.

Library of Congress Cataloging-in-Publication Data

Names: Kozel, Randy J., author.
Title: Settled versus right : a theory of precedent / Randy J. Kozel.
Other titles: Settled vs. right | Settled v. right
Description: Cambridge [UK] ; New York : Cambridge University Press, [2017] | Includes bibliographical references and index.
Identifiers: LCCN 2017006684 | ISBN 9781107127531 (hardback : alk. paper)
Subjects: LCSH: Stare decisis—United States. | Constitutional law—United States. | United States. Supreme Court—Decision making.
Classification: LCC KF429 .K69 2017 | DDC 347.73/001—dc23 LC record available at https://lccn.loc.gov/2017006684

ISBN 978-1-107-12753-1 Hardback
ISBN 978-1-107-56652-1 Paperback

Cambridge University Press has no responsibility for the persistence or accuracy of URLs for external or third-party internet websites referred to in this publication and does not guarantee that any content on such websites is, or will remain, accurate or appropriate.

For Abi, Kate Marie, and Hannah Jo

Contents

Acknowledgments	*page*	ix
Introduction		1
1 Framing the Study of Precedent		19
2 The Stakes of Deference		34
3 Strength of Constraint		60
4 Scope of Applicability		70
5 Precedent and Pluralism		92
6 Precedential Strength in Doctrinal Perspective		107
7 Precedential Strength in Structural Perspective		140
8 Compromise, Common Ground, and Precedential Scope		145
9 Implications and Transitions		161
Conclusion		175
Index		177

Acknowledgments

I wish to express my endless gratitude to my family: my amazing wife, Abi, and our wonderful daughters, Kate Marie and Hannah Jo. Together, they are my greatest joy and my source of strength. I have also been blessed with unyielding support from my parents, brothers, in-laws, and extended family.

This book is the product of countless exchanges with many friends who have shared their insights and suggestions over the years. A complete list is too lengthy to furnish, but they include Roger Alford, Amy Barrett, Will Baude, A. J. Bellia, Tricia Bellia, Barry Cushman, Erin Delaney, Justin Driver, Richard Ekins, Richard Fallon, Nicole Garnett, Richard Garnett, Michael Gerhardt, Erin Hawley, Bert Huang, Bruce Huber, John Inazu, Bill Kelley, Kurt Lash, Santiago Legarre, Jennifer McAward, John McGinnis, Mark McKenna, Jon Michaels, Michael Moreland, John Nagle, Aaron Nielsen, Lee Otis, Michael Stokes Paulsen, Jim Pfander, Andrea Pin, Jeff Pojanowski, Richard Re, Lawrence Solum, David Strauss, Jay Tidmarsh, Alex Tsesis, Adrian Vermeule, Chris Walker, and Paul Yowell. I am also indebted to my dean, Nell Newton, who graciously supported my scholarship from the moment I arrived at Notre Dame in 2011. And my thinking about precedent has been shaped by participants at many conferences, workshops, and colloquia, both at my home school of Notre Dame and elsewhere.

Laura Myers, Notre Dame Law School class of 2018, provided invaluable research and editorial assistance. Numerous other Notre Dame students made an impact on the book by enrolling in my seminars on the topic of legal change, which allowed us to discuss constancy and innovation across a variety of topics.

The team at Cambridge University Press – including Matt Gallaway, Kristina Deusch, and Fiona Allison – expertly moved the book through the publication process while improving it along the way.

Finally, no list of acknowledgments would be complete without a nod to my dear friend and faithful dog, Rally, who was by my side nearly every day as this book took shape.

The arguments developed in the book had their beginnings in a series of papers I published over the past six years. The citation information for each of them is listed below. Without exception, those papers were improved substantially by the tireless student editors who helped bring each paper to publication.

- *Stare Decisis in the Second-Best World*, 103 CALIFORNIA LAW REVIEW 1139 (2015)
- *Original Meaning and the Precedent Fallback*, 68 VANDERBILT LAW REVIEW 105 (2015)
- *The Scope of Precedent*, 113 MICHIGAN LAW REVIEW 179 (2014)
- *Settled Versus Right: Constitutional Method and the Path of Precedent*, 91 TEXAS LAW REVIEW 1843 (2013), republished as abridged in PRECEDENT ON THE U.S. SUPREME COURT 159–88 (Springer 2013) (with permission of Springer Nature)
- *Precedent and Reliance*, 62 EMORY LAW JOURNAL 1459 (2013)
- *Stare Decisis as Judicial Doctrine*, 67 WASHINGTON & LEE LAW REVIEW 411 (2010)

Introduction

The summer of 2005 was a time of transition at the US Supreme Court. Soon after the Court decided the last of its cases in June, Sandra Day O'Connor announced her plan to retire. Justice O'Connor had served on the Court since 1981. She made history as the first female justice, and her trademark pragmatism left a deep impression on American law. Around the halls of the Court, it is commonly said that any time a justice departs, the institution is made anew. With a jurist of Sandra Day O'Connor's stature on the cusp of leaving, that sentiment seemed as true as it had ever been.

Just two months after Justice O'Connor's announcement came the news that William Rehnquist had died. He had served on the Court since 1972, taking over as Chief Justice in 1986. His legacy extended beyond his legal decisions and into countless aspects of the Court's procedures and practices. Viewed alongside the retirement of Justice O'Connor, Chief Justice Rehnquist's passing foretold the end of one era and the dawn of another. Before 2005, the most recent departure from the Court had been that of Harry Blackmun, who retired in 1994. Now eleven years later, the Court faced the loss of two justices of enormous influence – who between them had served for more than fifty years – in the course of only a few months.

Initially, Justice O'Connor's seat on the Court was to be filled by John Roberts, who was serving at that time as a federal appellate judge. But after Chief Justice Rehnquist's death, President George W. Bush revised Judge Roberts's nomination. Judge Roberts would now take over as Chief Justice, with Justice O'Connor's successor – eventually, Samuel Alito – to be selected later.

Supreme Court justices earn their appointments based on their individual qualities and achievements. Upon their confirmation, however, they join a tribunal with two centuries of practices, customs, and decisions. A key issue for every new justice is how to balance respect for the Court's past with consideration of its future.

That issue would arise in illuminating fashion during Judge Roberts's confirmation hearing before the Senate Judiciary Committee. Like previous nominees, Judge Roberts was asked about the degree of respect that is owed to the Supreme Court's prior opinions – in other words, its precedents. In American legal culture, courts commonly describe precedents as carrying great weight. By respecting precedent, courts validate a time-honored principle: *stare decisis*, a Latin phrase meaning "to stand by things decided."[1] The phrase captures the idea that today's judges should not lightly disrupt the decisions of their predecessors. Even so, it is always *possible* for a court to overrule its precedents, so long as there is sufficient justification for doing so. The goal is to preserve the law's stable core without permanently entrenching every judicial mistake.

During an exchange with Judge Roberts, Senator Arlen Specter raised the topic of stare decisis in the context of *Roe v. Wade* (1973), the Supreme Court's landmark ruling on abortion rights. Yet the Senator's question went beyond *Roe* and addressed "principles of stare decisis" more generally. Judge Roberts responded in kind. He began with an appeal to history, explaining that America's founders "appreciated the role of precedent in promoting even-handedness, predictability, stability, [and] the appearance of integrity in the judicial process." He then turned to the Supreme Court's modern approach to precedent, which considers factors such as whether prior decisions have "proven to be unworkable" or "been eroded by subsequent developments."

Judge Roberts noted that to overrule a precedent is to give "a jolt to the legal system." At the same time, he cautioned that deference to precedent is only presumptive, not absolute. It is true that overruling precedent can tax the system. But sometimes "that's a price that has to be paid." He illustrated this point with the example of *Brown v. Board of Education* (1954), in which the Court broke from its past to make clear that racial segregation in public services violates fundamental constitutional precepts.[2]

The experience of Judge Roberts – now Chief Justice Roberts – was far from unique. His appointment was followed by those of Samuel Alito, Sonia Sotomayor, and Elena Kagan. The role of precedent arose during each of their confirmation hearings. All three of them offered explanations similar to that of then-Judge Roberts: The Court's precedents warrant meaningful deference, but such deference is not absolute.[3] And they have continued to endorse

---

[1] BLACK'S LAW DICTIONARY (10th ed. 2014).
[2] 109th Cong. 141–4 (2005).
[3] 111th Cong. 300 (2010) (J. Kagan); 111th Cong. 96–7 (2009) (J. Sotomayor); 109th Cong. 318–9 (2006) (J. Alito).

this understanding of precedent upon taking their positions on the Court. Indeed, every sitting justice has acknowledged the importance of deferring to precedent under certain circumstances. Each justice has also noted that precedent must sometimes yield. The question is *when*.

That question has been at the center of many of the Court's most controversial rulings. It was there when the Court upheld the central holding of *Roe v. Wade*. It was there when the Court rejected a challenge to the *Miranda* warnings that police officers must give to suspected criminals. More recently, it was there when the Court ruled that the First Amendment affords strong protection to political ads by corporations and labor unions – a decision President Barack Obama criticized during the 2010 State of the Union address not simply for being wrong, but for having "reversed a century of law." These disputes over precedent are pervasive and important. They are also deeply complex. The complexity reaches all the way down to the foundational issue of why a judge would ever willingly accept a ruling she believes to be wrong.

The study of precedent is the study of mistakes. Some past decisions were misguided from the outset. Others began sensibly enough but became shaky over time as facts changed. The issue in either case is what to do next. Should today's judges stand by prior decisions they view as incorrect? Or should they set the record straight and improve the law going forward?

At first glance the answer may seem obvious: Judges should never consciously repeat the mistakes of the past. But the calculus turns out to be complicated. People might have made investments and modified their behaviors as a result of past judicial decisions. There is also the worry that if judicial decisions are reversed too readily, the law will lose its durability and impersonality and be reduced to whatever today's judges say it is. And it is always possible that, notwithstanding the contrary belief of today's judges, the previous decision actually represents the more accurate interpretation of the law. In light of possibilities like these, maybe it is better – at least sometimes – to let things be.

As then-Judge Roberts noted during his confirmation hearing, the Supreme Court has offered a host of considerations to inform the choice between retaining and jettisoning a decision that is incorrect in the eyes of today's justices. Relevant factors include the precedent's procedural workability, the soundness of its factual premises, the extent to which subsequent decisions have eroded its foundations, and the reliance it has generated. Still, the justices continue to disagree over the role of precedent in particular cases. To some students of the Court, the best explanation for this disagreement is that stare decisis is really no principle at all. On that account, fidelity to precedent seldom (if ever) sways a justice from her preferred course. There is so much play in the joints that even as they talk about stare decisis, the justices manage to preserve the precedents they like and overrule the ones they don't.

These sentiments occasionally come from the justices themselves. Justice Scalia once criticized a majority opinion for using the doctrine of stare decisis as a "result-oriented expedient" rather than a consistent principle.[4] A decade earlier, Justice Marshall directed a comparable criticism at a majority opinion that upset settled doctrine. He concluded that "[n]either the law nor the facts" had changed; "[o]nly the personnel of this Court did." To Justice Marshall, the lesson was clear: "Power, not reason, is the new currency of this Court's decisionmaking."[5]

Comments like these reflect a tension in the Supreme Court's treatment of precedent. While there is widespread agreement among the justices about the factors that are potentially relevant to a dubious precedent's retention or overruling, there has been far less discussion of how stare decisis fits into various theories of judging. Nor has the Court devoted much attention to explaining why certain outcomes are so problematic as to trigger prompt overruling, while others should be tolerated in pursuit of values such as stability, continuity, and the protection of settled expectations. The lack of a comprehensive explanation can sometimes make it seem like the Court is being inconsistent in its treatment of precedent. The effect is especially pronounced within the realm of constitutional law, which draws the Court into debates over the protection of fundamental liberties and the essential structure of government. Some thirty years ago, Henry Monaghan described the problem in terms that remain resonant today: "Because a coherent rationale for the intermittent invocation of stare decisis has not been forthcoming, the impression is created that the doctrine is invoked only as a mask hiding other considerations. As a result, stare decisis seemingly operates with the randomness of a lighting bolt: on occasion it may strike, but when and where can be known only after the fact. A satisfactory theory of constitutional adjudication requires more than that."[6]

Without a meaningful role for precedent, the law sacrifices a share of its continuity, constraint, and impersonality. Decisions of the Supreme Court

---

[4] Lawrence v. Texas, 539 U.S. 558, 591 (2003) (Scalia, J., dissenting).
[5] Payne v. Tennessee, 501 U.S. 808, 844 (1991) (Marshall, J., dissenting).
[6] Henry Paul Monaghan, *Stare Decisis and Constitutional Adjudication*, 88 COLUM. L. REV. 723, 743 (1988).

become the products of fluctuating assemblages of justices who come and go from the bench rather than the outputs of an enduring institution that maintains its identity over time. The danger is not that the overruling of precedent will lead to rioting in the streets or widespread resistance to the Supreme Court's edicts. The costs are more in the nature of untapped potential. Time and again, the justices have underscored that deference to precedent promotes the rule of law. But those affirmations occur at the level of abstract theory. By translating them into practice, the Court can bolster the idea that its decisions flow from enduring legal principles rather than individual proclivities, and that the Constitution truly is more than "what five Justices say it is."[7]

Allow me to illustrate by reference to *Citizens United v. Federal Election Commission* (2010), about which I will have more to say in the pages ahead. In *Citizens United*, a five-justice majority voted to overrule precedent by enlarging the First Amendment liberties of corporations and labor unions. Four justices resisted that result, but they fell one vote short. For now, let us reserve judgment on whether the better argument was that of the five-justice majority or the four-justice dissent. Instead, think about the impact of the case going forward. Absent some presumption of deference to precedent, whether *Citizens United* remains the law of the land – which is to say, what the First Amendment means as applied to an important area of campaign finance regulation – depends on whether personnel changes at the Court turn the four-justice dissent into a five-justice majority. Nor does the cycle end there. Assume that *Citizens United* is reversed after a new justice arrives at the Court, but that in short order a member of the majority coalition retires and is replaced by a differently minded justice. Without a meaningful doctrine of stare decisis, the pendulum could just as easily swing back. All this despite the fact that the Constitution itself will not have changed a bit.

The *Citizens United* example sheds light on the connection between politics, judicial appointments, and the role of the Supreme Court in the constitutional order. In 2016, Lawrence Norden wrote in *The Atlantic* that "it is no exaggeration to say that the next appointments to the Supreme Court will have a profound impact on political power in the United States."[8] The underlying premise is clear: In modern constitutional law, the salient mechanism of change is not the formal amendment process, but rather the appointment of new justices to the Supreme Court.

---

[7] Lewis F. Powell, Jr., *Stare Decisis and Judicial Restraint*, 47 WASH. & LEE L. REV. 281, 288 (1990).
[8] Lawrence Norden, *The U.S. Supreme Court Can Still Take Big Money Out of Politics*, ATLANTIC, January 13, 2016.

This reality, I submit, is dispiriting and detrimental. Constitutional principles should be overarching and enduring. Deference to precedent advances the valuable ideal that it takes something more than a group of nine (or, in a split decision, five) individuals to revise what the Constitution requires. To be sure, the identity and interpretive predilections of individual judges will always matter. The composition of the courts will and should remain a topic of interest to political campaigns and social movements. But the fact that judges matter does not resolve the issue of *how much* they should matter. A meaningful doctrine of precedent asks the individual judge to subordinate – not always, but sometimes – her personal view of a case to the historical practice of her court as an institution. Judges still matter under a regime of stare decisis. They just matter less. And that is a valuable thing in a system that aspires to promote the rule of law as opposed to the rule of individual men and women.[9]

This book develops a theory of precedent designed to enhance the stability and impersonality of constitutional law. The problem with the Supreme Court's current approach to precedent is not that the justices are behaving in an unprincipled manner. The problem is that the modern doctrine of stare decisis is undermined by principled disagreements among justices acting in good faith. The doctrine's structure and composition all but guarantee that conclusions about the durability of precedent will track the justices' individual views about whether decisions are right or wrong and whether mistakes are harmful or benign. To rehabilitate the doctrine of stare decisis so it can bridge philosophical divides, we need to rethink the way in which precedent interacts with constitutional theory.

The starting point is recognizing the implications of a basic fact about US legal culture. The American legal system has not reached anything approaching consensus regarding the proper method for understanding and applying the Constitution. Rather, US law is home to pervasive disagreement over constitutional interpretation. That requires a theory of stare decisis attuned to the challenges of judicial disagreement and the value of precedent in overcoming them. It remains possible for stare decisis to play the vital role the Supreme Court has described for it in enhancing the continuity and impersonality of constitutional law. But for that to occur, we need to reconsider the doctrine from the ground up. The prevailing approach to precedent implies a greater degree of agreement about constitutional theory than actually exists. If stare decisis is to fulfill its promise, we must account for the unique challenges

---

[9] *Cf.* Monaghan, *Stare Decisis and Constitutional Adjudication, supra* note 6, at 752 ("A general judicial adherence to constitutional precedent supports a consensus about the rule of law, specifically the belief that all organs of government, including the Court, are bound by the law.").

posed by disagreements – good-faith, principled disagreements – about the proper ends and means of constitutional interpretation.

Having foreshadowed the conclusions toward which the book will build, allow me to explain the path it will take.

In the first part of the book, I aim to provide a descriptive and analytical account of precedent that is independent of the normative claims that will come later. Chapter 1 begins by distinguishing two common situations: those in which a court is considering the effect of its own prior decisions, and those in which a court must apply decisions from a tribunal of superior rank. The former scenario involves what are sometimes called horizontal precedents; the latter involves precedents that operate vertically, running from higher courts to lower courts. Though both situations deal with the impact of prior decisions on later courts, they are governed by different rules in the US federal system. While a court always has the power to reconsider its own past decisions, lower courts do not enjoy comparable discretion to revise the opinions of higher courts. The Supreme Court has insisted on this point, making clear that lower courts may never reject a Supreme Court decision – even if the decision is obviously flawed, has been eroded over time, or has been called into question by the justices themselves. These different rules require distinguishing between vertical and horizontal precedents, even while recognizing that some of the arguments for (and against) deference in the two contexts will overlap.

After drawing a line between vertical and horizontal precedents, Chapter 1 turns to another pivotal distinction, this one between precedential *strength* and precedential *scope*. In evaluating the role of precedent, it can be tempting to focus exclusively on the degree of constraint that prior decisions exert on future disputes. It is a precedent's strength that ultimately determines whether there is a sufficient justification for overruling it. Yet strength is only part of the equation. No matter how strong a precedent is deemed to be, it has no constraining force in situations it does not reach. There must be a threshold determination whether a prior decision applies to a later case. Sometimes it is quite clear that one case governs another, so the only valid options for the later court are to reaffirm or overrule. But in many other cases, whether a precedent applies to the case at hand is a thorny and contentious question. Keeping in mind these dual considerations of strength and scope is crucial to analyzing and, hopefully, improving the treatment of precedent.

Next, I introduce two more sets of distinctions that are helpful in understanding the law of precedent. The first is the type of case a court is called upon to resolve. Conventional wisdom holds that judicial interpretations of statutes are entitled to maximum deference going forward, whereas interpretations of the Constitution receive weaker deference. I offer some reasons for being skeptical about this distinction, and I argue that in all events, the fact that constitutional precedents receive relatively weak deference under existing law does not mean such deference is weak in absolute terms. Even if statutory cases receive the most insulation from overruling, that leaves a broad range of possibilities for how much deference should attach to constitutional decisions. The intricacies of constitutional stare decisis will be my focus for much of the book, though many aspects of my analysis will apply to statutory (and common law) decisions as well.

The remainder of Chapter 1 surveys the various functions that precedents serve in modern American law. Precedents are means of transmitting knowledge from past to present, so they can improve judicial decision-making even when there is no obligation to follow them. In some cases, though, it is not left to the later court to make up its mind about whether to follow precedent. Instead, the later court is duty-bound to stand by an earlier decision. This is easiest to see in the context of vertical precedent, as when a federal trial court is required to follow a Supreme Court decision despite reservations about that decision on the merits. Precedent can also constrain future iterations of the court that issued it. The Supreme Court is properly understood as constrained to follow its precedents under certain conditions: namely, when the Court's articulated criteria for overruling are not satisfied. This constraining function presents both the strengths and weaknesses of precedent-based judging in their starkest form. At its best, precedent limits the discretion of subsequent judges and contributes to a stable, consistent, and impersonal system of law. Yet a strong doctrine of precedent can also lead to the repetition and entrenchment of earlier judges' miscues. These are the stakes of the debate.

I elaborate on these stakes in Chapter 2, which begins by chronicling some of the commonly cited benefits of deference to precedent. They include the conservation of judicial resources, the protection of settled expectations, and the preservation of a stable environment to facilitate planning. They also include impersonality. A commitment to precedent can encourage the equal treatment of litigants, reducing the extent to which the idiosyncrasies of their situations affect the outcome of their disputes. At the same time, deference to precedent can allow the law to transcend the identity of the judge who happens to be presiding over a particular case. If a judge must follow precedent, her individual preferences and tendencies become less salient.

On the other side of the scale are the costs of abiding by precedent. Imagine that five justices of the Supreme Court conclude that a prior decision reflects an erroneous understanding of the Constitution. Those justices also happen to be stalwart proponents of stare decisis, for reasons including continuity and impersonality. They accordingly vote to reaffirm the decision, notwithstanding their misgivings about its rationale. While they believe themselves in possession of a sound basis for doing so, the justices relinquish the opportunity to replace (what they believe to be) an incorrect rule with a more accurate one. They consciously allow a mistake to go uncorrected. I will end up defending a meaningful doctrine of precedent despite these countervailing considerations. But the costs must be appreciated if the doctrine of stare decisis is to strike the appropriate balance between continuity and change.

Before closing the second chapter, I offer a few thoughts about the link between stare decisis and the Constitution. Issues of constitutional legitimacy are complicated and fascinating, but I do not dwell on them for the simple reason that they are uncontroversial in modern judicial practice. Justices of the Supreme Court vary in their readiness to overrule flawed decisions, but no justice has challenged the lawfulness of stare decisis. Still, a few commentators have raised such a challenge, so I briefly examine some possibilities for defending the legitimacy of stare decisis in constitutional cases. Those possibilities draw on the Constitution's text, the background understandings and practices in place at the time of the founding, the structure of the federal judiciary, and the need for judges to act in a collective, cooperative fashion notwithstanding their interpretive disagreements.

Chapters 3 and 4 unpack the complementary concepts of precedential strength and precedential scope. I explain how both concepts operate under the Supreme Court's existing approach to precedent, and I emphasize how they are shaped by underlying conclusions about the ends and means of constitutional interpretation.

To begin with precedential strength: Nearly a century ago, Justice Brandeis described the tension inherent in the doctrine of stare decisis as pitting the importance of leaving the law *settled* against the value of getting the law *right*.[10] This characterization has endured, and for good reason. In deciding whether to overrule a flawed decision, it is natural to inquire into the bad effects the decision has created and to predict the beneficial effects that would accompany a change of direction. But the factors that make a decision good or bad are neither static nor universal. They depend on the interpretive theory that a particular judge adopts. For some judges, a prior decision's moral implications shape whether it is harmful or benign. Other judges treat those considerations as legally irrelevant. Some judges measure the severity of a mistaken interpretation based on how sharply it departs from the Constitution's original meaning at the time of the founding. Others find the Constitution's original meaning to

---

[10] Burnet v. Coronado Oil & Gas Co., 285 U.S. 393, 406 (1932) (Brandeis, J., dissenting).

be less important than considerations such as a decision's pragmatic or moral ramifications.

The point is simply that judges rely, whether explicitly or implicitly, on their interpretive and normative commitments to determine whether a prior decision is correct in its reading of the Constitution. This can and does lead to principled disagreements. If some Supreme Court justices focus on the Constitution's original meaning while others focus on contemporary mores or policy judgments, it should be unsurprising when they part ways over the soundness of certain precedents. Those same variances in interpretive philosophy also inform the subsequent – and distinct – determination of precedential strength, which dictates whether a prior decision should be reaffirmed despite its flaws. Every judicial decision has a host of consequences, ranging from on-the-ground practical effects to broader implications for governmental design and political morality. Determining what types of consequences are legally relevant depends on a given judge's interpretive philosophy. In turn, assessing whether a prior decision is so problematic as to warrant overruling requires analyzing its legally relevant implications while excluding other matters. That enterprise is necessarily shaped by one's judicial philosophy.

The same is true of a precedent's scope of applicability, which I discuss in Chapter 4. Evaluating whether a prior decision is relevant to a newly arising dispute begins with figuring out what the prior decision means. In making that determination, a common step is to draw a line between judicial statements that were necessary to a case's resolution and statements that were dispensable, with the former representing the decision's *holding* and the latter mere *dicta*. That distinction informs the traditional definition of precedential scope: Holdings are entitled to deference in future cases, whereas dicta are nonbinding and may be accepted or rejected at the pleasure of the subsequent court.

Notwithstanding its historical pedigree, the holding/dicta distinction fails to explain existing federal practice, including at the Supreme Court. While the Court occasionally insists on a strict line between binding holdings and dispensable dicta, it regularly defers to aspects of its opinions – including sweeping rules and doctrinal frameworks – that range beyond the application of specific law to concrete fact. Whether this phenomenon should be lauded or jeered depends on underlying beliefs about the judicial role, the requirements of the Constitution, and the utility of precedent in constraining subsequent decision-makers. Some interpretive philosophies seek to minimize the extent to which judicial pronouncements displace factors such as the original meaning of the Constitution's text. On those theories, it is sensible to construe precedents narrowly. Other theories make greater use of precedent as a tool of judicial constraint or a source of common ground among differently minded judges, supporting the view that precedents should be defined in relatively broad terms. These are only two of several possibilities I will discuss, but they introduce the broader point. Just as attitudes toward the strength of precedent are bound up with underlying interpretive preferences, so too are accounts of precedential scope.

With the relationship between precedent and constitutional philosophy established, the book moves from *why* it is important to reconsider the role of precedent to *how* that reconsideration should proceed. In pursuing this inquiry, my focus is the operation of stare decisis at the US Supreme Court. Over the past three decades the justices have devoted considerable effort to discussing why precedent deserves presumptive respect and why that presumption must sometimes yield. In Chapters 5 and 6, I address the various factors the Court has enumerated to guide its applications of stare decisis. Of particular interest is the extent to which those factors possess objective content that does not depend on an individual judge's interpretive philosophy. Separating stare decisis from disputes over constitutional interpretation is vital if judicial responses to precedent are to transcend individual beliefs about how best to understand the Constitution's commands.

Stare decisis can bolster the stability and impersonality of constitutional law only if it sometimes requires a justice to accept an outcome she thinks is incorrect. If the pull of precedent gives way every time a justice concludes a prior decision is wrong, the impact of stare decisis dissipates. Yet that is precisely what we should expect from a doctrine that allows the interpretive philosophies of individual justices to dictate whether a prior decision is reaffirmed or overruled. As I explain in Chapter 5, because a justice's interpretive philosophy colors her determination of which considerations are legally relevant, it also goes a long way toward informing her applications of stare decisis under existing law.

This concern would be less pressing if there were widespread agreement about the proper ends and means of constitutional interpretation. Imagine a Supreme Court comprising nine justices who agree about how the Constitution ought to be interpreted, including which types of considerations are legally relevant and which are not. Imagine that the justices also agree about what makes a flawed precedent particularly bad – perhaps, for instance, that it creates serious injustice. That consensus would open the door for a consistent and systematic approach to precedent. *Plessy v. Ferguson* (1896), which validated racial segregation in public accommodations, would furnish a ready example of a flawed decision that was too unjust to tolerate.[11] By contrast, a

---

[11] 163 U.S. 537.

case like *National Bellas Hess v. Department of Revenue* (1967), which arguably misconstrued the authority of states to impose tax obligations on out-of-state sellers, might be retained; even if the decision is incorrect, it is difficult to construe as immoral.[12] More generally, the justices' conclusions about the durability of precedent would continue to depend on their theories of constitutional interpretation. But because those theories would be universally held – at the Court, at least – they would facilitate a consistent approach to precedent.

Now relax the assumption that the justices are in harmony, and assume instead that they are sharply divided over the appropriate methods of constitutional interpretation. The most obvious effect of disagreement is that they will split over whether certain precedents are wrong or right. But they will also disagree about another point: the factors that make a flawed precedent not simply wrong, but in need of overruling. That latter debate will tend to track the justices' differences of opinion over the appropriate principles for interpreting the Constitution. In other words, there will be two points of fracture. One relates to the characterization of a precedent as incorrect, and the other relates to the considerations that justify a flawed precedent's overruling. Yet both inquiries will be informed by the same methodological and normative priorities that divide the justices in the first place. Whether a precedent is overruled will depend, at base, on the interpretive philosophy that currently prevails at the Court.

This is not how stare decisis is supposed to work. The reason why the Supreme Court often links precedent to the rule of law is because deference to past decisions can unite justices of varying interpretive stripes. Two (or three, or nine) justices may disagree about how the Constitution should be interpreted but still share a common dedication to precedent. Stare decisis draws together justices who would otherwise disagree on the merits. But when the decision to overrule tracks the interpretive preferences of individual justices, the connection between stare decisis and judicial impersonality is severed. Precedent stops serving as common ground for overcoming philosophical disagreements. Invocations of stare decisis restate disagreements instead of bridging them.

A comparable analysis applies to the definition of a precedent's scope of applicability. Defining a precedent's contours depends in significant part on interpretive preferences: how much one values uniformity and guidance, one's approach to potential conflicts between decided cases and the Constitution's

---

[12] 386 U.S. 753.

text, and so on. Pervasive disagreements over constitutional theory create challenges in fashioning a consistent account of precedential scope.

The key to developing better approaches to precedential strength and precedential scope is acknowledging the impact of deep-seated disagreements among judges about the proper way to interpret the Constitution. In our world of pervasive interpretive disagreement, we need to think about the role of precedent differently than we would under conditions of widespread interpretive harmony. The question is no longer which factors are potentially relevant to a precedent's retention or overruling. The inquiry must be narrowed to include only those factors that are susceptible to principled application by justices across the philosophical spectrum. We need a second-best theory of stare decisis to complement our second-best world of interpretive disagreement.

This position may seem counterintuitive, for it requires ignoring certain considerations that would be relevant to a precedent's durability under conditions of interpretive harmony. Even so, disregarding some of those considerations and cabining others is necessary for stare decisis to overcome interpretive disputes instead of restating them. The objective of this reconceptualization is neither to increase nor decrease the power of precedent in any given case. It is to disentangle a precedent's correctness on the merits from its claim to deference notwithstanding its flaws.

Chapter 6 applies these principles to determinations of precedential strength. The approach I defend has some features in common with the doctrine of stare decisis that currently operates at the Supreme Court. Several factors loom large on both accounts: a decision's procedural workability, the accuracy of its factual premises, and the reliance it has yielded. Using precedent to bridge judicial disagreements means fine-tuning those factors to ensure that their invocation does not simply repackage disputes over interpretive philosophy.

While revising the inquiry into considerations such as workability and factual accuracy is important, the most significant change I propose relates to a precedent's substantive effects. As I have suggested, the relevance of such effects depends on one's theory of constitutional interpretation. Some theories prize matters of justice and morality, others pragmatic results, still others compatibility with founding-era understandings. If these are the drivers of whether a precedent is overruled, the application of stare decisis will track interpretive philosophies that differ from justice to justice. There is nothing unprincipled about such a regime. Each justice might make decisions about precedent that are consistent with her overall interpretive philosophy. Still, this vision of stare decisis relinquishes the ability to draw together justices who are sympathetic to different interpretive schools. In doing so, it gives away a large share of the promise of precedent.

Because their impact depends on contested matters of interpretive philosophy, substantive effects should generally be excluded from the stare decisis calculus. Allowing substantive effects to guide the analysis all but guarantees that the treatment of precedent will track deeper methodological disputes. Evaluating a precedent's substantive effects might be appropriate in a world of interpretive agreement, where the justices work from a shared set of assumptions to determine which of a prior decision's consequences are legally relevant. But that is not our world. In the second-best world of interpretive pluralism, a precedent's substantive effects should bear on its retention only in a small category of exceptional cases. The category comprises decisions that an individual justice views as not simply wrong or bad, but extraordinarily harmful. Of course, each justice must make that assessment based on her individual interpretive preferences. As a result, different justices will reach different conclusions about which precedents fit the bill. Once a justice decides that a mistaken precedent is responsible for causing extraordinary harm, she is justified in refusing to stand by that precedent for the sake of continuity. This exception coheres with the common understanding of stare decisis as meaningful but nonabsolute. Sometimes a precedent is too bad (from the perspective of an individual justice) to tolerate. In those cases, the pull of precedent gives way.

While the exception for extraordinary harm contemplates occasional situations in which individual attitudes toward constitutional interpretation are paramount, its narrowness reinforces the importance of compromise in the ordinary course. A robust doctrine of precedent regularly calls upon the justices to subordinate their individual conclusions in deference to the Court's institutional history. Disregarding a precedent's substantive effects goes hand-in-hand with the idea that it takes more than disagreement to justify a precedent's overruling. Only when a decision strikes a justice as so inordinately harmful that it cannot be tolerated does this principle yield.

The picture that emerges is one of precedent serving as a source of common ground among differently minded justices, thereby facilitating impersonal decision-making and coordinated action. This notion of common ground is certainly not unique to precedent. For example, the text of a statute or constitutional provision provides a useful source of common ground. There is no need for two justices to argue about whether, say, each state should have the same number of senators. The Constitution's clear text furnishes the answer. It will furnish the answer when there are five justices on the Court who give primacy to the Constitution's original meaning. It will furnish the same answer when there are five justices who view the Constitution as a living document that evolves over time.

Precedent can play a similar role. It allows some points to be taken as given rather than perpetually debated. And it does so in a fashion that is fundamentally neutral. To be sure, nearly every precedent has its backers and its critics. But the general practice of precedent-following does not work exclusively to the advantage of living constitutionalists, or originalists, or anyone else. Some precedents are consistent with the Constitution's original meaning. Others are consistent with living constitutionalism. This is important, because it limits what the individual justice sacrifices by committing herself to precedent. It is not as if a justice is asked to jettison her own interpretive philosophy and pledge fidelity to another. Rather, she agrees to defer to the Court's precedents, some of which she will favor and some of which she will not.

In emphasizing the basic neutrality of appeals to precedent qua precedent, I do not suggest that my theory is value-free. The argument that justices should promote continuity and aspire to impersonality is a normative claim, and I embrace it as such. Yet it is a normative claim that has been consistently endorsed by justices across the interpretive spectrum. For years, the Supreme Court has emphasized the importance of continuity and impersonality to the rule of law and the foundations of the constitutional order. As I will explain, I believe these aspirations to be normatively desirable. But even for those who disagree, the fact remains that as a matter of the Court's own expressions, there is no question about the centrality of continuity and impersonality in constitutional interpretation. My principal aim is to show how stare decisis can serve the objectives the Court itself has articulated.

I build upon these themes by considering more directly the decision-making process of the individual jurist. Up until this point, I defend second-best stare decisis on the assumption that the justices of the Supreme Court are jointly committed to maintaining a meaningful doctrine of precedent. I think this assumption is sound: As noted, a wide range of justices have urged the importance of stare decisis to a stable and impersonal rule of law, and I see no reason to doubt their sincerity or resolve. Even so, I relax this assumption and contend that a justice is well served to cast her lot with stare decisis irrespective of whether her judicial peers – present or future – follow suit. By adhering to precedent, even a single justice can promote continuity and impersonality while contributing to the establishment of stare decisis as an ongoing practice.

All of this depends on the effectiveness of attempting to limit the impact of factors such as a precedent's substantive effects. Chapter 7 discusses an alternative approach to precedential strength that is grounded not in the substance of stare decisis doctrine, but rather in the structure of Supreme Court decision-making. The proposal is to require a supermajority vote in order to overrule a precedent. The rationale is straightforward. The more votes it takes to overrule, the more likely it becomes that an overruling will require cooperation among justices who have different theories of constitutional interpretation. And the greater the likelihood that such cooperation is required, the lower the chances that a precedent will be jettisoned due to nothing more than personnel shifts – and accompanying changes in the Court's interpretive locus.

While a supermajority voting rule has the potential to enhance the impersonality of judicial decision-making, I will suggest that it is less promising than the doctrinal revisions to stare decisis described in Chapter 6. The supermajority rule operates by increasing the number of votes that are necessary to change the law. But it does not ask the individual justice to subordinate her own interpretive preferences to the role of the Court as an institution. That is a missed opportunity for reinforcing the prevalence of the rule of law over the rule of individual women and men.

In Chapter 8, I turn to the implications of interpretive disagreement for the definition of a precedent's scope of applicability. As a descriptive matter, debates over precedential scope cannot be reduced to distilling the holding of a case and separating it from the dicta. The Supreme Court commonly accords deference to aspects of its opinions that range far beyond the narrow application of law to fact. Determining whether that practice is legitimate and desirable depends on underlying beliefs about constitutional interpretation and judicial decision-making. The problem is familiar by now. Those underlying beliefs vary greatly from judge to judge and justice to justice, yet the doctrine of stare decisis must be grounded in considerations that steer clear of contestable interpretive and normative commitments.

In light of the challenges posed by interpretive pluralism, I defend a revised approach to precedential scope that leverages areas of agreement within existing law. With occasional exceptions, the Supreme Court's cases generally teach that judicial asides and hypotheticals are not entitled to deference in future disputes. It likewise is generally accepted that a judicial opinion can establish a precedent by setting forth a doctrinal rule or framework, even if that rule or framework obviously ranges beyond the facts presented. Given their widespread acceptance, these two principles provide building blocks for an approach to precedential scope that adds consistency while respecting what has gone before.

A more difficult question involves a prior court's statement of its reasoning. The Supreme Court sometimes treats decisional rationales as entitled to deference in future cases. At other times, it defers only to a decision's legal rule, characterizing expressed rationales as extraneous. In the face of this divide, I urge a compromise: The reasons offered in support of a decision do not warrant deference in all cases, but neither may they be discounted in a way that undermines the logic of the decision that announced them. This distinction, imperfect as it might be, responds to interpretive pluralism by walking the line between excessive deference to peripheral statements and inadequate respect for the considered expressions of prior courts.

Chapter 9 asks what the theory of second-best stare decisis means for leading schools of constitutional interpretation. I discuss the ways in which second-best stare decisis coheres with and complements certain interpretive philosophies, as well as the ways in which it challenges them. Leading methodologies such as living constitutionalism and originalism are compatible with second-best stare decisis in significant respects, including the use of precedent to guide and constrain future decision-makers. Yet tensions will inevitably arise. The living constitutionalist will sometimes be asked to stand by an originalist decision that she views as inconsistent with contemporary mores or sound policy judgments. The originalist will sometimes be asked to validate a decision that she views as having departed from the original meaning of the Constitution's text.

Despite these costs, deference to precedent is justified by the ideal of the Supreme Court as an enduring institution rather than the contingent product of individual predilections. There is also a more practical consideration at work: If living constitutionalists are unlikely to convince many originalists to join their cause, and if originalists are similarly unlikely to convince many living constitutionalists to come aboard, perhaps the best approach is one that gives something to – and asks something from – both.

The book concludes with some parting thoughts about the relationship between precedent, impersonality, and continuity in modern constitutional law. The reality of American law and politics is that constitutional change happens through judicial appointments, not formal amendments. The people elect their president, and each president tries to select Supreme Court justices who view the law in a particular way. This does not imply the Court is a "political" institution, at least if that word is taken to mean that the justices make their decisions based on political preferences. There is room for principled disagreement in the interpretation of the Constitution.

When some justices leave the Court and others arrive, the dynamics can change such that interpretive approaches that were formerly in the minority come to predominate. Again, this is unremarkable. Nor should it surprise us if a shift in the Court's interpretive locus leads to the reconsideration of precedents that reflect now-disfavored ways of understanding the Constitution. But ebb and flow is not the only way to design a system of constitutional adjudication. As an alternative, we can imagine a system in which constitutional law retains a stable, continuous core even as individual justices come and go. That is the world of stare decisis.

Legal continuity comes at a cost. Stare decisis means tolerating some interpretations that one believes to be mistaken. It also means declining some opportunities to innovate when the Court has already resolved an issue. Like the turtle adorning this book's cover – supporting a lamppost outside the Supreme Court in Washington, DC – a court that commits itself to stare decisis will proceed incrementally, deliberately, slowly in pushing the law forward. It will continue to fashion new rules in cases of first impression. But where the law is settled, it will tend to leave things as they stand. Legal change occurs not through the courts, but through other channels: channels like the enactment of state and federal legislation to protect important rights, and the proposal of constitutional amendments for national consideration and debate. Where the political process cannot or will not act, the law generally remains intact – even at the cost of enduring a past mistake.

The costs of continuity are real, but so are the benefits. Under a system of stare decisis, the potential vacillation of constitutional law following changes in judicial personnel is replaced by an abiding sense of stability and impersonality. By deferring to precedent, the justices subordinate their individual perspectives to the Court's institutional identity. They establish their commitment to an enduring institution that cannot be reduced to the tendencies of a sitting majority. And they make good on the promise of the Constitution as being more than what five justices say it is. The judges change, but the law remains the same.

1

Framing the Study of Precedent

This chapter introduces the concept of stare decisis and identifies four distinctions that are helpful in thinking about the role of precedent in judicial decision-making. One distinction relates to the sources of precedent, including whether a past decision was issued by a court of superior rank. Another involves the dual dimensions that define the impact of precedent: the strength or weakness of deference, and the breadth or narrowness with which past decisions are construed. A third distinction relates to the categorization of precedents as constitutional, statutory, or common law cases. And the final distinction arises from the variety of roles that precedents play, which range from gentle persuasion to genuine constraint.[1]

SOURCES OF PRECEDENT

In the business world, there are two types of requests: those that come from your boss and those that come from everyone else. The same goes for courts.

Judges pay close attention to precedents from courts of higher rank. Such *vertical* precedents are conclusive wherever they apply. For example, when the US Supreme Court issues an opinion interpreting federal law, that opinion is binding on all other courts, state and federal alike.[2] The lower courts have no authority to depart from the Supreme Court's instructions. Nor are they allowed to make predictions about whether the Supreme Court might have changed its mind in the years since it issued its decision. Even when some justices have called a precedent into doubt, the lower courts must keep

---

[1] A note on terminology: I will be using *the doctrine of precedent* and *the doctrine of stare decisis* interchangeably, and I will also use the term *precedents* more generally to refer to prior judicial decisions.

[2] *See, e.g.*, DIRECTV, Inc. v. Imburgia, 136 S. Ct. 463, 468 (2015).

on treating it as binding unless and until the Supreme Court instructs otherwise.[3] From the standpoint of a lower court judge, the existence of an applicable Supreme Court opinion marks the end of the case.

The rules are different for precedents issued by courts that are lower in the judicial hierarchy. The Supreme Court is not bound by the decisions of lower court judges. It is certainly true that the justices occasionally express approval of, and may even seem to track, decisions of the lower courts.[4] But if the justices behave in this way, it is because they agree with a lower court's decision, not because they are bound to follow that decision irrespective of whether they think it is correct. Lower courts influence higher courts by being persuasive. Higher courts influence lower courts by being higher. For the Supreme Court, being persuasive is just the icing on the cake.

So far we have considered two scenarios: A judge confronts a precedent issued by a higher court and a judge confronts a precedent issued by a lower court. Now let us introduce a third option, one that I will emphasize in the pages ahead. How should a judge treat precedents issued by her own court? This question is sometimes described as dealing with the *horizontal* implications of precedent, though it does just as well to think in terms of a court's relationship with its past self.

American litigation is awash in appeals to horizontal precedent. Consider the experience of the Supreme Court. When a justice picks up a brief to read about a new dispute that is awaiting resolution, she is sure to encounter arguments about how the Court's prior decisions should influence her analysis. Some decisions may be directly related to the case at hand, while others may be more attenuated. The decisions may be of recent vintage, meaning that the Court's current membership overlaps substantially with the membership that issued them. Or perhaps the Court made the relevant decisions long ago, with every justice having been replaced in the meantime. However these issues shake out, the question is what the Court's past means for its present (and future).

The impact of horizontal precedent is by no means limited to the Supreme Court. When a panel of three judges issues a decision on behalf of a federal court of appeals, that decision is generally binding on lower courts within the same region.[5] The decision is also binding on future three-judge panels of the court that issued it. It can be overruled only if the appellate judges agree to

---

[3] *See, e.g.,* State Oil Co. v. Khan, 522 U.S. 3, 20 (1997).
[4] *See generally* Aaron-Andrew P. Bruhl, *Following Lower-Court Precedent,* 81 U. CHI. L. REV. 851 (2014).
[5] Evan H. Caminker, *Why Must Inferior Courts Obey Superior Court Precedents?,* 46 STAN. L. REV. 817, 824 (1994).

rehear the case en banc (which usually means as a full court) or take other measures designed to ensure widespread support for a change of direction.[6] Without minimizing the important implications of horizontal precedent in the federal appellate courts, I will devote most of my attention to the US Supreme Court. The Supreme Court is distinctive in its internal dynamics, its resources, and its place in the constitutional order, so it provides a useful focal point for analyzing the path of precedent.

As a matter of existing practice, there are two basic principles that govern the Supreme Court's treatment of its own precedents. First, its precedents are entitled to deference, which seems to mean they receive the benefit of the doubt even if they are – in the view of a majority of today's justices – incorrect. Second, deference is not absolute, and all precedents may be reconsidered under the right circumstances. These two principles are straightforward enough. The difficulty is in applying them. The threshold question is how the Court should determine whether one (or more) of its precedents is relevant to the case at hand. If there is a relevant precedent on the books, the next question becomes whether to follow or overrule it. We can think of these inquires in terms of precedential scope and precedential strength, respectively.

SCOPE AND STRENGTH

Whether today's dispute is governed by yesterday's decision depends on the decision's scope of applicability. Sometimes a precedent's relevance to today's case is undeniable. When a court considers a case about a dog bite and finds a precedent on the books announcing that dog owners are strictly liable for their canines' actions, it makes no difference that the pending dispute involves a yellow dog while the prior case involved a red dog.[7] But there are many instances in which defining a precedent's scope of applicability is fraught and controversial. When the Supreme Court considered the constitutionality of laws restricting same-sex relationships, how much did it matter that the Court had previously invalidated an amendment to the Colorado Constitution that

---

[6] See id.; United States v. Collins, 415 F.3d 304, 311 (4th Cir. 2005). The decisions of federal district courts are commonly understood as lacking force as horizontal precedents in future cases. See, e.g., Ashcroft v. al-Kidd, 563 U.S. 731, 741 (2011).

[7] Cf. Frederick Schauer, Precedent, 39 STAN. L. REV. 571, 577 (1987). Professor Schauer adds that even in easy cases, "only the intervention of organizing theory, in the form of *rules of relevance*, allows us to distinguish the precedential from the irrelevant. Precedent depends upon such rules. And these rules themselves are contingent upon both time and culture." Id. at 578. Professor Schauer's analysis also illuminates the interaction between strength and scope, though he chooses not to focus on the issue of overruling. See id. at 594 n.47.

foreclosed special legal protections based on a person's sexual orientation?[8] When the Court considered a prohibition on false claims of military commendation, was it pertinent that the Court had denied the constitutional value of false speech in other contexts?[9] By articulating certain warnings that police officers should have given to a criminal suspect in a particular case, did the Court establish those warnings as binding law for all future interrogations?[10]

Questions of scope are critical to the role of precedent in judicial decision-making. Even if the bar for overruling a decision is quite high, future judges will have broad discretion to innovate if each precedent covers only a sliver of legal terrain.[11] If, however, past decisions are defined broadly, a strong norm of deference will make revisions and reconsiderations much harder to come by.

The classic account of precedential scope revolves around a stark dichotomy. A court's *holdings* receive deference in future cases. By contrast, the court's unnecessary *dicta* are relevant only to the extent that their reasoning is persuasive. But there is a great deal more to this story.[12] While the Supreme Court sometimes invokes the line between holdings and dicta, it frequently takes a capacious view of precedential scope. A vast array of judicial pronouncements – from underlying rationales to wide-ranging doctrinal frameworks – are treated as warranting deference in future cases. Lower court judges also tend to be generous in their readings of Supreme Court precedent, often deferring to the justices' statements regardless of whether they were strictly necessary to the decision that contained them. The point at this early stage of our inquiry is not to defend or criticize these practices, but merely to note that defining the scope of precedent can be a complex enterprise, with the traditional distinction between holdings and dicta reflecting only one consideration among many.

---

[8] *See* Lawrence v. Texas, 539 U.S. 558, 574–6 (2003) (discussing Romer v. Evans, 517 U.S. 620 (1996)).

[9] *See* United States v. Alvarez, 132 S. Ct. 2537 (2012).

[10] *See* Miranda v. Arizona, 384 U.S. 436 (1966), *reaff'd in* Dickerson v. United States, 530 U.S. 428 (2000).

[11] A precedent that is not strictly applicable to the case at hand can still exert what Ronald Dworkin called "gravitational force" by influencing "later decisions even when these later decisions lie outside its particular orbit." RONALD DWORKIN, TAKING RIGHTS SERIOUSLY 111 (1977). This effect could occur for any number of reasons. For example, it may reflect a general preference for consistency among legal rules, or agreement with the view that because "[a] precedent is the report of an earlier political decision," "the very fact of that decision, as a piece of political history, provides some reason for deciding other cases in a similar way in the future." Id. at 113. Whatever the explanation, exerting gravitational force is distinct from requiring future courts to reaffirm a decision notwithstanding their doubts about its soundness. That latter phenomenon is my primary interest.

[12] These issues are developed in Chapter 4.

Given the absoluteness of vertical precedent, issues of precedential scope are often dispositive in the lower courts. In the federal district and appellate courts, to find that a Supreme Court precedent applies is to find that it controls. But when we shift our gaze to a court's relationship with its past self, defining a precedent's scope of applicability is only the beginning. When today's justices determine that a Supreme Court precedent applies to a pending case, they must confront the further question of whether to stand by that precedent or overrule it.

The answer depends on the strength of precedent, meaning the degree of deference past decisions receive in future cases. If a court is almost never willing to overrule its past decisions even if it believes those decisions to be incorrect, the strength of precedent is great. At the other end of the spectrum, if a court is inclined to overrule nearly every precedent that it views as flawed, the strength of precedent is weak. The ambiguity arises in the middle, with courts recognizing that precedents are entitled to something less than absolute deference but something more than no deference at all. As we have seen, Justice Brandeis famously described the resulting tension as reflecting the competing values of leaving the law "settled" and getting the law "right."[13] Supreme Court justices continue to echo Justice Brandeis's sentiments while adding that excessive overruling could "threaten to substitute disruption, confusion, and uncertainty for necessary legal stability."[14] This abiding tension between legal correctness and legal continuity guides the Court's inquiries into the strength of precedent.

In mining the Supreme Court's opinions for a canonical account of precedential strength, one quickly comes to recognize the tendency to equate deference to precedent with the need for a "special justification" before overruling.[15] These statements do not take us very far, because there are countless ways to define the concept of a special justification. Nor have the justices offered a comprehensive definition of the term. To figure out what it means, we must look to the ways in which the Court has treated its precedents.

The Court has considered a variety of factors in determining whether there is a special justification for overruling precedent. One aspect of that analysis, which I will return to below, is worth foreshadowing. A major question in defining the strength of precedent is whether a decision's unsound reasoning

---

[13] Burnet v. Coronado Oil & Gas Co., 285 U.S. 393, 406 (1932) (Brandeis, J., dissenting).
[14] John R. Sand & Gravel Co. v. United States, 552 U.S. 130, 139 (2008); *see also* Citizens United v. FEC, 558 U.S. 310, 378 (2010) (Roberts, C. J., concurring) (describing the Court's duty to "balance the importance of having constitutional questions *decided* against the importance of having them *decided right*").
[15] *See, e.g., Dickerson*, 530 U.S. at 443.

and flawed result are themselves sufficient to warrant its overruling. The Court sometimes suggests that the answer is yes. Consider *Citizens United v. FEC* (2010), in which the majority began its discussion of stare decisis by noting that "[o]ur precedent is to be respected unless the most convincing of reasons demonstrates that adherence to it puts us on a course that is sure error."[16] Though it expresses respect for precedent, the Court's formulation implies that a decision's claim to deference rises or falls with the soundness of its reasoning as perceived by a majority of sitting justices. On this account, the function of stare decisis is to make sure that today's justices are confident that a decision is erroneous. The principle of stare decisis ought not dissuade the justices from correcting obvious mistakes, lest they inadvertently do more harm than good by propping up untenable decisions. One can detect a similar sensibility in Justice Brandeis's discussion of constitutional precedent in *Burnet v. Coronado Oil & Gas Company* (1932). Though he acknowledged the virtues of deference to precedent as a general matter, Justice Brandeis argued that within the sphere of constitutional law, the Court must be willing to "bow[] to the lessons of experience and the force of better reasoning" even at the expense of preserving the status quo.[17]

Yet the justices have offered numerous indications that disapproval of a decision's rationale and result are not enough to warrant its overruling. Justice Kagan recently noted that "the very point of *stare decisis*" is that "[t]he special justifications needed to reverse an opinion must go beyond demonstrations . . . that it was wrong."[18] Justice Sotomayor likewise has observed that "establishing that a decision was wrong does not, without more, justify overruling it."[19] A majority of justices made the same point in *Planned Parenthood of Southeastern Pennsylvania v. Casey* (1992), concluding that "a decision to overrule should rest on some special reason over and above the belief that a prior case was wrongly decided."[20] More recently, the Court noted in a statutory dispute that "an argument that we got something wrong – even a good argument to that effect – cannot by itself justify scrapping settled precedent. Or otherwise said, it is not alone sufficient that we would decide a case differently now than we did then."[21]

---

[16] *Citizens United*, 558 U.S. at 362 (majority op.).
[17] *Burnet*, 285 U.S. at 407–8 (Brandeis, J., dissenting); *see also* Payne v. Tennessee, 501 U.S. 808, 834 (1991) (Scalia, J., concurring) (criticizing "the notion that an important constitutional decision with plainly inadequate rational support *must* be left in place for the sole reason that it once attracted five votes").
[18] Harris v. Quinn, 134 S. Ct. 2618, 2652 (2014) (Kagan, J., dissenting).
[19] Alleyne v. United States, 133 S. Ct. 2151, 2164 (2013) (Sotomayor, J., concurring).
[20] 505 U.S. 833, 864.
[21] Kimble v. Marvel Entertainment, LLC, 135 S. Ct. 2401, 2409 (2015).

Statements like these suggest that an overruling must rest on more than disagreement with a precedent's reasoning or outcome. As Chief Justice Roberts explained during his confirmation hearing, "It is not enough that you may think the prior decision was wrongly decided. That really doesn't answer the question. It just poses the question."[22] Later I will contend that rejecting precedents based on their reasoning and results poses serious problems in a world of pervasive interpretive disagreement. If there were consensus (or something close to it) about the manner in which the Constitution should be interpreted, focusing on a decision's flawed reasoning or detrimental results could be a useful way of framing the analysis of precedent. But when the justices are divided over how the Constitution ought to be understood, there must be something more than a firm conviction of error to justify an overruling if stare decisis is to infuse the law with a sense of durability and impersonality that transcends interpretive debates.

STATUTES, THE CONSTITUTION, AND THE COMMON LAW

The Supreme Court commonly describes its interpretations of statutes as entitled to strong deference going forward. This practice is grounded in Congress's ultimate authority over statutory matters. Because Congress has the power to pass new legislation that responds to – and overrides – the Supreme Court's interpretations of statutes, the Court has been reluctant to revisit its own judgments. Instead, "critics of our ruling can take their objections across the street, and Congress can correct any mistake it sees."[23] The Court has also suggested that Congress's failure to revise a judicial interpretation might be a form of acquiescence. On that understanding, the Court's overruling of precedent could contravene Congress's (implicit) wishes.[24] And there is a related concern that while the courts must play some role in settling statutory disputes, that role should not include vacillating after an issue has been settled.[25]

Each of these arguments is subject to challenge.[26] Congress's failure to amend a statute might be for reasons other than its agreement with the judiciary's interpretation, such as the limited capacity of the legislative agenda.[27]

---

[22] 109th Cong. 144 (2005).
[23] *Kimble*, 135 S. Ct. at 2409; *see also* STEPHEN BREYER, MAKING OUR DEMOCRACY WORK: A JUDGE'S VIEW 151–2 (2010).
[24] *See, e.g., Kimble*, 135 S. Ct. at 2410.
[25] *See* Boys Markets, Inc. v. Retail Clerks Union, Local 770, 398 U.S. 235, 257–8 (1970) (Black, J., dissenting).
[26] *See, e.g.,* William N. Eskridge, Jr., *Overruling Statutory Precedents*, 76 GEO. L.J. 1361, 1409 (1988).
[27] *See Kimble*, 135 S. Ct. at 2418 (Alito, J., dissenting); Johnson v. Transportation Agency, 480 U.S. 616, 672 (1987) (Scalia, J., dissenting).

Moreover, even if a failure to act is taken as implying congressional acquiescence, it reflects the position of *today's* Congress. It not clear why that position should matter to a court charged with interpreting a statute that was enacted by a *prior* Congress. Presumably it is the latter whose understanding is most relevant to disputed questions of statutory interpretation.[28] Finally, it is at least debatable whether a proper conception of the judicial role requires today's court to endorse, for the sake of continuity, an interpretation that it views as misconstruing the legislature's intentions.

Notwithstanding these challenges, the Supreme Court insists that its statutory precedents are entitled to a uniquely powerful form of deference. Some scholars have suggested that this practice represents a fairly recent innovation, beginning to appear only in the twentieth century.[29] Others have questioned whether the Court's statements are really borne out in practice. A recent study contends that other factors (such as the amount of criticism a precedent has received) are stronger predictors of deference than whether the precedent dealt with statutory law rather than constitutional law.[30] Still, the Court continues to describe statutory interpretation as a domain in which stability and continuity are especially important.

The Court has taken a modified approach to statutes such as the Sherman Act, which forbids unlawful restraints on trade.[31] According to the Court, the statute's broad language suggests a central role for the judiciary in crafting rules of its own rather than simply interpreting congressional commands.[32] In serving this function, the Court is willing to revisit its decisions in light of "modern understanding and greater experience."[33] But most statutes envision a more limited role for the judiciary, reinforcing the Court's hesitance to reconsider its prior interpretations.

---

[28] *See Johnson*, 480 U.S. at 671 (Scalia, J., dissenting); Lawrence C. Marshall, *"Let Congress Do It": The Case for an Absolute Rule of Statutory Stare Decisis*, 88 MICH. L. REV. 177, 194–5 (1989).

[29] *See* Thomas R. Lee, *Stare Decisis in Historical Perspective*, 52 VAND. L. REV. 647, 735 (1999).

[30] Lee Epstein, William M. Landes, & Adam Liptak, *The Decision to Depart (or Not) from Constitutional Precedent: An Empirical Study of the Roberts Court*, 90 N.Y.U. L. REV. 1115, 1118 (2015). For an earlier recognition of the limits of the "super-strong presumption against overruling statutory precedents," see Eskridge, *Overruling Statutory Precedents, supra* note 26, at 1363 ("A given statutory precedent is particularly vulnerable to modification or overruling if the Court's original discussion of the issues is procedurally unsatisfactory, if the statute being interpreted is generally worded and has not been the subject of extensive legislative tinkering, and/or if subsequent legislative developments have undercut the rationale of the decision and private parties have not extensively relied on it.").

[31] Leegin Creative Leather Products, Inc. v. PSKS, Inc., 551 U.S. 877, 899 (2007).

[32] Eskridge, *Overruling Statutory Precedents, supra* note 26, at 1377.

[33] *Leegin*, 551 U.S. at 899.

Let us turn next to the Constitution. There is some basis for contending that constitutional precedents should be entitled to the most powerful form of deference, given their importance to the architecture of government and their impact on the fundamental relationship between sovereign and citizen. The rationale is that if stability and continuity are important anywhere, they are important in cases that interpret the Constitution. At very least, the argument goes, constitutional rules should receive no less deference than other legal rules.[34] A related argument is that if the Court is to retain its power to "rein in the forces of democratic politics" through constitutional interpretation, it must demonstrate that it is "implementing 'principles . . . founded in the law rather than in the proclivities of individuals.'"[35] This concern suggests that the Court should be leery of revisiting its constitutional decisions, lest it be viewed as announcing the conclusions of five individuals rather than the judgment of an enduring institution.

Notwithstanding arguments like these, the Supreme Court has not characterized its constitutional precedents as possessing the durability that attaches to statutory decisions. While the Court leaves it to the legislative process to fix mistaken interpretations of statutes, the justices have described themselves as more willing to revisit their constitutional decisions. Constitutional precedents receive some deference, but not the "superpowered" deference that most statutory precedents enjoy.[36]

From the interpretation of statutes and constitutional provisions, we come finally to judge-made rules of the common law. Some thirty years ago, William Eskridge described the Court as placing common law decisions somewhere between constitutional decisions and statutory decisions in the deference they receive.[37] This classification remains instructive. Still, the description of constitutional precedents as weak in relative terms should not be taken to mean such deference is inconsequential in absolute terms. The Court has emphasized the importance of deferring even to constitutional precedents in order to promote values such as stability and impersonality. Indeed, it has invoked the doctrine of stare decisis en route to upholding some of its most high-profile constitutional decisions.[38]

---

[34] *See* Frank H. Easterbrook, *Stability and Reliability in Judicial Decisions*, 73 CORNELL L. REV. 422, 431 (1988).
[35] *Payne*, 501 U.S. at 853 (Marshall, J., dissenting) (quoting Vasquez v. Hillery, 474 U.S. 254, 265 (1986)).
[36] *Kimble*, 135 S. Ct. at 2410 (majority op.).
[37] *See* Eskridge, *Overruling Statutory Precedents*, *supra* note 26, at 1362; Amy Coney Barrett, *Statutory Stare Decisis in the Courts of Appeals*, 73 GEORGE WASH. L. REV. 317, 321 (2005).
[38] *See Casey*, 505 U.S. at 833 (upholding the core holding of Roe v. Wade, 410 U.S. 113 (1973)); *Dickerson*, 530 U.S. at 428 (upholding *Miranda*, 384 U.S. at 436); *cf.* Frederick Schauer, *Has*

I have noted that my analysis in the pages that follow will revolve around the Supreme Court (while carrying some implications for other courts). In addition, it will deal primarily, though not exclusively, with the Court's constitutional decisions. The Court's most extensive and controversial discussions of precedent have arisen in the constitutional context, which makes for a useful topic of study. I hope to shed light on the role of constitutional precedent under existing law, and to suggest revisions designed to make the doctrine of stare decisis more effective in a legal system characterized by deep disagreements over the best way to interpret the Constitution. My theory might be taken to imply that the strength of deference should remain constant regardless of whether a precedent deals with constitutional law, statutory law, or the common law. Yet while I do not necessarily reject that claim, I will not defend it here. I will focus instead on analyzing the dynamics and implications of constitutional precedent, in hopes that such an analysis may also provide a useful starting point for evaluating the function of precedent in statutory and common law cases.

TYPES OF LEGAL RULES

The Supreme Court regularly reminds us that the pull of precedent is strongest in the domains of property rights, contractual obligations, and commercial transactions. The rationale is that "parties are especially likely to rely on such precedents when ordering their affairs."[39] The Court summarized its thinking over a century ago by noting that when it sets down a property rule, "every one would suppose . . . he might safely enter into contracts, upon the faith that rights thus acquired would not be disturbed."[40] Upsetting the law could disrupt the reasonable expectations of those who made deals and plans against the backdrop of an established legal rule.

Consider the plight of two companies that haggle for months to write a detailed contract only to have the Supreme Court alter its case law in a way that turns their deal on its head. Or consider the person who buys a beachfront home after receiving assurances from his lawyer that his path to the ocean will remain clear, but who learns after a judicial reversal that the government

---

Precedent Ever Mattered in the Supreme Court?, 24 GEORGIA STATE UNIV. L. REV. 381, 393–4 (2007) (discussing cases in which "a Justice voted contrary to his or her precedent-independent beliefs solely because of the current felt obligation to follow precedent," but concluding that such cases "are few and far between").

[39] *Kimble*, 135 S. Ct. at 2410; *see also Payne*, 501 U.S. at 828 (majority op.).
[40] *The Genesee Chief v. Fitzhugh*, 53 U.S. 443, 458 (1851).

now holds title to the land between him and the water.[41] Stare decisis is a way to avoid situations like these by protecting people's reasonable expectations about commercial relationships, interests, and transactions.

Notwithstanding the Court's emphasis on expectations surrounding contract and property rights, reliance interests extend beyond the domain of commercial activities. They can also attach to decisions involving other rights, such as the freedom of speech and the protection against unreasonable searches and seizures. In emphasizing the role of precedent in cases relating to property and contract, the Court has not implied that tangible expectations are more significant than expectations involving these other types of rights. Nor should we infer from the Court's statements that contract and property rules are unimportant, such that allowing judicial mistakes to linger is of little concern.

The better way to understand the Court's teachings is that cases involving tangible rights and commercial investments often present the clearest examples of reliance on existing legal rules. As we will see, reliance interests are always relevant to the Court's determination whether to overrule a past decision. Whether a decision deals with contracts or property or speech or privacy, the protection of expectations is a reason why the Court might choose to retain a precedent despite its flaws. The difference is that decisions involving contract and property rights tend to generate the most evident and concrete sorts of reliance in the form of commercial transactions, financial investments, and the like. To say that settled expectations are especially resonant in the fields of contract and property is simply to say that, though the Court must always consider whether an overruling would disrupt reliance interests, those interests are easiest to see and evaluate when commercial interests are on the line. This does not mean every precedent involving contracts or property would be extremely disruptive if overruled. Likewise, it leaves open the possibility that cases outside the domains of contract and property might themselves carry significant reliance implications.

Here, then, is a clunkier but more accurate formulation of the relationship between precedent and the rules of contract and property: People and organizations often rely on contract and property rules, and courts should think twice before disrupting that reliance by overruling a past decision. But every contract and property case will involve a different degree of reliance: sometimes greater, sometimes lesser. And some cases that have nothing to do with contracts or property will generate significant reliance that an overruling

---

[41] *Cf.* Stop the Beach Renourishment, Inc. v. Florida Department of Environmental Protection, 560 U.S. 702 (2010).

would upset. The singling out of cases involving contracts and property is merely a shortcut, not a rigid rule of judicial decision-making.

THE FUNCTIONS OF PRECEDENT

Appeals to precedent serve a variety of purposes. They can frame the terms of a debate, connect an argument with historical practice, enlist the credibility of previous decision-makers, and more. This is true in all walks of life. Judicial decision-making is no exception.

My primary concern in this book is the use of precedent as a constraint. In serving this role, precedent acts as a buffer between the interpretive tendencies of today's judges and the resolution of constitutional disputes. Before reaching the issue of constraint, I offer a brief overview of other uses of precedent in American law.

Control. Courts at one level of the judicial hierarchy can use precedents to control the decision-making of courts at lower levels. For example, after the Supreme Court issues an opinion interpreting a provision of the Constitution, every judge in the country has a binding obligation to treat that decision as controlling. The obligation remains intact even if a judge concludes that the Supreme Court was wrong, and even if she believes that the justices are likely to reverse course in the immediate future. The effect is to give the Supreme Court considerable power to guide the decision-making of judges throughout the nation.[42]

Persuasion. A court's prior decisions can affect future adjudicators by means of persuasion. Even if a later court is not required to follow the opinion in question, it can study the opinion's reasoning and benefit from the analytical work done by other judges. The later court can also examine whether its predecessors' empirical assumptions and projections have been borne out over time. But sooner or later, a court that looks to precedent for its persuasive force must gauge the soundness of the precedent's reasoning. As Justice Scalia once noted, "If one has been persuaded by another, so that one's judgment accords with the other's, there is no room for deferral – only for agreement."[43]

Looking to precedent for its persuasive value is different from treating precedent as infused with formal authority irrespective of its soundness. Unlike the use of precedent for hierarchical control, the persuasive function does not portray the fact of a decision's existence as carrying independent significance. The point of consulting precedents for their persuasive value is to

---

[42] *See, e.g.,* Richard H. Fallon, Jr., *Constitutional Constraints*, 97 CAL. L. REV. 975, 1008 (2009).
[43] Kasten v. Saint-Gobain Performance Plastics Corp., 563 U.S. 1, 24 n.6 (2011) (Scalia, J., dissenting).

assist today's court in understanding and evaluating competing positions. The lawyers before a court might not make an argument in its strongest form. Even if they do, they might not present the argument with the same emphasis or in the same terms as prior courts have done. Grappling with the relevant precedents allows judges to better understand the claims before them. A judge who is facing a difficult case will naturally be interested in how other courts have resolved the issue even if she is not obliged to follow them.

The corollary is that, notwithstanding its utility, the persuasive function of precedent never requires a court to issue a ruling whose soundness it doubts. A judge who consults prior decisions for their persuasive value need not embrace a presumption in favor of the status quo. She may simply seek a fuller understanding of the relevant arguments before reaching her own conclusion. A judicial decision that is treated as persuasive has no force beyond that which might emerge from an amicus curiae brief or a scholarly treatise. If the relevant proposition is correct, it will carry the day. If it is incorrect, it will fall by the wayside.

Stage Setting. What looks like the use of precedent for its persuasive value often reveals itself as something different: an exercise in stage setting. Judges, like the attorneys who argue before them, use precedents as a means of framing and bolstering their positions. The implication is not that today's court *must* follow the precedents being invoked. Nor is it that the precedents warrant consideration due solely to the persuasiveness of their reasoning. Instead, a court uses precedents to show that its ruling is an unremarkable application of established principles. Though the prior decisions might not have addressed the precise question under review, they are depicted as setting the doctrinal stage and suggesting the proper result by analogy or modest extension.[44] Stage setting is the "Nothing to see here!" of judicial craftsmanship.

Like the persuasive function of precedent, the use of precedent for stage setting is discretionary. A court that describes past decisions as supporting today's ruling does not necessarily indicate that its ruling would have been different but for those decisions. The court might simply agree with the decisions' reasoning, meaning that it would have reached the same result even if they had

---

[44] *Compare* National Federation of Independent Business v. Sebelius, 132 S. Ct. 2566, 2590 (2012) ("Our precedents recognize Congress's power to regulate 'class[es] of *activities*,' not classes of *individuals*, apart from any activity in which they are engaged.") (internal citation omitted) (quoting Gonzales v. Raich, 545 U.S. 1, 17 (2005)), *with* id. at 2609 (Ginsburg, J., concurring in part, concurring in the judgment in part, and dissenting in part) ("Since 1937, our precedent has recognized Congress' large authority to set the Nation's course in the economic and social welfare realm."), *and* id. at 2646 (Scalia, J., dissenting) ("At the outer edge of the commerce power, this Court has insisted on careful scrutiny of regulations that do not act directly on an interstate market or its participants.").

not been on the books. To be sure, stage setting affects the composition of judicial opinions. It may even supply an element of "lawyerly authenticity" by connecting a ruling with longstanding judicial practice.[45] But it does not change the bottom line by requiring a judge to accept a position notwithstanding what she thinks is faulty reasoning.

Braking. Precedent can act as a braking mechanism by encouraging judges to be moderate and gradual in their rulings. By avoiding conflicts with existing law, judges express their respect for precedent. The objective is to preserve a court's established rules while developing the law at the margins. Even if the court eventually decides to overrule its prior decisions, the resulting delay will have slowed the pace of legal change. There will have been more debate and deliberation at the court and outside it, and stakeholders will have had more time to plan for the possibility of an overruling.

Though the braking function of precedent leads to narrower decisions, it does not cause a judge to announce a ruling she believes to be incorrect. The point of the braking function is to allow the judge to issue a decision that she thinks is right, even as she avoids unnecessary or premature conflicts with settled law. Braking is a means of delaying and mediating change, not reaffirming mistakes.

Constraint. This brings us to the most dramatic and controversial role of precedent in American law. The scenario is familiar. The Supreme Court is asked to review a case, and it concludes that one of its past decisions has already furnished an answer. But there is a wrinkle: The Court believes its prior decision is wrong. That puts the justices to a choice. They can overrule the precedent and set the law straight, or they can reaffirm it, notwithstanding its shortcomings.

If the justices choose the latter course, they will accept a result based on what a majority of them believe to be flawed reasoning. In doing so, they will have treated the precedent as a source of constraint. When a case's result would have come out differently but for the existence of a precedent, the constraining function of precedent is on full display. It is one thing for the Court to develop the law gradually to avoid changing too much too soon. That practice might reflect some degree of constraint, in that the Court may have gone further without the relevant precedent on the books. But the constraining effect of prior decisions reaches its apex when the justices rely on principles of stare decisis to accept a decision they otherwise would have rejected.

---

[45] Steven G. Calabresi, *Text, Precedent, and the Constitution: Some Originalist and Normative Arguments for Overruling* Planned Parenthood of Southeastern Pennsylvania v. Casey, 22 CONST. COMMENT. 311, 329 (2005).

A precedent's persuasive force flows from its logic and exposition. The constraining function of precedent works differently. What matters is not just the precedent's reasoning, but the fact that it was issued prior in time and has stood as binding law ever since. Having come first, the precedent acts as a "fundamental restraint" on later judges' ability to resolve cases as they would otherwise see fit.[46]

At the same time, precedential constraint need not be absolute. It is a separate question whether the presumptive constraint of precedent should give way to the need for revision or innovation. We can imagine a regime in which the Supreme Court has no discretion at all to overrule its past decisions. Upon finding a precedent to be controlling, the Court would be bound to follow it.[47] Any changes to the law would need to come through channels outside the judiciary. Yet the Supreme Court has never treated its precedents that way. It gives presumptive deference to its prior decisions, but it recognizes that the presumption can be rebutted – which is to say, precedents can be overruled – under appropriate circumstances. Defining those circumstances will occupy a great deal of our attention in the pages ahead. For now, it is enough to highlight the central question that arises in discussions about the constraining function of precedent: When should a court uphold a past decision despite its flaws, and when should a court break from the past? Or, to harken back to Justice Brandeis: How does a court determine whether it is more important for the law to be settled or right?

---

[46] United States v. Lopez, 514 U.S. 549, 574 (1995) (Kennedy, J., concurring).
[47] The UK House of Lords described its approach along these lines during the first part of the twentieth century, though there is debate over whether the formal description was always borne out in practice. *See* NEIL DUXBURY, THE NATURE AND AUTHORITY OF PRECEDENT 104, 127 (2008).

2

The Stakes of Deference

The story of precedent is old and new. Writing in the late eighteenth century, William Blackstone noted the role of precedent in preventing a judge from rendering decisions "according to his private sentiments."[1] Not long after, Alexander Hamilton described precedent as an antidote to judges' "arbitrary discretion" in his defense of the proposed US Constitution.[2] James Madison likewise took up the topic, arguing that "the good of society requires that the rules of conduct of its members should be certain and known, which would not be the case if any judge, disregarding the decision of his predecessors, should vary the rule of law according to his individual interpretation of it."[3] And these commentators were far from the first to take up the topic of precedent. Debates about the role of prior cases in judicial decision-making can be traced back long before the American founding.[4]

The Supreme Court also has a lengthy history of engaging with precedent. In 1827, for example, Justice Washington explained that while he possessed a particular view of the bankruptcy power, he had come to accept that his view

---

[1] WILLIAM BLACKSTONE, COMMENTARIES ON THE LAWS OF ENGLAND *69 (1765); *see also* id. ("[H]e being sworn to determine, not according to his own private judgment, but according to the known laws and customs of the land . . ."). Blackstone recognized an exception "where the former determination is most evidently contrary to reason; much more if it be contrary to the divine law." Id. at *69–70.
[2] THE FEDERALIST NO. 78 (Alexander Hamilton).
[3] Letter from James Madison to Charles Jared Ingersoll (June 25, 1831), *in* THE MIND OF THE FOUNDER: SOURCES OF THE POLITICAL THOUGHT OF JAMES MADISON 390, 391 (Marvin Meyers, rev. ed. 1981).
[4] *See generally* GERALD J. POSTEMA, *Some Roots of our Notion of Precedent*, *in* PRECEDENT IN LAW (Laurence Goldstein, 1987) (describing the views of Coke, Hale, Hobbes, and Hume, among others); *cf.* PHILIP HAMBURGER, LAW AND JUDICIAL DUTY 228–34 (2008) (discussing debates over the authority of judges to expound the law by issuing opinions); NEIL DUXBURY, THE NATURE AND AUTHORITY OF PRECEDENT 9 (2008) (noting that "the common law existed as a form of customary law long before there was a doctrine of precedent").

"was, and is incorrect, since it stands condemned by the decision of a majority of this Court, solemnly pronounced."[5] A few years earlier, Chief Justice Marshall had offered his thoughts about the scope of precedent and the limits of deference. He reasoned that judicial statements that "go beyond the case . . . may be respected, but ought not to control the judgment in a subsequent suit when the very point is presented for decision."[6] Related questions of precedential strength and scope remain salient to this day.

While legal thinkers have debated the role of precedent for centuries, the Supreme Court's attempt to create a formalized, systematic doctrine of stare decisis is of more recent vintage. In 1991, the Supreme Court overruled two decisions on its way to concluding that victim-impact evidence may be introduced during the sentencing phase of capital trials. In explaining its break with the past, the majority highlighted the fact that deference to precedent is a defeasible principle rather than "an inexorable command."[7] That explanation was unconvincing to Justice Marshall, who wrote that the majority's willingness to depart from precedent made plain that "[p]ower, not reason, is the new currency of this Court's decisionmaking."[8] The stage was set for renewed debate over what makes a precedent worth preserving despite its flaws, and what renders it susceptible to being overruled.

The crescendo came the very next year. The case was *Planned Parenthood of Southeastern Pennsylvania v. Casey* (1992), which dealt with the regulation of abortion. The justices split five-to-four in reaffirming the portion of *Roe v. Wade* (1973) that recognized a constitutional right to nontherapeutic abortion in certain circumstances. The lead opinion in *Casey* noted that any doubts the authors might have had about *Roe* were overcome by the importance of stare decisis.[9] More generally, the opinion devoted considerable attention to the operation of stare decisis as a legal doctrine encompassing a defined set of considerations and principles.

Discussions of stare decisis continue to arise with regularity in the Court's constitutional cases. Sometimes the importance of deference looms especially large. For example, the Court invoked the power of precedent when it reaffirmed the well-known *Miranda* warnings that police officers must give to criminal suspects.[10] The Court also appealed to precedent in refusing to reconsider its longstanding approach to determining whether the Bill of Rights is

---

[5] Ogden v. Saunders, 25 U.S. (12 Wheat.) 213, 264 (1827) (Washington, J.).
[6] Cohens v. Virginia, 19 U.S. (6 Wheat.) 264, 399 (1821).
[7] Payne v. Tennessee, 501 U.S. 808, 828 (1991).
[8] Id. at 844 (Marshall, J., dissenting).
[9] 505 U.S. 833, 861.
[10] Dickerson v. United States, 530 U.S. 428, 444 (2000).

binding against states and localities.[11] And some justices discussed the value of deference when the Court rebuffed a request to overrule *Buckley v. Valeo* (1976), a major case dealing with the regulation of campaign contributions and expenditures.[12]

On the other hand, in 2003 the Court showed no hesitation in overruling a decision that had effectively permitted the criminalization of same-sex relationships.[13] Nor could the pull of precedent prevent the Court in *Citizens United v. FEC* (2010) from overruling its past decisions by enlarging the constitutional protections for corporate political speech.[14] These illustrations only scratch the surface. The Court has also pondered the role of precedent in cases dealing with everything from labor unions to automobile searches, from criminal sentencing to the right to counsel, and well beyond.

This chapter surveys leading arguments for why the Court might defer to its past decisions even if it views those decisions as flawed. I also describe countervailing arguments for why deference to flawed precedents is unwise or illegitimate. In considering the arguments for and against deference, the chapter is informed by recent case law and commentary, as well as longstanding debates about the role of precedent in judicial decision-making.

Parsing the reasons for deferring (or not deferring) to precedent helps to explain how the Court's doctrine of stare decisis ended up in its current form. It will also provide a backdrop for evaluating the doctrine in later chapters. To discover ways in which the treatment of precedent can be improved, we must begin by analyzing what is gained and lost by privileging the past.

THE CASE FOR PRECEDENT

There are numerous reasons why it might be wise to defer to precedent. Among them are promoting decisional efficiency, protecting settled expectations, and finding common ground among judges who are inclined to see the world differently. In the pages that follow, I introduce leading justifications for deferring to prior decisions even at the cost of allowing flawed interpretations to persist.

Judicial Economy and Resource Conservation. The Supreme Court has noted that "[t]he obligation to follow precedent begins with necessity."[15] The law is too vast, and society too complex, to start from scratch in every dispute.

[11] McDonald v. City of Chicago, 561 U.S. 742, 758 (2010) (plurality op.).
[12] Randall v. Sorrell, 548 U.S. 230, 244 (2006) (Breyer, J.).
[13] Lawrence v. Texas, 539 U.S. 558 (2003).
[14] 558 U.S. 310.
[15] *Casey*, 505 U.S. at 854.

If judges could not treat some issues as settled, they might be obliged to spend immense amounts of time revisiting foundational issues over and over again. Hence the Court's statement that no legal system "could do society's work if it eyed each issue afresh in every case that raised it."[16]

The economies of precedent are easiest to spot when a higher court's decision is being applied by a lower court. When, for example, a federal court of appeals concludes that a pending case is covered by a Supreme Court precedent, it has no choice but to follow suit. Irrespective of whether the precedent rests on flawed reasoning or has led to bad (however defined) consequences, the court of appeals must do what the Supreme Court has instructed. Some judges may find this obligation frustrating, but there is a silver lining. The duty to follow vertical precedents spares judges from considering issues the Supreme Court has already resolved. Likewise, parties and lawyers need not argue over settled matters. Costs are saved and litigation is streamlined.

Savings can also arise when a court defers to its own past decisions. By treating certain issues as settled, a court makes its docket easier to manage and focuses attention on new and unresolved questions. Instead of starting from first principles, today's judges pick up where their predecessors left off. There is no need to begin sentencing hearings by asking whether the Eighth Amendment applies to the states (it does), or to begin defamation cases by asking whether slander against private individuals is governed by the same rules as slander against public officials (it is not). When background principles are stable, today's judges can cut to the chase. What is more, parties may be more inclined to settle their disputes privately, and cost-effectively, rather than pressing ahead with expensive litigation in the hopes of convincing a court to revisit its prior approach.[17] Of course, even if there were no doctrine of stare decisis, lawyers naturally would feature some arguments over others based on calculations about their probability of success. Adding a doctrine of precedent influences those calculations by making certain arguments – namely, those that require the overruling of settled precedent – harder to win.

In courts that control their own dockets, deference to precedent carries additional benefits for case selection. The Supreme Court rarely explains its refusal to hear cases. But it is fair to assume that the Court frequently rejects petitions for review because their arguments are inconsistent with settled precedent, which the justices see no need to upset. If this assumption were incorrect, we would expect the Court to devote a far greater share of its time to reconsidering its past pronouncements.

[16] Id. (citing BENJAMIN N. CARDOZO, THE NATURE OF THE JUDICIAL PROCESS 149 (1921)).
[17] See HENRY M. HART, JR. & ALBERT M. SACKS, THE LEGAL PROCESS: BASIC PROBLEMS IN THE MAKING AND APPLICATION OF LAW 568 (William N. Eskridge, Jr. & Philip P. Frickey, 1994).

One wrinkle in assessing the efficiency of stare decisis is that the Supreme Court always possesses the power to overrule its past decisions. Abiding by precedent is itself the product of a judgment that sometimes follows an elaborate inquiry into the Court's doctrine of stare decisis. The more in-depth the Court's analysis of whether it should depart from precedent, the less efficiency it gains by deferring rather than considering issues afresh.

There is another drag on the efficiency of precedent-based systems, one that arises irrespective of whether precedent is being applied horizontally by the court that issued it or vertically by a court of lower rank. I have been positing situations in which a particular precedent is indisputably relevant to the facts at hand. And, indeed, that is sometimes true. But in other cases, a precedent's relevance will itself be a difficult and contentious issue. That means there must be an initial analysis of whether the precedent applies before issues of overruling are even on the table. To the extent that debates over a precedent's scope of applicability are challenging and time-consuming, the efficiency savings of precedent-based judging are reduced.

A powerful argument remains that deference to precedent creates some resource savings at all levels of the judiciary. Forcing courts to start from scratch in every case would be a significant burden, and forcing litigants to cover every issue would be costly. Even so, we should keep in mind that a system of precedent creates some demands of its own as judges endeavor to understand and apply the governing principles of stare decisis.

Individual Limitations and Collective Wisdom. No judge is infallible. That goes for the judges of past and present alike. Stare decisis responds to this reality by encouraging judges to think about legal reasoning as a collective enterprise that spans generations. The hope, as David Strauss has explained, is to combine "humility about the power of individual reason" with recognition of "the collective wisdom of other people who have tried to solve the same problem." Prior decisions are like natural experiments whose results can inform the decision-making of future judges. What emerges is "a kind of rough common sense" that is "based in experience." Professor Strauss connects this approach with the writings of Edmund Burke, who cautioned against "put[ting] men to live and trade each on his own stock of reason," given that "this stock in each man is small."[18]

Treating precedent with respect is a way of acknowledging our individual limitations and our collective potential. That is all well and good in the abstract. The harder question is whether judges should put the principle into

---

[18] DAVID A. STRAUSS, THE LIVING CONSTITUTION 41 (2010) (quoting EDMUND BURKE, REFLECTIONS ON THE REVOLUTION IN FRANCE 251 (J.C.D. Clark, Stanford University Press, 2001) (1790)).

practice by standing by precedents they believe to be wrong. Some critics charge that to defer to a past decision despite confidence in its wrongness is to abdicate the judge's duty to interpret the law correctly.[19] But this is not the only way to understand the dynamics of deference. An alternative view is that today's judge is within her rights to acknowledge that her well-considered conclusions sometimes may be mistaken.

There is also the possibility that a judge on the verge of blazing a new trail might relent for fear of unforeseeable problems. Far safer, the argument goes, to keep faith with past practice. This is true of the judge who harbors doubts about his conclusions in a particular area of law, even if he believes that, on balance, those conclusions are correct. It may likewise be true of the judge who is confident about the correctness and consequences of his determination. As Deborah Hellman has explained, so long as other judges sometimes make mistakes and misunderstand the effects of their decisions, a judge who is fully confident about her own conclusions might plausibly support deference to precedent as a general rule.[20] The confident judge occasionally may need to endure precedents she views as problematic, but the legal system will benefit if the practice of deferring to precedent leads to fewer errors in the aggregate.

The benefits are compounded to the extent that deferring to established bodies of case law tends to improve legal interpretation by creating a presumption against discarding the accumulated wisdom of past generations. And even short of that improvement, requiring judges to meaningfully engage counterarguments can increase the likelihood that the bases for and implications of selecting one rule instead of another are fully understood.[21]

In influencing the operation of stare decisis, the limitations of individual decision-makers are more resonant in some contexts than others. For example, if a given constitutional rule emerged in a single decision and then fell off the

---

[19] See, e.g., Michael Stokes Paulsen, *The Intrinsically Corrupting Influence of Precedent*, 22 CONST. COMMENT. 289, 290 (2005).

[20] See Deborah Hellman, *An Epistemic Defense of Precedent*, in PRECEDENT IN THE UNITED STATES SUPREME COURT 66–9 (Christopher J. Peters, 2013).

[21] See id. at 73 ("The doctrine of stare decisis provides a built-in structure requiring today's judges to seriously consider alternative viewpoints – at least in those cases in which their view about the correct resolution of a case differs from the view of past judges. It creates an artificial conversation across time and space in which the judge in the precedent case gets to play 'devil's advocate,' challenging the judgment and intuitions of the judge in the case under consideration."). Of course, a good judge will always consider opposing viewpoints. But as Professor Hellman notes, "a realistic appraisal of human behavior tells us that we tend to be overly confident in our own views and to dismiss too easily the conclusions of those with whom we disagree. If this is right, then from a systemic perspective, we would do well to force decision-makers to take opposing views seriously." Id. Stare decisis serves that function.

judicial agenda for decades, we might doubt whether the court that issued the decision was any more likely to be correct than today's judges, who are reviewing the issue afresh. By contrast, if a decision has been reaffirmed by numerous judges across multiple cases, we might be more inclined to think deference is appropriate. There is good reason to draw distinctions such as these if deference to precedent is grounded in beliefs about individual limitations and the collective wisdom of the ages.

Uniformity. Judges often note the value of treating like cases alike.[22] Part of that value relates to the sense of injustice a person can experience when others receive more favorable treatment in similar situations. Another part stems from the principle that courts must decide cases based on overarching legal principles rather than the characteristics of the parties before them. Deference to precedent helps to ensure that people in comparable circumstances will receive equivalent treatment under the law. Principled consistency across cases may also enhance a court's credibility, and with it the status of the judiciary as a steady, impersonal institution.[23]

While treating like cases alike can promote consistency and equality, it also raises concerns. For one thing, if a prior decision was incorrect or unjust, replicating that decision exacerbates the problem.[24] For another, the comfort of knowing you will be treated consistently with past litigants can be offset by the frustration of having a good argument rejected because today's judges are wary of upending settled law. Finally, determining whether two cases are alike can be complex and controversial. Without a workable set of rules for explaining when cases are alike and when they are different, there is a danger that appeals to precedent might be perceived as exercises in rhetoric rather than articulations of established principles.

Notwithstanding these concerns, the value of consistency remains a prominent justification for deferring to precedent.[25] Few would contend that doubling down on a serious injustice is something to applaud. Yet there is value in separating legal principles from the personal characteristics of parties and causes. Deference to precedent keeps that distinction intact. Following precedent demonstrates that legal rules can endure even as parties change.

These benefits can arise even in cases of first impression, when there is no applicable precedent on the books. Operating within a precedent-based system encourages judges to treat each case as emblematic of something larger.

---

[22] *See, e.g.,* Pepper v. United States, 562 U.S. 476, 510 (2011) (Breyer, J., concurring in part and concurring in the judgment); Martin v. Franklin Capital Corp., 546 U.S. 132, 139 (2005).
[23] *See* Frederick Schauer, *Precedent*, 39 STAN. L. REV. 571, 600 (1987).
[24] *See* Larry Alexander, *Constrained by Precedent*, 63 SOUTHERN CAL. L. REV. 1, 11 (1989).
[25] *See, e.g.,* Michigan v. Bay Mills Indian Community, 134 S. Ct. 2024, 2036 (2014).

Precedent "raises the stakes" by shifting the focus away from "the merits of the litigants as individuals" and toward "the merits of the underlying legal question to be decided."[26] Awareness that a decision will serve as a precedent in future cases can encourage judges to treat individual disputes as recurring problems that require generalizable solutions.[27] Though it is possible for judges to adopt this mentality irrespective of whether future decision-makers treat past decisions with presumptive respect,[28] the mentality is promoted by widespread commitment to stare decisis as an important norm.

Impersonality and Constraint. So far I have emphasized consistency from the standpoint of the parties to litigation: Similarly situated parties should be treated alike. Who you are should not affect the legal protections you receive.

A distinct type of consistency relates to the resolution of similar issues by different judges. Shared fidelity to Supreme Court decisions reduces opportunities for lower-court judges to reach divergent conclusions based on their individual philosophies. Even if a federal judge in California and a federal judge in New York have competing views about the best interpretation of a constitutional provision, their disagreement is beside the point when the Supreme Court has already spoken. Precedent unifies the judiciary, making judge-specific characteristics less salient in determining legal rights.

When the Supreme Court confronts its own past decisions, consistency arises in another way. Instead of uniting judges across regions, horizontal precedent works to unite the justices across time. A case comes out the same way today as it did ten or twenty or fifty years ago, despite the fact that the justices who issued the opinion have been replaced in the meantime. This feature is implicit in the Court's descriptions of precedent as facilitating "impersonal and reasoned judgments"[29] and contributing to a system in which "bedrock principles are founded in the law rather than in the proclivities of individuals."[30] To follow the decisions of one's predecessors is to embrace

---

[26] Geoffrey R. Stone, *Precedent, the Amendment Process, and Evolution in Constitutional Doctrine*, 11 HARV. J. L. & PUB. POL'Y 67, 70 (1988).

[27] For a different take, see Adrian Vermeule, *Veil of Ignorance Rules in Constitutional Law*, 111 YALE L. J. 399, 416–7 (2001) (noting the argument that "interpreters will reason impartially if they anticipate that the decision may be invoked in future cases whose valence in terms of the decisionmakers' future interests is unpredictable," but responding that "it is hardly clear that durability successfully dampens decisionmakers' self-interest").

[28] *Cf.* Jeremy Waldron, *Stare Decisis and the Rule of Law: A Layered Approach*, 111 MICH. L. REV. 1, 20 (2012) (arguing that the rule of law requires a judge "to derive her particular decisions from an identified and articulated general norm," and noting that this obligation would persist "[e]ven if she knew that no one would follow her").

[29] Moragne v. States Marine Lines, Inc., 398 U.S. 375, 403 (1970).

[30] Vasquez v. Hillery, 474 U.S. 254, 265 (1986).

"a conception of a court continuing over time."[31] By deferring to precedent, a justice highlights her membership in a larger institution that predates her and that will continue long after she is gone.

Fidelity to precedent ensures that the law is not reduced to the preferences and personalities of a particular group of justices assembled at a particular moment in time. This is another way of saying the *rule of law* prevails over the rule of men and women. Stare decisis is especially valuable when a court is marked by deep philosophical disagreements among its members. The Supreme Court is a paradigmatic example. Though interpretive disputes abound, the justices' fidelity to precedent "moderates ideological swings and thus preserves both the appearance and the reality of the Court as a legal rather than a purely political institution."[32] Calendar pages turn and political winds shift, but the law is still the law.

Constraint via prior decisions pushes back against the exercise of "an arbitrary discretion"[33] and the resolution of disputes according to a judge's "private sentiments."[34] Precedents stand in the way of a judge's inclination, even a good-faith and reasonable inclination, to refashion the law in the manner she thinks best. Stare decisis reinforces the principle that all government officials, including judges, are bound by rules.

Constraints work best when the public knows about them and can insist on compliance. That is why it is so important for a precedent-based system to ensure that judicial decisions are widely accessible. It is possible to imagine a Supreme Court that keeps all its opinions secret while going to great lengths to respect precedent in its internal deliberations. Even so, the constraining effect of precedent is likely to be more potent if the community of judges, lawyers, and private citizens is brought into the mix. When precedents are publicly accessible, there is a "basis of legal accountability for the power" that judges exercise.[35] Publicity exerts a disciplining function by increasing the chances that judges will be called upon to explain why they have chosen to depart from precedent. It also provides judges with opportunities to demonstrate that their discretion is limited and that their legal interpretations are not the same as their ideological or philosophical preferences.

Fidelity to precedent is not the only path to constraint. Judges can also be constrained by enacted law, such as statutes and constitutional provisions.

[31] Michael C. Dorf, *Prediction and the Rule of Law*, 42 U.C.L.A. L. Rev. 651, 683 (1995).
[32] *See* Stone, *Precedent, the Amendment Process, and Evolution in Constitutional Doctrine*, *supra* note 26, at 70.
[33] The Federalist No. 78 (Alexander Hamilton).
[34] Blackstone, Commentaries on the Laws of England, *supra* note 1, at *69.
[35] *See* Waldron, *Stare Decisis and the Rule of Law*, *supra* note 28, at 3.

But consulting those sorts of provisions is not always enough to resolve a dispute. The language at issue may be vague or ambiguous, or the concepts may be defined at a high level of generality – think "freedom of speech" or "equal protection of the laws" – which leaves multiple options on the table. Precedent is a way to fill the gaps. It can constrain a judge's discretion where enacted law leaves off.

Mechanisms of constraint are clearest when a judge is dealing with the decisions of a superior court. If the judge disregards those decisions, she faces the prospect of reversal. By contrast, when a court is dealing with its own past decisions, there is no threat of judicial reversal. The Supreme Court might choose to follow its precedents or it might choose to overrule them, but in neither event will its decision be overturned by a superior tribunal. How, then, can the Court's precedents be said to constrain it?

There are a few possible answers to this question. At the outset, it is worth noting that while the Supreme Court cannot be reversed for paying scarce attention to precedent, neither can it be reversed for paying scarce attention to the text of a statute or constitutional provision. One might respond that although impeaching a justice based on her treatment of statutes or constitutional provisions currently seems close to unthinkable, an impeachment on those grounds is still easier to imagine than an impeachment for disavowing the Court's prior decisions. That is true enough. Yet it seems underwhelming to argue that the constraining force of enacted text comes from the threat of impeachment being nearly unthinkable as opposed to entirely unthinkable.

The reality is that the impeachment power is neither the only nor the most important check on Supreme Court discretion. The more meaningful sources of constraint begin with each justice's conscience. If a justice believes sound interpretation of the Constitution entails scrupulous fidelity to its original meaning, the document's original meaning can constrain her. If she believes her role sometimes requires her to adapt constitutional principles to keep pace with contemporary mores, those mores can constrain her. And if she believes the proper discharge of her duties occasionally demands that she uphold her predecessors' decisions despite her disagreement, those decisions can constrain her, too.

There are external constraints as well. They begin with the justices' explanations of their decisions in written opinions. Judges within a precedent-based system face a heightened burden of explaining themselves when they break from settled law.[36] Overturning precedent without good reason risks subjecting

---

[36] See Duxbury, The Nature and Authority of Precedent, *supra* note 4, at 21 (arguing that "[w]hen judges follow precedents they do so not because they fear the imposition of a sanction, but because precedent-following is regarded among them as correct practice, as a norm,

a court's decisions to criticism for being outcome-oriented or ad hoc. Hasty or ill-explained overrulings might lead to "a diminution in esteem within the legal profession, if not in the eyes of the broader public."[37] What is more, if an individual justice insists on disregarding precedent even as her colleagues defer, she may find herself without "the privilege of speaking authoritatively" for the Court by writing majority opinions.[38]

I have been talking about constraint in terms of a prior decision's insulation from overruling. This is a matter of precedential strength. But the value of constraint is also intertwined with a precedent's scope of applicability. If precedents are too malleable, such that later courts have sweeping discretion to define the precedents' contours, the notion of constraint becomes illusory.

Defining the scope of precedent can be complicated and contested. But these challenges need not turn precedents into Rorschach tests in which judges can glimpse whatever they wish. Sometimes a precedent clearly applies to the facts at hand, and any efforts at distinguishing it will be unpersuasive. Frederick Schauer puts the point nicely when he explains that "[p]recedent rests on similarity, and some determinations of similarity are incontestable within particular cultures or subcultures." Similarity thus provides another source of constraint: "If the available characterizations constitute a closed and often rather limited set, requiring a decisionmaker to follow some earlier result can substantially affect decisions."[39] A legal system can bolster this effect by articulating rules to define a precedent's scope of applicability. Those rules can both guide the efforts of future judges and make any deviations apparent to interested onlookers. The clearer our rules for defining a prior decision's lessons for future cases, the more constraint a system of precedent can provide.

Irrespective of how the scope of precedent is defined, being constrained does not mean deferring in every instance. It may be true that repudiating certain principles, such as the lawfulness of paper money, would test the Court's ability to have its decisions accepted and implemented. But in most cases the Court can overrule precedent without creating a meaningful risk of official opposition. The real question is how often the Court can depart from

---

deviation from which is likely to be viewed negatively"); id. at 165 ("Precedent, particularly accumulated precedent, can place a significant justificatory burden on those minded to decide differently on the same facts.").

[37] Richard H. Fallon, Jr., *Constitutional Constraints*, 97 CAL. L. REV. 975, 1000 (2009).
[38] Id. at 1022.
[39] Schauer, *Precedent*, supra note 23, at 587; see also DUXBURY, THE NATURE AND AUTHORITY OF PRECEDENT, supra note 4, at 114.

precedent while maintaining a body of constitutional law that is essentially stable and impersonal.[40]

Common Ground. Precedent furnishes common ground among justices who disagree about the best way to interpret the Constitution. The Supreme Court fills out the constitutional framework by resolving disputes and issuing opinions. It provides guidance for future courts and for those who live under the law, making norms "thicker" and rules of conduct clearer.[41] It also provides a basis for coordinated action going forward. Two justices might part ways over the best reading of a constitutional provision, but they might nevertheless agree that (at least in some cases) it is acceptable to leave matters settled by reaffirming precedent. In doing so, they follow "norms that favor leaving existing arrangements intact if they seem satisfactory, even if they are not optimal, especially if unsettling those arrangements could be costly."[42] This is not only a benefit to the justices. It is a benefit to the legal system as a whole. If too much were up for grabs – if, for example, constitutional principles were in constant flux based on the interpretive philosophies of a majority of Supreme Court justices at any given time – the law would be less comprehensible and predictable. Stare decisis provides unity to the law.

Precedent is not the only, or even the most obvious, source of common ground in constitutional disputes. That honor goes to the Constitution's text, which furnishes the justices (and everyone else) with shared commitments and common purposes that transcend individual theories of interpretation. But the constitutional text is, by design, too sparse and abstract to resolve every case and controversy. There must be something else to flesh out the document's implications for a complex society. That is where judicial opinions come in. They transform broad principles into concrete applications and shape what the Constitution means in practical terms.

Cooperation is particularly important for multimember institutions like the Supreme Court. The Court generally decides cases as a body by majority vote. Yet the justices often disagree. Sometimes their disagreements arise from divergent applications of a common methodology, as when two justices view the historical evidence as pointing toward different understandings of a constitutional provision's original meaning. In other cases the disagreement reflects

---

[40] *Cf.* Richard H. Fallon, Jr., *Constitutional Precedent Viewed through the Lens of Hartian Positivist Jurisprudence*, 86 N.C. L. Rev. 1107, 1156 (2008) (arguing that Supreme Court justices "feel constrained from overturning too many past decisions . . . by an apprehension that the public would find too much instability in constitutional law to be unacceptable").

[41] Thomas W. Merrill, *The Conservative Case for Precedent*, 31 Harv. J. L. & Pub. Pol'y 977, 980 (2008).

[42] David A. Strauss, *Foreword: Does the Constitution Mean What It Says?*, 129 Harv. L. Rev. 1, 55 (2015).

competing interpretive methodologies. Whatever the source of the impasse, precedent provides a path forward. Justices who cannot agree on a first-order question of constitutional interpretation may be able to agree on a second-order commitment to precedent.[43]

Part of precedent's appeal as a unifying force is its neutrality.[44] Some precedents point in favor of outcomes that are ideologically liberal, while others support outcomes that are ideologically conservative. Some emphasize the Constitution's original meaning, while others give original meaning little role to play. Some reflect fairly explicit judgments about morality, while others treat such judgments as peripheral or even out of bounds. The embrace of stare decisis transcends methodological and normative premises. And the neutrality of the doctrine is underscored by looking to the future. In thinking about the path of precedent going forward, today's justices are faced with something akin to a Rawlsian veil of ignorance, not knowing which way future precedents will tend to lean.[45] Adherence to a system of stare decisis will insulate some bad decisions (however "bad" is defined) as well as the good ones.

A commitment to stare decisis is a commitment to what has come before, regardless of the ideological valence of its result or the methodological cast of its rationale. Stare decisis does not ask the living constitutionalist to forsake her theory in favor of original-meaning textualism, nor does it ask the originalist to soften her resistance to morality and practical effects as components of constitutional interpretation. Instead, the doctrine asks justices to defer to existing law, whatever the principles and preferences it might reflect in a given situation, precisely because it is existing law.

A multimember court does not strictly need to find common ground in order to go about its business. Supreme Court justices can choose to publish individual concurrences and dissents irrespective of the positions taken by their colleagues. As disagreements become more pervasive, the justices can simply issue more concurrences and partial dissents.

The virtues and vices of separate opinions have garnered scholarly attention for decades, and thoughtful commentators have lined up on both sides of the issue.[46] For present purposes, I wish to isolate one component of the debate to

---

[43] See RICHARD H. FALLON, JR., IMPLEMENTING THE CONSTITUTION 103 (2001) ("The phenomenon of reasonable disagreement provides a potent reason for maintaining a principle of stare decisis in constitutional adjudication.").

[44] Cf. John Harrison, The Power of Congress over the Rules of Precedent, 50 DUKE L. J. 503, 540 (2000).

[45] Cf. JOHN RAWLS, A THEORY OF JUSTICE 11 (1971).

[46] Compare David L. Shapiro, In Defense of Judicial Candor, 100 HARV. L. REV. 731, 743 (1987), with Henry Paul Monaghan, Stare Decisis and Constitutional Adjudication, 88 COLUM. L. REV. 723, 755 n.184 (1988).

highlight its implications for stare decisis. Whatever their benefits, fractured decisions can impair the ability of lower courts, lawyers, and other citizens to understand the law and plan their actions with confidence. Some might view these effects as antithetical to a core purpose of law, but one need not go so far in order to conclude that coordinated and internally coherent judicial decisions offer benefits that fractured opinions cannot match. Richard Fallon puts the point nicely: "Apart from being truth tellers, the Justices have an obligation to produce clear, workable law. In service of this aim, they must sometimes accommodate each other's views in order to produce 'opinions of the Court' instead of a collection of individual essays."[47] If a Supreme Court justice accepts this rationale as justifying the general practice of seeking coordination in judicial decision-making, the question is not whether to look for common ground, but where to find it. Precedent is part of the answer.

One might respond that there is no need to resort to precedent, because the Constitution's original meaning fleshes out the implications of its text. Original meanings, the argument goes, are a ready source of common ground that can guide our understandings of constitutional law. The interplay between stare decisis and originalism is important, and I will return to it repeatedly in the chapters ahead. At this stage in our analysis, the issue is not whether precedent is the best option for furnishing common ground among legal decision-makers. The point is simply that precedent is one such option. The role of precedent in promoting predictability and facilitating coordinated action is another potential reason why a legal system might commit itself to a meaningful doctrine of stare decisis.

Reliance. The Supreme Court's discussions of precedent commonly address the reliance of those who took actions and made plans based on the existing legal regime. A prominent rationale for deferring to precedent is protecting the "legitimate expectations of those who live under the law."[48] If precedents are too unsteady, it becomes difficult for parties to organize their affairs and for lawyers to offer sound guidance. That is why the Court considers the "cost of a rule's repudiation as it would fall on those who have relied reasonably on the rule's continued application" before it overrules a decision.[49] Reliance is not always enough to prevent an overruling, but it is a "significant reason to adhere" to precedent.[50]

---

[47] FALLON, IMPLEMENTING THE CONSTITUTION, *supra* note 43, at 4–5.
[48] Hubbard v. United States, 514 U.S. 695, 716 (1995) (Scalia, J., concurring in part and concurring in the judgment); *see also* ANTONIN SCALIA & BRYAN A. GARNER, READING LAW: THE INTERPRETATION OF LEGAL TEXTS 412 (2012).
[49] *Casey*, 505 U.S. at 855.
[50] Leegin Creative Leather Products, Inc. v. PSKS, Inc., 551 U.S. 877, 906 (2007).

The underlying premise is that when the Court issues an opinion, people modify their behaviors in response. This applies to commercial activities like the formation of contracts, the allocation of investments, and the organization of business operations. It also applies to actions within the government, such as a legislature's effort to write a statute that complies with constitutional limits. And even people who do not take discrete action based on a judicial opinion might draw on that opinion to inform their understandings about the content of the law.

The flip side is that judicial reversals are disruptive by nature. After an overruling, commercial arrangements that once seemed ingenious can be undermined. Hard-fought and extensively researched legislation can be invalidated, with the law-makers sent back to the drawing board for another sapping of public resources. Widespread understandings about the legal backdrop can be challenged, sometimes marginally and sometimes substantially. By deferring to its past decisions, the Court can limit these disturbances.

While the importance of reliance is established in the Court's cases, its role in particular disputes can be divisive. One area of uncertainty is the amount of evidence needed to prove a precedent's effects on reliance expectations.[51] There is also controversy surrounding the types of reliance that are relevant to the overruling calculus. As I explained in Chapter 1, the justices pay attention to tangible activities such as forming a contract or setting up a business. More debatable is whether the Court should also take note of widespread social understandings that would need to be revised following an overruling. I take up these issues in Chapter 6. For now, I merely observe that notwithstanding the points of contention, the Court has left no doubt that, as a general matter, reliance on precedent is worthy of protection.[52]

Though it is undeniable that reliance is a component of the Supreme Court's inquiry into stare decisis, it is worth asking whether that ought to be the case. There is a plausible argument that reliance on a flawed precedent should be treated as a calculated risk. The Court has made clear that all precedents are potentially subject to reconsideration, whether or not they have led to substantial reliance; fidelity to precedent is not an "inexorable command."[53] Sometimes the Court goes to great lengths to emphasize just how vulnerable its past decisions can be. A good example is *Payne v. Tennessee* (1991), which characterized overrulings as a familiar feature of Supreme Court practice: "[T]he Court has during the past 20 Terms overruled in whole or in part 33 of

---

[51] *See, e.g.,* Quill Corp. v. North Dakota, 504 U.S. 298, 331–2 (1992) (White, J., concurring in part and dissenting in part).

[52] *See, e.g.,* Montejo v. Louisiana, 556 U.S. 778, 792–3 (2009).

[53] *Payne,* 501 U.S. at 828.

its previous constitutional decisions."[54] Deference to precedent is important, the Court explained, but it is not absolute.

That recognition carries potential implications for the relationship between precedent and reliance. The Court has been clear about the defeasibility of precedent. It has rejected any claim that deference to precedent is an unyielding requirement, and it has acted on that understanding by overruling some of its past decisions. Given the Court's words and actions, one might conclude that people should not rely whole-heartedly on the continuing vitality of its prior decisions. Instead, they should take precautions to protect themselves in case the Court changes its mind.[55] If we assume people are taking their own precautions against legal change – or making calculated decisions to roll the dice – maybe the Court can forget about reliance when it is considering whether to overrule a past decision. The Court has reserved the option to overrule itself. How could the exercise of that option subvert anyone's reasonable expectations?

The Court apparently has rejected this unforgiving approach to reliance, though it has not explained its position in much detail. Part of the rationale may be that predicting the path of the law is so difficult that it would be unfair to punish people for making bad bets. Another part may flow from the premise that stability and continuity are crucial to a well-functioning legal system. The costs of uncertainty and vacillation cannot be avoided through public notice that all laws are subject to change. Even if the legal system's architects disclaim any fidelity to the past, frequent overhaul at the expense of settled expectations would undermine the stable core that the rule of law requires. Overrulings also create transition costs that are (all else being equal) in society's best interest to avoid. That is an additional reason why judges might be willing to stand by precedents whose repudiation would cause significant disruption.

The common theme among these defenses of the reliance inquiry is that while accurate interpretation of the Constitution is a central goal of the judicial branch, the pursuit of accuracy can carry severe costs when prior decisions have come out the other way. Focusing on reliance helps to identify the precedents that would be most disruptive to overrule – which is to say, the precedents that carry the highest price of correction.

---

[54] Id.
[55] Cf. Louis Kaplow, *An Economic Analysis of Legal Transitions*, 99 HARV. L. REV. 509, 525–6 (1986) ("Perceptive investors will typically act on probability estimates of possible changes in the legal regime, just as they will take into account the probabilities of changes in relevant market conditions . . ."); Michael Stokes Paulsen, *Abrogating Stare Decisis by Statute: May Congress Remove the Precedential Effect of Roe and Casey?*, 109 YALE L. J. 1535, 1554 (2000) ("Rational actors should rely on a decision's remaining the rule only to the extent that it can be predicted that the courts will adhere to the decision as correct.").

THE CASE AGAINST PRECEDENT

Having examined leading justifications for deferring to precedent, we turn now to the other side of the ledger. While my discussion of the arguments against deference will be briefer than the foregoing discussion of the arguments in precedent's favor, this should not be taken to imply anything about the weight of the respective positions. The reason why we can be briefer in stating the case against stare decisis is because its central plank is so forceful and clear: The job of judges is to interpret the law correctly.

Error, Unsoundness, and Injustice. Deferring to precedent can lead a judge to get the law wrong. As the Supreme Court recently noted in *Kimble v. Marvel Entertainment* (2015), "Respecting *stare decisis* means sticking to some wrong decisions."[56] *Kimble* was a statutory case, but the principle is general. In the context of constitutional law, the concern is that stare decisis "would have judges apply, in preference to the Constitution, that which is not consistent with the Constitution."[57]

The judge who defers to precedent may end up standing by a decision she views as having been misguided from the outset. Or the deferring judge might find herself compelled to ignore the lessons of experience in order to keep faith with the past. Neil Duxbury provides a vivid illustration of this latter point in explaining how arguments from precedent and arguments from experience can come into conflict:

> When my youngest daughter made her case for my buying her a mobile phone on her eleventh birthday, she reasoned from precedent: her elder sister received a mobile phone for her eleventh birthday. When I refused to buy my youngest daughter a mobile phone on her eleventh birthday, I reasoned from the experience of her sister's inability to be a responsible mobile-phone owner at the age of eleven.[58]

Abiding by precedent sometimes means continuing down a path that one suspects, based on experience, is likely to yield poor results. It can also mean tolerating the fruits of an interpretive approach – be it originalism, living constitutionalism, or otherwise – that one believes is faulty or misguided.

These are serious costs, and they go a long way toward explaining some challenges to stare decisis. The mobile phone example shows the pervasiveness of the problem, which extends beyond the law to other modes of

---

[56] 135 S. Ct. 2401, 2409.
[57] Paulsen, *The Intrinsically Corrupting Influence of Precedent*, supra note 19, at 291.
[58] Duxbury, The Nature and Authority of Precedent, supra note 4, at 2.

decision-making. But the mundaneness of that illustration stands in contrast to the stakes of modern constitutional law.

When the Supreme Court issued its recent decisions on corporate electioneering and same-sex relationships, its rulings were made possible only by its determination that settled law must yield.[59] By contrast, the Court suggested that the famous warnings set forth in *Miranda v. Arizona* (1966), which define the rules of engagement between police officers and arrestees, might not have remained law but for the doctrine of stare decisis.[60] And when the Court reaffirmed the central holding of *Roe v. Wade* (1973), it left open the possibility that some members of the majority may have harbored doubts about *Roe* on the merits.[61] Whether or not decisions like *Miranda* or *Roe* were correct as an initial matter, the Court's references to stare decisis in the course of reaffirming them highlight the potential costs of deference. If the Court declines to overrule an erroneous constitutional decision, it reinforces a separation of the *actual* interpretation of the law from its *proper* interpretation. The effect may be to entrench rights that ought not be entrenched. Or it may be to leave unprotected rights that warrant safeguarding. Erroneous results are validated, and deserving parties turned away, for the preservation of the status quo.

The concern is not just for the substance of particular rules. Misconstruing the Constitution can affect democratic government. Deferring to erroneous precedents risks undermining "the collective judgments that our representatives have authoritatively expressed."[62] Misinterpretation creates a wedge between the law as properly understood and the law as applied. When the Supreme Court declines the opportunity to eliminate the dissonance, the system bears a cost.

Concerns about mistaken interpretations have a procedural dimension as well. When the Court concedes that a precedent is flawed but nevertheless opts to follow it, the losing party may feel the sting of injustice. After all, he could have won his case but for the Court's prior mistake. The implication is similar, though subtler, when the Court stops short of confessing error. For example, the Court might note that a precedent has come under challenge.

[59] See *Citizens United*, 558 U.S. 310; *Lawrence*, 539 U.S. 558.
[60] *Dickerson*, 530 U.S. at 443–4.
[61] See *Casey*, 505 U.S. at 853; *see also* RONALD DWORKIN, FREEDOM'S LAW: THE MORAL READING OF THE AMERICAN CONSTITUTION 124 (1996) ("[W]hatever reservation one or more members of the three-justice group [that authored the lead opinion in *Casey*] might have had about *Roe*'s central holding, if he or she were free to think about the matter on a clean slate, the group was united in thinking that a sound respect for *stare decisis* – the legal tradition that a court ought not lightly to alter its own past decisions – barred any reconsideration of that holding now.").
[62] Caleb Nelson, *Stare Decisis and Demonstrably Erroneous Precedents*, 87 VA. L. REV. 1, 62 (2001).

It might even express doubts about the precedent's soundness. But it might nevertheless decline to offer a definitive conclusion about the precedent, explaining that any doubts are outweighed by the importance of deferring to settled law. Again, the losing party may feel aggrieved, though what he has been denied in this scenario is not the protection of a substantive rule that should work in his favor. Instead, the losing party's complaint is that he was denied resolution of whether his asserted right actually exists. From his perspective, deference to precedent has short-circuited the adjudicative process, leaving a dent in the rule of law. Even if we conclude that deference to precedent provides substantial benefits to the legal system, we must forgive our disappointed litigant for his frustration. It is reasonable to be dismayed when one's arguments are rejected without a full vetting of the merits.[63] There is also a systemic concern: If too much of the legal landscape is covered by unyielding precedents, we might worry about people's ability to agitate effectively for legal change.[64]

Here it is worth reiterating that deference to precedent does not always come at the expense of accurate interpretation. I noted above that the faithful application of constitutional text is sometimes insufficient to resolve a dispute. In those situations, certain justices might believe that proper interpretation requires the invocation of a default rule that, for example, defers to the political branches or prioritizes individual freedom from governmental mandates. But other justices might conclude that the proper rule is stare decisis.

The gulf between deference to precedent and accurate interpretation shrinks further when issues of humility and individual limitations are taken into account. Imagine that the Supreme Court mistakenly concludes that a prior decision is wrong when it is actually right. If the Court defers to the precedent despite its misgivings, its case law will be more accurate than it otherwise would have been. If we generalize this phenomenon and assume that individual judges and justices make mistakes with some regularity, it is at least possible that a practice of precedent-following may enhance the accuracy of law by limiting misguided attempts at innovation.

These considerations of ambiguity and humility are useful reminders that the tension between precedent and accuracy will not always be as pitched as it initially may seem. Even so, it remains true that a robust doctrine of stare decisis will sometimes call upon a justice to tolerate a decision that she believes,

---

[63] *Cf.* Amy Coney Barrett, *Stare Decisis and Due Process*, 74 U. COLO. L. REV. 1011, 1012 (2003) ("[W]hen viewed from the perspective of an individual litigant, stare decisis often functions like the doctrine of issue preclusion – it precludes the relitigation of issues decided in earlier cases.").

[64] *See* Jeremy Waldron, *The Concept and the Rule of Law*, 43 GA. L. REV. 1, 7–9 (2008).

confidently and accurately, to be incorrect. Acknowledging the costs of error is vital to analyzing a system of precedent.

Overreaching. A system of precedent can create benefits even in cases of first impression. The knowledge that decisions will be relevant to future disputes can encourage judges to employ general principles that contribute to an impersonal rule of law.[65] But the effects are not all to the good. Some judges might be inclined to overreach in drafting their opinions, in hopes of affecting as much of the legal landscape as they can. While this impulse may exist even without a system of precedent, it is amplified when judges know prior decisions receive presumptive deference precisely because they came first. To the extent one sees virtue in restrained judging, a powerful doctrine of precedent may create some troubling incentives.

This concern is significant, but there are ways to address it. The first is the principle of judicial restraint. In interpreting statutes and constitutional provisions, the restrained judge generally leaves innovation to the people and their representatives.[66] In cases of first impression, restraint entails resolving a case without sweeping more broadly than is necessary. Such a mentality will have a narrowing effect on the crafting of opinions. The more general point is that stare decisis does not work alone. It is part of a set of tools that combine to define the judicial role.

A second check against overreaching comes from the fact that every precedent must be interpreted by future courts. If judges construe precedents narrowly, overreaching is less of a concern, and courts will be limited in their ability to issue sweeping proclamations. Those limitations soften when future judges interpret precedents broadly. As the scope of precedent widens, so too does the authority of courts in cases of first impression. Within a precedent-based system, the question becomes how to promote benefits of continuity and impersonality without giving earlier judges too much power to bind their successors. By focusing on tomorrow, the rules of precedent influence what happens today.

A WORD ABOUT LEGITIMACY

Scrutinizing the costs and benefits of deference is beside the point if stare decisis is unlawful. Some commentators have taken this position, describing stare decisis as illegitimate in constitutional cases. The core of their argument

---

[65] *See generally* Waldron, *Stare Decisis and the Rule of Law, supra* note 28.
[66] *Cf.* Thomas B. Colby, *The Sacrifice of the New Originalism,* 99 GEO. L. J. 713, 751 (2011) (distinguishing between judicial restraint, which entails "deference to legislative majorities," and judicial constraint, which is a tool "to narrow the discretion of judges").

is that if a Supreme Court decision misinterprets the Constitution, future justices are not authorized to reaffirm it. To do so would be to elevate the Court's pronouncements over the Constitution itself. There is no room to consider the disruptiveness of overruling or the implications for stability and impersonality. The justices must do as the Constitution instructs.

This is a provocative argument, and versions of it have been skillfully developed by scholars such as Gary Lawson, Michael Paulsen, and Randy Barnett.[67] So far the courts have been unreceptive. The Supreme Court regularly emphasizes the importance of abiding by its constitutional decisions absent a special justification for changing direction. When dissenting justices take issue with the treatment of precedent in a particular case, they do not question the legitimacy of stare decisis as a general matter.

The commentators who challenge the lawfulness of stare decisis do not dispute any of this. Their point is that the justices are wrong about the legitimacy of deference to erroneous constitutional precedents. The project of this book is different. It is to examine the role of precedent in modern constitutional law. In pursuing that project, I follow the Supreme Court in accepting stare decisis as lawful even in constitutional disputes, and even when it leads a justice to accept a result she does not view as reflecting the best interpretation of the Constitution. Nevertheless, before moving on I wish to sketch a few possible responses to arguments that challenge the legitimacy of constitutional stare decisis.

Judicial Power. The Constitution vests the "judicial Power" of the United States "in one supreme Court, and in such inferior Courts as the Congress may from time to time ordain and establish." If we understand the judicial power in reference to current practice, it seems to include the power to defer to precedent. The Supreme Court commonly invokes precedent even in constitutional cases, and it treats those invocations as not only permissible but indispensable. For commentators such as Richard Fallon who would interpret constitutional text with an eye toward established practice, "Article III's grant of 'the judicial Power' authorizes the Supreme Court to elaborate and rely on a principle of stare decisis and, more generally, to treat precedent as a constituent element of constitutional adjudication."[68] Michael Gerhardt reaches a similar conclusion by emphasizing Article III's extension of the judicial power

---

[67] See generally Randy E. Barnett, *Trumping Precedent with Original Meaning: Not as Radical as It Sounds*, 22 CONST. COMMENT. 257 (2005); Gary Lawson, *The Constitutional Case Against Precedent*, 17 HARV. J. L. & PUB. POL'Y 23 (1994); Paulsen, *The Intrinsically Corrupting Influence of Precedent*, supra note 19.

[68] Richard H. Fallon, Jr., *Stare Decisis and the Constitution: An Essay on Constitutional Methodology*, 76 N.Y.U. L. REV. 570, 577 (2001).

to "Cases" and "Controversies." For him, the "plain implication" is that judicial decisions are "legitimate exercises" of authority that may receive weight in future cases.[69]

Along with Professors Fallon and Gerhardt, a host of other scholars have analyzed the implications of Article III for the role of precedent. Many of their efforts have been historical, focusing on the meaning of the Constitution at the time of the founding. Some scholars contend that Article III's reference to judicial power was originally understood as encompassing some degree of respect for precedent. Others reject that conclusion, denying that deference to precedent has a hook in the original meaning of the Constitution's text. Our present concern is not to take sides in those debates, but simply to note that certain interpretations of the judicial power vested in the federal courts might authorize the doctrine of stare decisis.

Common Law. Even if one thinks the Constitution's text does not expressly authorize deference to precedent, nothing in the Constitution expressly forbids such deference. That leaves the door open for other arguments about the legitimacy of stare decisis. One such argument is that judicial reliance on precedent was an accepted practice around the time of America's founding. While the practice may not have been written into the Constitution, it carried forward as part of the common law background.[70] Caleb Nelson has developed this type of argument in suggesting that the country's founders "may have thought that custom and reason gave interpreters an obligation to follow settled understandings of indeterminate provisions in written laws."[71] John Harrison likewise contends that "[t]he norms of precedent as the federal courts know them consist mainly of unwritten principles that are characterized as binding law but that reflect substantial judicial input, custom, and practice."[72] Scholars such as Michael Rappaport and John McGinnis also emphasize the status of precedent as "an important part of Anglo-American law for centuries before the enactment of the Constitution" and a concept "the Founding generation expected . . . to apply to, and continue after, the Constitution."

---

[69] MICHAEL J. GERHARDT, THE POWER OF PRECEDENT 58–9 (2008). Professor Gerhardt adds another dimension to his textual argument by contending that "[t]he exercise of Article III judicial power entails deliberating over how it ought to be exercised," and that "[d]eciding cases entails determining how much weight to accord to precedent and other sources of constitutional meaning." Id. at 59.

[70] See, e.g., William Baude, *Is Originalism Our Law?*, 115 COLUM. L. REV. 2349, 2359–60 (2015); Stephen E. Sachs, *Constitutional Backdrops*, 80 GEO. WASH. L. REV. 1813, 1865 (2012).

[71] Caleb Nelson, *Originalism and Interpretive Conventions*, 70 U. CHI. L. REV. 519, 552 (2003).

[72] Harrison, *The Power of Congress over the Rules of Precedent*, supra note 44, at 529.

For them, this historical background creates a "strong presumption for interpreting the Constitution in a way that permits precedent."[73]

The depiction of precedent as part of the Constitution's common law background raises a host of complex questions. Among the most important is whether Congress could decide to override the Supreme Court's preferred approach to precedent. That question does not arise in the same way if deference to precedent is understood as hardwired into the Constitution itself. Notwithstanding uncertainties such as these, focusing on the background principles against which the Constitution was enacted is a potential means of explaining how the Supreme Court may legitimately defer to flawed precedents. Treating deference to precedent as an exercise in common law decision-making also coheres with the Court's modern approach to stare decisis, which tends to focus on judicial practice and policy judgments rather than forays into constitutional history.[74]

Individual Limitations and Collective Wisdom, Redux. I have already discussed the argument that precedents embody the collective wisdom of generations. The stock of wisdom in established precedents is a potential reason for deferring to them. On this rationale, judges ought to respect precedent based on the "counsel of humility and the value of experience."[75]

This argument can be recast as suggesting not simply that deference to precedent is sensible, but that it is valid and legitimate. To illustrate, let us go back in time to 2009, when the Supreme Court was considering the constitutional protection of campaign-related speech by corporations. Imagine that after reading the parties' briefs, listening to oral arguments, and researching the issues, a justice determines the First Amendment is best understood as protecting corporate electioneering. Yet the justice also notes that the Court's precedents allow restrictions on campaign-related speech by corporations. In other words, she acknowledges that her predecessors disagreed with her reading of the First Amendment. At this point one might conclude that the justice has an obligation to vote to overrule precedents she views as inconsistent with the Constitution's true meaning.

But let us also assume that our justice makes the reasonable assumption that even her well-considered views are sometimes wrong. In the case at hand, she is confident about her rightness. Then again, so were her predecessors, whom she has now deemed to be mistaken. Mulling over all these considerations,

---

[73] John O. McGinnis & Michael B. Rappaport, Originalism and the Good Constitution 154–5 (2013).

[74] *See Casey*, 505 U.S. at 854.

[75] David A. Strauss, *Common Law Constitutional Interpretation*, 63 U. Chi. L. Rev. 877, 879, 902 (1996).

the justice ultimately decides that she will defer to precedent. She still thinks her reading is the better one. Nevertheless, being realistic about the limits of individual reason, and being optimistic about the soundness of collective wisdom, she decides to defer to past practice.

Perhaps what our justice has done is wise, or perhaps it is foolish. The more pressing question for now is whether her action is legitimate. I submit the answer is yes. The justice's obligation is to render decisions according to law. One way to discharge that obligation is by voting in light of her individual understanding of the constitutional provision under consideration. But this is not the only way for her to behave lawfully. In light of her views on individual limitations and collective wisdom, the justice may reason that the law is best served by decision-makers who leave open the possibility of deferring to precedents with which they disagree. This is particularly true if she believes her commitment to precedent will help to establish a broader practice of deference among her judicial colleagues, present and future.[76] At that point, it is not only her own capacity for error she is providing against; it is also the fallibility of her fellow judges. Of course, her predecessors – the judges who issued the relevant precedents – might themselves have been mistaken. But it is permissible for a justice to conclude that in some cases, prior decisions are more likely to reflect accurate interpretations than abrupt changes-of-course favored by a majority of today's Court.[77]

Our justice might temper her deference by voting to overrule under certain circumstances: for example, when important facts have changed or a rule has proved unworkable to administer. She might also hold open the possibility of overruling decisions whose reasoning she thinks is not just wrong but thin and hasty, or whose consequences she perceives as disastrous. Considerations such as these relate to the content of the doctrine of stare decisis. Regardless of how they are handled, they do not affect the threshold issue of whether it is legitimate to defer to a constitutional decision despite one's conclusion that it is probably wrong on the merits.

Common Ground, Redux. As I explained above, deferring to past decisions is a way for judges to come together, notwithstanding their different theories about how the Constitution should be interpreted. The need for coordinated action among differently minded justices also furnishes another argument in favor of the legitimacy of constitutional stare decisis. To speak with one voice,

---

[76] *Cf.* Hellman, *An Epistemic Defense of Precedent, supra* note 20, at 68 ("The individual judge has good reason to accord weight to (or follow) precedent if that is what the norms of judicial decisionmaking dictate within our system, whether or not deference to precedent is justified for epistemic reasons or any other reasons.").

[77] *See id.* at 74–5; Strauss, The Living Constitution, *supra* note 18, at 41–2.

a multimember court must have mechanisms for overcoming disagreement. In some cases the Constitution's plain text will serve this role. The document leaves no doubt that the Senate includes two members from every state and the president must be at least thirty-five years old. In many other cases the Constitution's text gives rise to serious disagreements. What is meant by open-ended phrases like "cruel and unusual punishments"? Does the concept of "due process of law" refer only to procedural protections, or does it also include some substantive rights – and, if the latter, where do we find those rights? The disputes are familiar and legion.

One reaction to textual uncertainty is for every justice to vote for the reading she thinks is best in light of her own interpretive theory. But some justices might view this individualistic conception as undermining the Court's coherence as a unified institution. In response, they might seek mechanisms that can draw together jurists who disagree about first principles. Precedent is one such measure, and it gives rise to the argument that stare decisis is legitimized by the Court's need for coordinated action. A justice may adapt her individual approach to the reality that she is one among many.

Structural Inference. A final argument for the legitimacy of stare decisis involves the implications of judicial discretion. Deference to precedent is justified as an effective way to guide the action of federal judges who are asked to interpret a document that is often uncertain and who are insulated from official and electoral control.

The argument begins with the Constitution's structure, which makes judicial power distinct from the authority exercised by legislative and executive actors. This separation suggests a vision of judges as engaged in a different style of decision-making than their political peers. The same understanding is reinforced by Article III's description of the judicial power as extending to discrete cases and controversies. Unlike the political branches, which lead the polity forward, the judiciary is designed to react. To draw on Alexander Hamilton's famous depiction, the courts' prerogative is not to mimic the legislature by searching for social problems in need of resolution or "prescrib[ing] the rules by which the duties and rights of every citizen are to be regulated." Nor is it to mimic the executive by "hold[ing] the sword of the community."[78] The judiciary is meant to answer questions that are posed to it.

The distinctiveness of judicial power is underscored by the independence of federal judges. Article III provides that judges "shall hold their Offices during good Behaviour." The article also prevents reductions in judges' pay. The combined effect is to protect what Chief Justice Roberts has called "the

---

[78] THE FEDERALIST No. 78 (Alexander Hamilton).

constitutional birthright of Article III judges" to resolve cases without political interference.[79] That includes official pressure of the sort that might be applied by the legislative and executive branches. It likewise includes electoral pressure exerted by the people casting their ballots. In its design of the legislative and executive branches, the Constitution emphasizes the role of political accountability and periodic reconsideration. Legislative officials stand for regular reelection. The president does, too. The nature of the judiciary is different. It is defined by durability and constancy rather than accountability and change.

Independence is a double-edged sword. A court that is not bound by politics invites questions as to what it *is* bound by.[80] The obvious answer is the Constitution's text. While the document sometimes speaks in specific terms, and while it always takes certain options off the table, at many points it is too vague or ambiguous to fully resolve a contested question. The doctrine of stare decisis responds by enlisting precedent as a tool of constraint. Even as federal judges and justices enjoy insulation from official and electoral pressures, stare decisis gives effect to general, publicly accessible principles that emerged in prior decisions. Precedent supplements the constitutional framework by preventing judicial independence from turning into unchecked discretion. It fends off the "arbitrary discretion" that might otherwise prevail when life-tenured judges are asked to apply a charter containing numerous areas of uncertainty.[81]

This has been a brief and preliminary overview of some possibilities for defending the legitimacy of stare decisis. A comprehensive analysis of the issue would fill the remainder of this book. But while the legitimacy of deference is an important and fascinating issue, it is not in serious dispute at the modern Supreme Court. The more pressing questions deal with the manner in which precedents are understood and applied. I turn now to those questions, beginning with what it takes to overrule a precedent that stands in the way of getting the law right.

---

[79] Wellness International Network, Ltd. v. Sharif, 135 S. Ct. 1932, 1951 (2015) (Roberts, C.J., dissenting) (quoting Plaut v. Spendthrift Farm, Inc., 514 U.S. 211, 219 (1995)).
[80] *See* Adrian Vermeule, Judging Under Uncertainty 238 (2006) ("Life tenure and salary protection liberate the judges to pursue whatever version of constitutionalism they find attractive.").
[81] The Federalist No. 78 (Alexander Hamilton).

3

Strength of Constraint

If the first rule of precedent is that prior decisions warrant respect, a close second is that no decision is untouchable. The Supreme Court has emphasized that deference to precedent is a sound practice rather than an unyielding obligation.[1] But the recognition that precedent is not absolute only gets us so far. We need more details about the strength of the Court's commitment to prior decisions even if those decisions rest on reasoning that is flawed (from the perspective of today's justices, that is).

The Court has not disappointed. On numerous occasions it has discussed the criteria for overcoming the presumption of fidelity to precedent. Its opinions offer an array of factors to inform the choice between retaining or overruling a dubious decision. We will examine those factors in depth in Chapter 6. Before doing so, it is useful to step back and think about precedential strength in more general terms.

I have framed the issue of precedential strength using Justice Brandeis' famous dichotomy between leaving matters settled and getting decisions right. There are always costs to disrupting expectations and replacing a legal rule. There are also costs to leaving a flawed precedent on the books. What I want to emphasize is the complexity that surrounds the question of how problematic a flawed precedent really is. The reasons for this complexity go beyond challenges of calculation. The more fundamental difficulty is that different interpretive theories lead to different conclusions about the types of consequences that are relevant to the stare decisis calculus.

Every theory of interpretation implies choices about which considerations are legally relevant. From some perspectives, constitutional interpretation

---

[1] *See, e.g.*, Citizens United v. FEC, 558 U.S. 310, 377–8 (2010) (Roberts, C.J., concurring) ("[S]*tare decisis* is neither an 'inexorable command' nor 'a mechanical formula of adherence to the latest decision,' especially in constitutional cases . . . [N]one of us has viewed *stare decisis* in such absolute terms.") (citations omitted).

is about finding solutions that are sensible and effective in pragmatic terms. A problematic decision is one that leads to impractical or inefficient outcomes. On other accounts, the pivotal considerations are contemporary notions of fairness and morality, such that decisions are most insidious when they fall dramatically out of step with modern ideals. Still other perspectives emphasize the centrality of popular sovereignty to American law and politics. If a judicial decision stands in the way of self-government, it is a prime candidate for being overruled. The list goes on and on, and the takeaway is always the same: Commitment to any interpretive methodology has crucial implications for the status of precedent. The fact that a judge dislikes a particular statute does not mean the statute is unconstitutional. Likewise, the fact that a judge is bothered by the consequences of a prior decision does not mean those consequences are relevant to whether the decision should be overruled.

If theories of precedent are derivative of broader theories of constitutional interpretation, debates over the durability of precedent collapse into debates about which interpretive approach is best. Once that happens, stare decisis loses the ability to bring together judges of different predilections and to imbue constitutional law with a sense of continuity that transcends interpretive debates. To avoid such a result, I will suggest that the better practice is to shake off the trappings of constitutional theory in pursuing a doctrine of stare decisis that operates independently of any interpretive methodology.

Before rethinking the connection between precedent and interpretive theory, we must bring that connection to the surface. In this chapter, I explore ways in which a judge's preferred methodology of constitutional interpretation can affect her conclusions about the strength of precedent. I also contend that thinking in terms of methodology is only the first step. Different judges can arrive at the same methodology through distinct normative commitments. Those commitments – the underlying choices that explain why someone has adopted a given approach to legal interpretation – play a significant role in defining the relevant costs of judicial error and determining when a precedent should be overruled.[2] My hope is to situate debates over precedential strength within the context of competing interpretive methodologies and the normative commitments that drive them.

---

[2] Generally speaking, I will use *interpretive methodology* to mean a particular procedure for deriving answers to constitutional questions. I will use *interpretive theory* and *interpretive philosophy* to encompass not just questions of methodology, but also underlying normative commitments that lead a judge to a given methodological approach. That said, I do not mean for anything to depend on these labels. The important step is to recognize that methodological commitments and normative commitments work together in constitutional adjudication. Both concepts have implications for the treatment of precedent.

CONSTITUTIONAL INTERPRETATION AND LEGAL RELEVANCE

In exploring the connection between precedent and interpretive methodology, a natural starting point is constitutional originalism. That is because recent years have witnessed an outpouring of scholarship regarding originalism's compatibility with stare decisis. This phenomenon owes in part to the rising profile of originalism as an interpretive approach. It also reflects a response to originalism's critics, some of whom contend that a focus on the Constitution's original meaning is incompatible with wide swaths of the Supreme Court's case law, including heralded decisions like *Brown v. Board of Education* (1954).[3]

As it is commonly understood, originalism encompasses the belief that the meaning of constitutional terms was "determined at the time the text was written and adopted."[4] What exactly that meaning entails, and how it is gleaned, is subject to debate. Some originalists seek to discern the intentions of the Constitution's authors or ratifiers. Others look to the public understanding of the Constitution's text during the framing era. And even those who agree on the proper inquiry can differ about the best way to undertake it.

For the moment, let us put these differences aside and begin with a version of originalism that is especially resistant to constitutional precedent – a version introduced by Chapter 2's discussion of the legitimacy of stare decisis. Gary Lawson asserts that the judiciary's power to invalidate actions of the political branches exists only because the Constitution is "hierarchically superior to all other claimed sources of law."[5] It follows, he contends, that the Supreme Court may not defer to judicial precedents that misinterpret the Constitution. Along with Professor Lawson, Michael Paulsen has articulated a vision of originalism that is at odds with the preservation of judicial mistakes. In Professor Paulsen's words, deferring to flawed constitutional precedents "undermines – even refutes – the premises that are supposed to justify originalism."[6] We might think of these arguments as reflecting a *structural* version of originalism grounded in beliefs about how the structure of American government, as defined by the original meaning of the Constitution's text, affects the nature of judicial decision-making.

For a Supreme Court justice who follows commentators like Professors Lawson and Paulsen in emphasizing the Constitution's superiority to its judicial

---

[3] 347 U.S. 483.
[4] Lawrence B. Solum, *Faith and Fidelity: Originalism and the Possibility of Constitutional Redemption*, 91 TEXAS L. REV. 147, 154 (2012).
[5] Gary Lawson, *The Constitutional Case against Precedent*, 17 HARV. J. L. & PUB. POL'Y 23, 26 (1994).
[6] Michael Stokes Paulsen, *The Intrinsically Corrupting Influence of Precedent*, 22 CONST. COMMENT. 289, 289 (2005).

gloss, the role of precedent is straightforward: Flawed constitutional decisions must be overruled. It makes no difference whether an overruling would be disruptive or whether a precedent has come to enjoy widespread support in the legal community and society at large. To elevate a flawed decision over the Constitution's original meaning is to exceed the Court's lawful authority.

If adherence to mistaken constitutional precedents is illegitimate, no weighing of countervailing considerations is necessary. The flawed precedents must be abandoned and the proper constitutional balance restored. To the structural originalist, the relevant cost of an erroneous precedent is the very fact that it deviates from the Constitution's original meaning. The costliness of such mistakes is always too great to tolerate in the name of preserving the status quo. It makes no difference whether a mistaken precedent involves taxation power, or the freedom of speech, or abortion rights. Every departure from the Constitution's original meaning is in need of correction. The cost of judicial error is constant – and decisive.

Compare the structural originalist position with an interpretive approach that treats the Constitution's meaning as subject to change in light of emerging problems and contemporary norms. That latter approach is often described as *living constitutionalism*. Like originalism, living constitutionalism is a label that covers a variety of approaches, which differ in meaningful ways. Some of the differences relate to matters of technique, and some deal with more foundational issues, such as the optimal pace of legal evolution.

Among the leading advocates of living constitutionalism is David Strauss, who defends a *common law* approach to constitutional interpretation whereby "the requirements of the Constitution evolve over time."[7] Evolution is not the same as revolution, and common law constitutionalism gives significant regard to precedent as a source of collective wisdom and common ground. Yet precedent must yield when it becomes too great an impediment to progress. Deference gives way "[i]f one is quite confident that a practice is wrong – or if one believes, even with less certainty, that it is terribly wrong."[8]

The contrast between common law constitutionalism and structural originalism is stark. Because structural originalism treats all decisions that depart from the Constitution's original meaning as irredeemable, there is no need to distinguish between erroneous precedents to determine which are the most costly. From the perspective of common law constitutionalism, by contrast, distinguishing between flawed precedents is crucial. Some erroneous precedents

---

[7] David A. Strauss, *Legitimacy, "Constitutional Patriotism," and the Common Law Constitution*, 126 HARV. L. REV. FORUM 50, 55 (2013).

[8] David A. Strauss, *Common Law Constitutional Interpretation*, 63 U. CHI. L. REV. 877, 895 (1996).

are indeed too harmful to tolerate, but others should endure. The cost of standing by flawed precedents varies depending on the nature of their mistakes.

Comparing structural originalism with living constitutionalism demonstrates the more general connection between interpretive philosophy and judicial precedent. For adherents of structural originalism, precedents that depart from the Constitution's original meaning must be overruled. By definition, those precedents are too costly to tolerate. That is not true of living constitutionalism. For the common law constitutionalist, whether a flawed precedent should be overruled depends on considerations such as morality and policy. There must be an inquiry into the specific consequences of a given constitutional mistake. Only then can today's judges determine how costly it is for the law to remain settled and how important it is for the law to be right.

In drawing distinctions among flawed decisions, common law constitutionalism reveals itself as more complicated than structural originalism in its relationship with precedent. This is not necessarily a weakness. If one believes precedents occasionally should be preserved despite their flaws, some complexity is to be expected. But the debate between structural originalism and common law constitutionalism need not detain us. The point I wish to highlight is that whatever the precedent under review, the perceived cost of leaving it on the books can vary greatly depending on the interpretive methodology that one adopts. Interpretive methodology determines the relevant costs of enduring a flawed decision.

FROM INTERPRETIVE METHODOLOGY TO NORMATIVE COMMITMENTS

No one is born an originalist. Nor is anyone born a living constitutionalist. A jurist who comes to embrace a particular methodology does so based on an underlying set of normative commitments that guide her approach to the law.

Those normative commitments add another dimension to the interplay between precedent and judicial decision-making. So far I have argued that evaluating the costliness of a flawed precedent requires judges to consult an interpretive methodology to determine which consequences are legally relevant. But a complete understanding of the costs of error must go beyond interpretive methodology. We must also be sensitive to the normative commitments that lead judges to prefer one methodology to another.

Normative commitments are the paths to interpretive methodology. Still, there is no universal set of normative commitments for every methodological approach. Even within a particular school such as originalism or living constitutionalism, differences in normative underpinnings dramatically alter the perceived gravity of constitutional mistakes – and, as a result, the determination whether a dubious precedent ought to be retained.

Return to the example of originalism. I already described a version of structural originalism that emphasizes the Constitution's hierarchical superiority to, among other things, judicial precedents. But there is more than one way to be an originalist. Some proponents of originalism look to other values to justify their methodological choice. Those values, in turn, inform the treatment of precedent.

To illustrate, consider the work of John McGinnis and Michael Rappaport, who defend a theory of *consequentialist originalism*. They argue that interpreting the Constitution in light of its original meaning is the best approach from the perspective of maximizing human welfare. Professors McGinnis and Rappaport do not dwell on the welfare effects of specific constitutional rules. They focus instead on the process by which the Constitution became law. Their central claim is that because the Constitution and its amendments required supermajority approval, constitutional rules will tend to perform well in promoting welfare so long as the document is interpreted in light of its original meaning. Professors McGinnis and Rappaport also cite other consequentialist advantages of originalism in the form of legal clarity, judicial restraint, and the channeling of efforts at revision through the formal amendment process. Ultimately, though, the most distinctive feature of their theory is the connection between supermajority processes and desirable results.

Consequentialist originalism presumes that the Constitution's original meaning should be implemented, but the theory allows for the elevation of precedent over original meaning under certain circumstances. For example, when a flawed (in originalist terms) precedent has come to receive supermajority support, courts ought to preserve it. Following such precedents is presumed to be beneficial given their widespread support, thus overmatching any benefits of changing the law to make it more consistent with the Constitution's original meaning.[9] Likewise, if a precedent's overruling would generate extraordinary costs, the precedent may be retained, notwithstanding its deviation from the Constitution's original meaning. As these exceptions suggest, the driving objective for consequentialist originalism is not to privilege original meanings for their own sake. It is to maximize welfare through an approach that gives presumptive fidelity to original meanings but that leaves space for deferring to flawed precedents under specified conditions. The aspiration is "to use the original meaning when it produces greater net benefits than precedent and to use precedent when the reverse holds true."[10]

---

[9] *See* John O. McGinnis and Michael B. Rappaport, Originalism and the Good Constitution 182 (2013).
[10] Id. at 177.

The need to determine which flawed precedents are most problematic marks an important difference between consequentialist originalism and its structuralist cousin. Structural originalism does not countenance the preservation of flawed precedents based on considerations such as acceptance or reliance; the judiciary cannot be spared the duty of correcting its constitutional mistakes. Consequentialist originalism takes a different approach by accepting the legitimacy and soundness of retaining certain decisions notwithstanding their deviation from the Constitution's original meaning. The very considerations that consequentialist originalists use to defend their methodology, including a focus on welfare maximization and a belief in the presumptive wisdom of supermajorities, also justify the preservation of some decisions that departed from the Constitution's original meaning.

The difference between the structuralist and consequentialist approaches flows from the theories' underlying normative commitments. For those who accept the structural originalists' claims about constitutional design and the illegitimacy of stare decisis, it makes sense to renounce the idea of preserving flawed constitutional decisions. If, by contrast, one agrees with the premises of consequentialist originalism, it is perfectly natural to acknowledge the possibility of retaining mistaken decisions that have garnered widespread support or whose overruling would be extremely disruptive. This distinction shows why it is not enough to talk about the relationship between precedent and "originalism." The originalist school is too diverse and wide-ranging to be reduced to a single, universal perspective on precedent.

The role of normative premises can be crystallized by introducing a third version of originalism, this one motivated by considerations of *popular sovereignty*. As described by scholars such as Kurt Lash, the popular sovereignty account maintains that constitutional rules are uniquely capable of embodying the will of the people. Preserving that connection requires fidelity to original meanings to ensure the "entrenchment of fundamental law expressed in a written constitution."[11] The basic reason why judges and justices should apply the Constitution's original meaning is respect for the will of the people.

A focus on popular sovereignty also implies that some departures from the Constitution's original meaning are more harmful than others. For proponents of popular sovereignty originalism, the costliness of a mistaken precedent depends on its interference with the democratic process. The most troubling episodes are those in which courts have recognized a right that the

---

[11] Kurt T. Lash, *Originalism, Popular Sovereignty, and Reverse Stare Decisis*, 93 VA. L. REV. 1437, 1441 (2007).

Constitution does not actually protect. Once a right is recognized, it can be removed only through the onerous process of constitutional amendment.

By comparison, a judicial decision that improperly withholds constitutional protection can be addressed through the enactment of ordinary legislation. Passing a law is not easy, but it is easier than amending the Constitution. In some situations, the possibility of a legislative fix is insufficient to neutralize the threat to popular sovereignty. For example, a decision that denies protection to political speech might undermine the very mechanism through which legislative solutions are supposed to emerge.[12] In other cases, the judiciary's withholding of constitutional protection leaves open the possibility of a legislative solution if the people are inclined to pursue one.

What this implies for the doctrine of stare decisis is that some departures from the Constitution's original meaning are more problematic than others. Decisions that improperly recognize constitutional rights are deeply harmful and should be rectified; their interference with the will of the people is too great to bear. Yet the same result does not necessarily follow for decisions whose offense is a failure to safeguard rights that the people can protect via ordinary legislation. Those cases give rise to the possibility of standing by a flawed precedent without doing too much damage to popular sovereignty.[13] Popular sovereignty originalism thus provides another illustration of how a theory's normative premises can affect the determination of which precedents are tolerable and which are too harmful to preserve.

Though I have drawn on examples from the originalist school, the role of normative premises is equally important for other interpretive methodologies. Let us return to the living constitutionalist approach, which I introduced using David Strauss's theory of common law constitutionalism. Professor Strauss argues that overrulings are justified when precedents become too problematic on metrics such as "fairness and social policy."[14] Even so, he emphasizes the importance of maintaining continuity over time through an incremental, common law approach to judging. The goal is for constitutional law to evolve, but (usually) to do so step by step. This mentality reflects concerns about the risks of disregarding the collective wisdom of generations. It also coheres with the belief that fidelity to settled law is a valuable means of showing respect to fellow citizens: "Even among people who disagree about an issue, it is a sign of respect to seek to justify one's position by referring to premises that are shared by the others."[15]

---

[12] Cf. Kurt T. Lash, *The Cost of Judicial Error: Stare Decisis and the Role of Normative Theory*, 89 NOTRE DAME L. REV. 2189, 2217 (2014).
[13] See Lash, *Originalism, Popular Sovereignty, and Reverse Stare Decisis*, supra note 11, at 1475.
[14] DAVID A. STRAUSS, THE LIVING CONSTITUTION 45 (2010).
[15] Strauss, *Common Law Constitutional Interpretation*, supra note 8, at 908.

As compared with common law constitutionalism, some other versions of living constitutionalism place less value on continuity and more emphasis on innovation and responsiveness. Justin Driver, for example, argues that a Supreme Court whose approach is too "backward-looking" cannot be expected to "bring legally subordinated groups into the constitutional fold." Far better for the justices to "make affirmative choices to distance themselves from the framework of prior judicial decisions before setting out in a fresh jurisprudential direction, venturing into uncharted judicial territory."[16] This theory shares with common law constitutionalism a commitment to progressivism and the morality of constitutional rules. It also shares a belief that the Constitution's original meaning is not always suitable for resolving modern disputes. Yet the two approaches have different normative emphases, which lead to different depictions of precedent. The more urgent version of living constitutionalism has a greater tendency to treat perceived injustice as a cost the legal system should not accept, even temporarily, in the name of keeping faith with the past. By contrast, the common law approach is more inclined to treat some flawed constitutional rules as tolerable while the process of incremental revision and case-by-case evolution runs its course. This is not always the case; Professor Strauss makes clear that some results are so problematic that they should be corrected without hesitation.[17] But generally speaking, common law constitutionalism is more likely to opt for gradualism and incrementalism, even if it means delaying the achievement of sound constitutional outcomes.

Another illustration of the connection between methodology and normative commitments straddles the line between originalism and living constitutionalism. Jack Balkin argues that the Constitution should be interpreted in light of its original meaning for reasons including respect for popular sovereignty. He also contends that the text "does not settle most disputed questions of constitutional interpretation." This, in his view, is a good thing. The unsettled areas allow each generation to adapt the Constitution to its own values. A primary role of the judiciary is to safeguard the people's authority to "build out" the constitutional framework "over time."[18] Here again we see popular sovereignty looming large, but in a new way. Under Professor Balkin's theory, popular sovereignty is continually renewed as the people fill out the constitutional

---

[16] Justin Driver, *The Significance of the Frontier in American Constitutional Law*, 2011 SUP. CT. REV. 345, 350–1.

[17] *See* Strauss, *Common Law Constitutional Interpretation*, *supra* note 8, at 895.

[18] Jack M. Balkin, *The New Originalism and the Uses of History*, 82 FORDHAM L. REV. 641, 649 (2013); *see also* JACK M. BALKIN, LIVING ORIGINALISM 3 (2011) (describing a theory of "framework originalism" that "views the Constitution as an initial framework for governance that sets politics in motion, and that Americans must fill out over time through constitutional construction").

framework in ways that are clearly and unapologetically driven by contemporary judgments and mores.

On the topic of precedent, Professor Balkin suggests that courts should sometimes tolerate flawed constitutional decisions. Still, decisions should not continue to hang around after they have been rendered "obsolete" by "changes in demographics, economics, technology, social customs, or other features of social life," or when they are "deeply unjust or unworkable."[19] The costliness of a mistaken precedent depends in significant part on its congruence with values and realities of modern society. This approach to precedent reflects and follows from Professor Balkin's broader theory of constitutional interpretation.[20] If it is vital for the Constitution to keep pace with the evolving sensibilities of rising generations, it is understandable that the most problematic precedents, and those in most urgent need of overruling, should be ones that are out of step with contemporary thinking and modern life. It is likewise understandable for constitutional mistakes that do not stand in the way of progress and self-government to be treated as tolerable, notwithstanding their flaws. The line that begins with the theory's underlying premises continues all the way to its vision of stare decisis.

By drawing distinctions within the originalist and living constitutionalist schools, I do not mean to downplay the areas of common ground. There are important similarities among theories that treat the Constitution's meaning as evolving with society's understandings and practices. Likewise, there are important similarities among theories that reject such evolution and give primacy to the Constitution's original meaning.

It is also worth noting that some judges resist comprehensive interpretive theories of any sort, choosing to tailor their methodological approach to the case at hand. For now, suffice to say that whether or not the theories I have described find full-throated acceptance in the practice of any particular court or judge, they help to illustrate an essential point about the status of flawed precedents. Determining how costly it would be to uphold a precedent depends on underlying methodological and normative conclusions. Those conclusions tell us which sorts of implications are relevant to the interpretation of the Constitution. There is no universal explanation for why it is important for the law to be right or why it is problematic for the law to be wrong. A theory of precedent must never lose sight of this fact.

---

[19] BALKIN, LIVING ORIGINALISM, *supra* note 18, at 124.
[20] *See, e.g.*, id. at 54 ("Courts have neither the first word nor the last word on the interpretation of the Constitution. Instead, courts work in the middle of a long process of shaping and modifying constitutional constructions; both public protest and public acceptance of court decisions are crucial to the development of constitutional doctrine in the United States.").

4

Scope of Applicability

In designing a system of precedent, the strength of constraint is only half the story. There is also the matter of determining which parts of a judicial opinion are binding in future cases. This inquiry into precedential scope is often framed by the distinction between necessary holdings and dispensable dicta. The holding/dicta dichotomy is a useful starting point, but it creates difficulties in practice. It also has trouble explaining modern American law. While the federal courts, including the Supreme Court, occasionally insist on maintaining the line between holdings and dicta, in other cases they construe the scope of precedent broadly.

This chapter contends that just as the strength of precedent is bound up with matters of interpretive methodology and normative commitment, so too is a precedent's scope of applicability. It is not enough to consider concepts like holding and dicta in isolation. Whether precedents should be construed narrowly or broadly also depends on factors such as the capabilities of courts, the structure of the federal government, and the constitutional limits on judicial authority.

STARTING POINTS

It is a truth universally acknowledged that a judge who is asked to decide a thorny dispute must be presented with competing arguments from precedent. One party will claim the case law demands, or at least strongly suggests, a certain outcome. The opposing party will contend the proper inference from the case law is actually quite the contrary. And so the meaning of precedent will be placed before the judge for resolution.

The threshold question is how to determine what the relevant precedents stand for. I noted in Chapter 1 that the most common answer revolves around the difference between holdings and dicta. To recap, a holding is "[a] court's determination of a matter of law pivotal to its decision" or "a principle drawn from such a decision." Dicta, by comparison, are comments that are unnecessary to a decision "and therefore not precedential."[1]

This framework defines a precedent's scope of applicability as commonly described. Holdings receive deference in future cases. Dicta do not; they are relevant only to the extent future judges find them persuasive. Chief Justice Marshall made the point nearly two centuries ago in noting that while expressions that "go beyond the case ... may be respected," they do not control "in a subsequent suit when the very point is presented for decision."[2] Concrete rulings that are necessary to resolve a case command deference from future courts. Asides and hypotheticals are the stuff of dicta.

The distinction between holding and dicta continues to pepper the Supreme Court's opinions. The justices have made clear that unnecessary dicta are generally dispensable. An illustrative statement from 2013 explains that "we are not necessarily bound by dicta should more complete argument demonstrate that the dicta is not correct."[3] Elsewhere the justices have added that repeating dicta over time does not change their nonbinding character, leaving future judges at liberty to discard dicta they find unpersuasive.[4] Only a case's rule of decision and its "preceding determinations" command formal deference going forward.[5] Whenever a court treats a proposition as unworthy

---

[1] BLACK'S LAW DICTIONARY (10th ed. 2014). The quoted language is drawn from the definition of *obiter dictum*. *Black's* offers a separate entry for *judicial dictum*, which it defines as an "opinion by a court on a question that is directly involved, briefed, and argued by counsel, and even passed on by the court, but that is not essential to the decision." A related term is *ratio decidendi*, which can be described as either "[t]he principle or rule of law on which a court's decision is founded" or "[t]he rule of law on which a later court thinks that a previous court founded its decision." Id.; *see also* NEIL DUXBURY, THE NATURE AND AUTHORITY OF PRECEDENT 67 (2008) ("Judicial reasoning may be integral to the *ratio*, but the *ratio* itself is more than the reasoning, and within many cases there will be judicial reasoning that constitutes not part of the *ratio*, but *obiter dicta*."). These concepts have generated a wealth of probing analysis stretching back for many years. For insightful syntheses and commentaries, see, for example, Professor Duxbury's book, as well as Larry Alexander, *Constrained by Precedent*, 63 SOUTHERN CAL. L. REV. 1 (1989). Notwithstanding the historical importance of these terms, in analyzing the operation of precedent at the modern Supreme Court I will avoid any distinction between obiter and judicial dicta. I will also avoid the term ratio decidendi, though I will discuss the underlying issue of which aspects of a precedent's rationale ought to receive deference in future cases.

[2] Cohens v. Virginia, 19 U.S. (6 Wheat.) 264, 399 (1821).

[3] Kirtsaeng v. John Wiley & Sons, 133 S. Ct. 1351, 1368 (2013); *see also* Arkansas Game & Fish Commission v. United States, 133 S. Ct. 511, 520 (2012) (calling the *Cohens* language a "sage observation"); Central Virginia Community College v. Katz, 546 U.S. 356, 363 (2006) ("For the reasons stated by Chief Justice Marshall in [*Cohens*], we are not bound to follow our dicta in a prior case in which the point now at issue was not fully debated.").

[4] *See* Gonzales v. United States, 553 U.S. 242, 256 (2008) (Scalia, J., concurring in the judgment).

[5] Tyler v. Cain, 533 U.S. 656, 663 n.4 (2001).

of deference because it ventured beyond "the narrow point actually decided," the holding/dicta distinction is at work.[6]

The impact of the distinction is especially apparent when the Supreme Court depicts its past statements as peripheral or overbroad. Take the Court's recent decision in *United States v. Alvarez* (2012). *Alvarez* struck down a federal statute that prohibited certain lies about one's military service. A plurality of justices reasoned that the Constitution treats some false statements as intrinsically valuable and worthy of robust First Amendment protection. Before reaching its conclusion, the plurality had to confront the Court's language in prior opinions supporting the contrary view that false claims have no inherent worth. According to the plurality, the opinions that had described false speech as valueless involved "defamation, fraud, or some other legally cognizable harm . . . such as an invasion of privacy or the costs of vexatious litigation." Those opinions accordingly did not offer any insight into the treatment of false speech in the case at hand.[7]

It made no difference to the *Alvarez* plurality that the Court's precedents contained broad language indicating that false statements lack constitutional worth. Only the Court's applications of its rule to causes of action such as defamation and fraud warranted deference going forward. By drawing a rigid line between fact-intensive rulings and nonbinding judicial exposition, the *Alvarez* plurality highlighted the importance of separating holdings from dicta.

To similar effect is *United States v. Stevens* (2010). That case dealt with a federal statute aimed at depictions of animal cruelty. In defending the statute's constitutionality, the government pressed an argument grounded in cost–benefit analysis: Because depictions of animal cruelty have meager social value but impose significant social harm, they should be treated as a categorical exception to First Amendment protection. The government's argument drew on previous cases in which the Supreme Court had described this type of cost–benefit analysis as relevant to constitutional protection. But *Stevens* dismissed the prior endorsements of cost–benefit analysis as merely "descriptive." According to the majority, the Court's prior statements linking First Amendment coverage to cost–benefit analysis were peripheral. The statements did not "set forth a test that may be applied as a general matter."[8] *Stevens* explained that historical practice, not cost–benefit analysis, determines whether speech falls into a categorical exception to protection. Though the historical approach might conflict with some of the Court's *language*, the

---

[6] Humphrey's Executor v. United States, 295 U.S. 602, 626 (1935).
[7] 132 S. Ct. 2537, 2544–5 (plurality op.).
[8] 559 U.S. 460, 471.

majority found the approach consistent with the *rule* embodied in the Court's prior decisions.

The Court evinced a comparable view of precedential scope in *Planned Parenthood v. Casey* (1992), which continues to represent the justices' most controversial engagement with precedent. When the Court addressed the constitutional implications of abortion in *Roe v. Wade* (1973), it ventured beyond the facts at hand to articulate a framework for assessing abortion regulations based on the trimester of pregnancy.[9] That framework was not essential to *Roe*'s disposition, nor was it an application of law to specific, concrete facts. Rather, it served as a general set of instructions for analyzing and resolving future cases. In *Casey*, the Court reaffirmed *Roe*'s protection of a woman's constitutional right "to terminate her pregnancy in its early stages."[10] At the same time, a plurality of justices rejected *Roe*'s trimester framework, which they described as unnecessary and therefore expendable.[11] The plurality thus distinguished central holdings from peripheral statements – even statements manifestly intended to guide the resolution of disputes going forward.

Cases like *Alvarez*, *Stevens*, and *Casey* provide some basis for characterizing the Supreme Court as adopting a relatively narrow approach to precedents' scope of applicability, one that insists on preserving the line between holdings and dicta. On this view, no deference is due to unnecessary statements, regardless of whether they were meant as guidance for future courts. Those sorts of statements may or may not be convincing on the merits, but in no event do they warrant deference beyond their persuasive force. Such deference is reserved for the targeted application of law to actual, concrete facts.

BEYOND HOLDINGS AND DICTA

Given these illustrations of the divide between holding and dicta, one might infer that federal courts customarily define the scope of precedent in narrow fashion. Yet judicial opinions, including those of the Supreme Court, are commonly filled with justifications, reflections, and prescriptions for the future. It seems clear that this is often intentional rather than incidental. As Justice Stevens once observed, "[v]irtually every one of the Court's opinions announcing a new application of a constitutional principle contains some explanatory language that is intended to provide guidance to lawyers and

---

[9] 410 U.S. 113, 163–6.
[10] Planned Parenthood of Southeastern Pennsylvania v. Casey, 505 U.S. 833, 844 (1992).
[11] *See id.* at 873 (plurality op.).

judges in future cases."[12] As we shall see, federal judges and justices frequently respond by giving binding effect to propositions that sweep far beyond a decision's narrow holding. To illustrate, I will address four features of Supreme Court opinions – hypotheticals and asides, doctrinal frameworks, codifying statements, and supporting rationales – that do not fit neatly into the conventional definition of a decision's holding but that nevertheless play a significant role in the trajectory of constitutional law.

Hypotheticals and Asides. Judicial musings about situations not currently presented for review are dicta in the most familiar sense. Such statements do not resolve, or even attempt to resolve, a pending dispute. Instead, they are suggestions about how the law should or will apply in future cases. This type of dicta-as-hypothetical has a close cousin in the form of judicial asides. Asides may be related to the case at hand, but they are attenuated from, and unnecessary to, the court's ruling.

Yet the Supreme Court sometimes invokes its prior statements even as it acknowledges them as unnecessary dicta. In *Rivera v. Illinois* (2009), for example, the Court noted it had previously disavowed language from a prior opinion, "albeit in dicta."[13] Chief Justice Roberts offered similar sentiments in a 2010 concurrence that treated certain statements as worth citing notwithstanding their status as dicta.[14] A comparable example is *Kappos v. Hyatt* (2012), in which the Court considered a party's ability to introduce new evidence when contesting the denial of a patent. The Court had previously described subsequent challenges as independent of patent applications, meaning new evidence could be introduced. It made those statements in an 1884 case called *Butterworth v. United States*. Looking back more than a century later, the *Kappos* Court gave deference to *Butterworth*'s statements about subsequent challenges even though those statements were "not strictly necessary to *Butterworth*'s holding." The Court explained that while the pertinent statements in *Butterworth* were technically dicta, they were "not the kind of ill-considered dicta that we are inclined to ignore." On the contrary, the *Butterworth* discussion reflected a "careful[] examin[ation]" of the statutory context and relevant decisions of the lower courts. The Court had also "reiterated *Butterworth*'s well-reasoned interpretation . . . in three later cases." The dicta were therefore entitled to some deference going forward.[15]

[12] Carey v. Musladin, 549 U.S. 70, 79 (2006) (Stevens, J., concurring in the judgment).
[13] 556 U.S. 148, 160.
[14] South Carolina v. North Carolina, 558 U.S. 256, 282 (2010) (Roberts, C. J., concurring in the judgment in part and dissenting in part) (endorsing a point the Court had "strongly intimated in other decisions (albeit in dictum)").
[15] Kappos v. Hyatt, 132 S. Ct. 1690, 1699 (2012) (discussing Butterworth v. United States *ex rel.* Hoe, 112 U.S. 50 (1884)).

It is hard to tell exactly how much deference the *Butterworth* dicta received, because the *Kappos* Court also found them convincing on the merits. The key point is the recognition of distinctions among different types of dicta. By separating "ill-considered dicta" from dicta that ought not be "ignor[ed]," *Kappos* makes a subtle but significant revision to the divide between holdings and dicta. The case implies that even dicta can be worthy of deference under the right circumstances.

For one final example, consider *Parents Involved in Community Schools v. Seattle School District No. 1* (2007), a case dealing with the racial demographics of school districts.[16] At issue was the districts' authority to consider students' race in deciding which school they would attend. The Supreme Court concluded the districts' practices violated the Equal Protection Clause of the Fourteenth Amendment.

Justice Breyer dissented on behalf of himself and three others. Among his points of disagreement with the lead opinion was its treatment of *Swann v. Charlotte-Mecklenburg Board of Education* (1971). In *Swann*, the Court described the "broad discretionary powers of school authorities" as encompassing the ability to promote racial diversity within schools in order to "prepare students to live in a pluralistic society."[17] The lead opinion in *Parents Involved* characterized the relevant portion of *Swann* as inapposite, outmoded, and nonbinding dicta. Justice Breyer took issue with that depiction in his dissent. Though he acknowledged that the relevant statement was not part of *Swann*'s holding, he countered that the Court had "set forth its view prominently in an important opinion joined by all nine justices, knowing that it would be read and followed throughout the Nation." *Swann*'s statement had also come to enjoy "wide acceptance in the legal culture." And "it reflected a consensus that had already emerged among state and lower federal courts." In light of these facts, Justice Breyer found the plurality's "rigid distinctions between holdings and dicta" to be misguided. He concluded that if the plurality wanted to revisit *Swann*, it should have acknowledged an obligation to "explain to the courts and to the Nation *why* it would abandon guidance set forth many years before."[18]

Justice Breyer's treatment of *Swann* cannot be explained by the traditional distinction between holdings and dicta. While he recognized the pertinent portion of *Swann* as dicta, he nevertheless contended that the statement warranted some degree of deference above and beyond its persuasiveness on the merits. This conclusion owed in part to what Justice Breyer perceived to be

[16] 551 U.S. 701.
[17] 402 U.S. 1, 16.
[18] Id. at 827, 831 (Breyer, J., dissenting).

the intention of the *Swann* Court, and in part to the role *Swann's* statements had come to play over time in the wider "legal culture." Dicta or not, the statements were "authoritative legal guidance."[19]

Justice Breyer's assumptions run parallel with those of the majority in *Kappos*, the case involving lawsuits following patent denials. Both opinions imply that in certain situations, judicial statements warrant deference despite having been unnecessary to the decision that contained them. From the outset, then, we can see some complexity in the traditional divide between binding holdings and dispensable dicta.

Doctrinal Frameworks. The Supreme Court regularly builds frameworks to guide the resolution of future disputes. By their nature, these frameworks sweep beyond the facts at hand to address situations not currently before the Court. Yet while the justices occasionally refuse to accept the validity of doctrinal frameworks with which they disagree,[20] in many cases the frameworks are taken as given, with the real differences concerning their application to particular sets of facts. The Court's assessments of racial classifications assume that the proper starting point is whether the government has narrowly tailored its approach to serve a compelling interest.[21] The Court's applications of the Ex Post Facto Clause give canonical force to a multi-part test dating back to 1798.[22] The Court's forays into administrative law are frequently governed by the two-step protocol set forth in the famous case of *Chevron U.S.A. Inc. v. Natural Resources Defense Council, Inc.*[23] In situations like these, doctrinal frameworks appear to exert binding force.

For a further illustration, consider the Supreme Court's treatment of the right to bear arms. In *District of Columbia v. Heller* (2008), the Court interpreted the Second Amendment as protecting an individual's right to own a gun, at least insofar as the Amendment prohibits bans on firearm possession in one's home.[24] The Court accordingly struck down a District of Columbia law. Among the questions raised by the Court's decision was whether it would apply to state and local laws in the same way it applies to federal laws of the sort that govern the District of Columbia. The question was made more complicated by the fact that the Second Amendment is understood as applying only to the federal government. If state and local governments are

[19] Id.
[20] See, e.g., State Farm Mutual Automobile Insurance Co. v. Campbell, 538 U.S. 408, 429 (2003) (Scalia, J., dissenting).
[21] See, e.g., Grutter v. Bollinger, 539 U.S. 306, 326 (2003); id. at 378 (Rehnquist, C. J., dissenting).
[22] See, e.g., Peugh v. United States, 133 S. Ct. 2072, 2081 (2013) (citing Calder v. Bull, 3 U.S. (3 Dall.) 386, 390 (1798)).
[23] 467 U.S. 837 (1984).
[24] 554 U.S. 570, 635 (2008).

limited in their regulatory power over firearms, those limits must come from a different source.

One possible source is the Fourteenth Amendment's Privileges or Immunities Clause. The Clause instructs that "[n]o State shall make or enforce any law which shall abridge the privileges or immunities of citizens of the United States." In the *Slaughter-House Cases* (1873), the Supreme Court described those privileges and immunities as extending only to "rights 'which owe their existence to the Federal government, its National character, or its laws.'"[25] Such rights touch upon issues like traveling to "the seat of government to assert" a claim upon it, but they do not sweep in the restrictions on governmental power set forth in the Bill of Rights.[26]

Over the years, many commentators have criticized the Court as misconstruing the Privileges or Immunities Clause. Properly understood, the critics claim, the Clause incorporates the protections of the Bill of Rights against state and local governments. But whether it is right or wrong, the prevailing interpretation of the Privileges or Immunities Clause has not left people unprotected against state and local action. Rather, they receive extensive protection via the Fourteenth Amendment's Due Process Clause, which prevents states from depriving "any person of life, liberty, or property, without due process of law."

This approach has been controversial in its own right. There are some who believe the Due Process Clause deals only with procedure, not substance. On this reading, the Clause does not protect any substantive rights, including those encompassed within the Bill of Rights.[27] Some critics of the Court's approach also worry that by recognizing a substantive dimension to the Due Process Clause, the justices open up the possibility of creating new rights that have little or no grounding in the Constitution's text or history.[28]

The application of the Bill of Rights to state and local action moved to the foreground in *McDonald v. City of Chicago* (2010). In *McDonald*, the Court considered the validity of local laws against handguns. The challengers in *McDonald* wanted the laws invalidated, but they also asked the Court to deviate from its customary approach. Rather than emphasizing the Due Process Clause, the challengers asked the Court to recognize the right to bear arms as protected by the Privileges or Immunities Clause. Such a revision,

---

[25] McDonald v. City of Chicago, 561 U.S. 742, 754 (2010) (quoting the Slaughter-House Cases, 83 U.S. 36, 79 (1873)).
[26] *See id.* at 755 (quoting the *Slaughter-House Cases*, 83 U.S. at 79).
[27] *See id.* at 811 (Thomas, J., concurring in part and concurring in the judgment).
[28] *See id.*

they contended, would be true to the proper understanding of the Fourteenth Amendment.

Ultimately, the Court ruled that states and localities must respect citizens' rights to bear arms. Yet it declined the invitation to invoke the Privileges or Immunities Clause. Instead, a plurality stuck with the Court's tried-and-true reliance on the Due Process Clause. The plurality acknowledged the extensive criticism the Court's approach had received from legal scholars. Even so, it "decline[d] to disturb the *Slaughter-House* holding."[29]

The *McDonald* approach is interesting on several fronts, but the most notable implication for present purposes involves the issue of precedential scope. The plurality depicted the Court's prior interpretations of the Fourteenth Amendment as settled law entitled to deference. It offered no conclusions about whether incorporating the Bill of Rights via the Due Process Clause reflects the best reading of the Constitution. Instead, the plurality indicated that whether or not the Court's prior interpretations were correct, they warranted respect given their prevalence "[f]or many decades."[30] The plurality treated the preexisting standard for incorporation as entitled to deference – which is to say, as falling within the relevant precedents' scope of binding authority.

To one who is immersed in the classical distinction between binding holdings and dispensable dicta, this approach might be surprising. The Court's position on incorporation emerged through cases involving issues like police searches and the freedom of speech. Those cases had nothing to do with gun rights. Nevertheless, the *McDonald* plurality accepted the Court's prior decisions as applying in full measure to the right to bear arms. In effect, the plurality recognized that cases involving certain constitutional rights can serve as binding precedents in future cases involving entirely different rights. This type of doctrinal transcendence is difficult to square with a vision of precedential scope that is defined by the targeted application of narrow rules to concrete facts.

The Court's treatment of abortion laws provides a similar illustration in a different context. As noted above, when the Court decided *Roe v. Wade*, it ventured beyond the dispute at hand to articulate a framework for assessing regulations based on the trimester of pregnancy. When the Court returned to *Roe* in *Planned Parenthood v. Casey*, it preserved what it described as *Roe's* core holding relating to the constitutional status of abortion rights and the government's countervailing interests. At the same time, three of the five justices who voted to reaffirm a constitutional right to abortion went on to reject *Roe's*

---

[29] See id. at 758 (plurality op.); *see also* id. at 791 (Scalia, J., concurring) (noting his acquiescence in the Court's existing approach notwithstanding his "misgivings about Substantive Due Process as an original matter").

[30] Id. at 758 (plurality op.).

trimester framework. Instead of focusing on the trimester of pregnancy, they described the proper question as whether "state regulation imposes an undue burden on a woman's" right to an abortion.[31] The justices also explained that "[r]egulations which do no more than create a structural mechanism" for "express[ing] profound respect for the life of the unborn are permitted," so long as "they are not a substantial obstacle to the woman's exercise of the right to choose."[32]

Again, our immediate interest is what the *Casey* approach reveals about the scope of precedent. On the one hand, the plurality's withholding of deference from *Roe*'s trimester framework lends support to the distinction between essential holdings and peripheral dicta. On the other hand, the plurality saw fit to announce its own wide-ranging, forward-looking test based on whether a regulation creates an undue burden on abortion rights. And it made clear the new standard was one it intended "to adhere to" going forward.[33]

Perhaps the *Casey* plurality merely wanted to provide some guidance about its (nonbinding) aspirations for the path of the law. But it seems more likely the plurality thought it was articulating a legal standard that would be controlling in future cases. In the lower courts, such deference would be absolute. As for the Supreme Court itself, it would always retain the power to reconsider its approach, just as the *Casey* plurality had departed from *Roe*'s trimester framework. Even so, the undue-burden standard would be entitled to some degree of deference, and it would furnish the appropriate framework of review unless and until the Court recognized a special justification for overruling it. What started out looking like a restrictive approach to precedential scope – one that reserved deference for a decision's core holding as opposed to its peripheral instructions – gave way to a more capacious view, which treats wide-ranging doctrinal frameworks as entitled to respect.

Another species of doctrinal framework has been called a "codifying decision[]."[34] Codifying decisions set forth legal requirements in detailed and elaborate terms. A prominent example is *Miranda*, which considered "procedural safeguards" for custodial interrogations of suspected criminals. The *Miranda* Court went far beyond determining whether any constitutional rights had been violated in the case before it. It described the warnings that would be required in future cases, including the right to remain silent, to the presence of an attorney, and so forth.[35]

---

[31] *Casey*, 505 U.S. at 874 (plurality op.).
[32] Id. at 877.
[33] Id. at 876.
[34] Faheem-El v. Klincar, 841 F.2d 712, 730 (7th Cir. 1988) (en banc) (Easterbrook, J., concurring).
[35] 384 U.S. 436, 444–5.

A court's willingness to issue codifying decisions implies a broad understanding of the scope of precedent. Notwithstanding the Supreme Court's determined effort at elaboration, the *Miranda* warnings would carry limited force in a system that withholds deference from peripheral and nonessential statements. As Judge Frank Easterbrook has noted, because the suspect in *Miranda* "had not been given any warning," there was no need for the Supreme Court to set forth a defined set of *four* warnings.[36] Nevertheless, the Court did not limit itself to what was necessary. And subsequent courts followed its lead, treating the *Miranda* warnings as settled law. Indeed, when the Supreme Court was asked to overrule *Miranda* in 2000, it explained that "[w]hether or not we would agree with *Miranda*'s reasoning and its resulting rule, were we addressing the issue in the first instance, the principles of *stare decisis* weigh heavily against overruling it now."[37]

Like doctrinal frameworks, codifying decisions float free of any particular dispute. Their aim is to guide judicial actions when new facts emerge and new disputes arise. Nevertheless, while they reflect broad statements of guiding principles, codifying statements can exert binding force as a matter of federal practice.

Supporting Rationales. The reasons offered to support a judicial ruling are distinct from the ruling itself. Some definitions of precedential scope are broad enough to give binding effect to supporting reasons.[38] For example, Judge Pierre Leval has defined the concept of dicta as encompassing propositions that do not affect "the court's judgment and the reasoning which supports it."[39] On other accounts, however, decisional rationales should not receive deference when they are exported to new factual contexts. This debate has been with us for decades. In 1928, Herman Oliphant lamented that "we are well on our way toward a shift from following decisions to following so-called principles, from *stare decisis* to ... *stare dictis.*"[40] Some sixty years later, Justice Kennedy explained that deference extends "not only to the holdings of our prior cases, but also to their explications of the governing rules of law."[41]

---

[36] *Faheem-El*, 841 F.2d at 730.
[37] Dickerson v. United States, 530 U.S. 428, 443 (2000).
[38] *See, e.g.*, 18 MOORE'S FEDERAL PRACTICE § 134.03.
[39] Pierre N. Leval, *Judging Under the Constitution: Dicta About Dicta*, 81 N.Y.U. L. REV. 1249, 1256 (2006).
[40] Herman Oliphant, *A Return to Stare Decisis*, 14 A.B.A. J. 71, 72 (1928).
[41] County of Allegheny v. ACLU, 492 U.S. 573, 668 (1989) (Kennedy, J., concurring in the judgment in part and dissenting in part); *see also* Local 28, Sheet Metal Workers' International Association v. EEOC, 478 U.S. 421, 490 (1986) (O'Connor, J., concurring in part and dissenting in part).

More recently, the Supreme Court has stated that a "well-established rationale upon which the Court based the results of its earlier decisions" is entitled to deference in future cases.[42] But the Court has not been entirely consistent in embracing this position. In *Stevens*, the Court drew a sharp distinction between rules of decision and "descriptions" of those rules. The latter, descriptive components might furnish the underlying rationales that drove prior decisions – for example, by explaining that a category of speech has been denied constitutional protection based on an evaluation of its costs and benefits. Even so, the Court rejected the claim that descriptions are entitled to deference.[43] A plurality took a similar position in *Alvarez*, which raised questions about the constitutional value of false speech. Though the Court had previously reasoned that false speech is unworthy of constitutional protection, the *Alvarez* plurality declined to defer to that rationale, focusing instead on the particular examples of false speech that had arisen in its prior cases.[44]

We are thus left in a zone of uncertainty. Sometimes the Supreme Court insists on a firm line between rules and rationales in determining the forward-looking effect of precedent. In other cases, the lesson seems to be that decisional rationales are entitled to deference even if future courts disagree with them.

One way to resolve this uncertainty is to recognize the difference between a rationale that is expressed within a particular opinion and a rationale that is reconstructed by a court looking back over its prior decisions. When the Supreme Court considers its cases within a given field, it sometimes perceives an overarching rule that links them together. The Court might defer to such a rule even if it would not be inclined to defer to the statements of rationale contained in the decisions themselves. This understanding arguably explains cases like *Stevens* and *Alvarez*, both of which deduced a new rationale by focusing on the facts of the relevant precedents rather than the articulated reasons. Those cases support the view that in defining a precedent's future application, its express statements of reasoning are less important – sometimes, at least – than underlying rationales reconstructed by later courts.

PRECEDENT IN THE LOWER FEDERAL COURTS

Judges occasionally emphasize the need for interpreting precedents, even Supreme Court precedents, in relatively narrow terms. Judge Danny Boggs, for instance, has noted that "the holding/dicta distinction demands that

---

[42] Seminole Tribe of Florida v. Florida, 517 U.S. 44, 66–7 (1996).
[43] *Stevens*, 559 U.S. at 460.
[44] *Alvarez*, 132 S. Ct. 2537 (plurality op.).

we consider binding only that which was necessary to resolve the question before the [Supreme] Court."[45] Likewise, Judge Pierre Leval has explained that Supreme Court dicta are "not law."[46] The implication is not merely that judges should feel free to depart from dicta. The idea is that a judge who treats dicta as binding fails to discharge her duty. Judge Ruggero Aldisert took a similar position in contending that "[t]he common-law tradition requires starting with a narrow holding and, then . . . either applying it or not applying it to subsequent facts."[47]

Others take a different approach to the scope of Supreme Court precedent. As Frederick Schauer notes, it often seems as though in "interpretive arenas below the Supreme Court, one good quote is worth a hundred clever analyses of the holding."[48] And, indeed, many lower courts describe Supreme Court statements as entitled to deference regardless of whether those statements were made in dicta. The strength of deference varies from court to court. There are opinions that describe Supreme Court dicta as akin to Supreme Court holdings, and opinions contemplating an intermediate approach whereby dicta carry some force, though not as much as holdings. The common thread is that Supreme Court dicta warrant respect above and beyond their persuasiveness on the merits.[49]

Here again we have a particular vision of the scope of precedent, one that eschews strict adherence to the line between holdings and dicta. Rather than being denied any weight beyond their persuasiveness, Supreme Court dicta receive substantial, and sometimes controlling, deference in many lower courts. A recent empirical study by David Klein and Neal Devins underscores the point by confirming the "frequent decisions" among lower courts "to abide by statements from higher courts even though they are recognized as dicta."[50] The contrast between holding and dicta makes far less difference if judges are in the habit of according strong deference to Supreme Court pronouncements of any type.[51] In practical terms, the lesson is that while the holding/dicta distinction is integral to understanding the scope of precedent

---

[45] Grutter v. Bollinger, 288 F.3d 732, 787 (6th Cir. 2002) (en banc) (Boggs, J., dissenting).
[46] Leval, *Judging Under the Constitution, supra* note 39, at 1274.
[47] Ruggero J. Aldisert, *Precedent: What It Is and What It Isn't; When Do We Kiss It and When Do We Kill It?*, 17 Pepp. L. Rev. 605, 610 (1990); *cf. In re* American Express Merchants' Litigation, 681 F.3d 139, 147 (2d Cir. 2012) (Jacobs, J., dissenting from denial of rehearing en banc).
[48] Frederick Schauer, *Opinions as Rules*, 53 U. Chi. L. Rev. 682, 683 (1986).
[49] *See* Randy J. Kozel, *The Scope of Precedent*, 113 Mich. L. Rev. 179, 198–9 (2014).
[50] David Klein & Neil Devins, *Dicta, Schmicta: Theory Versus Practice in Lower Court Decision Making*, 54 Wm. & Mary L. Rev. 2021, 2044 (2013).
[51] Of course, a court might construe Supreme Court precedents broadly even while preserving the line between holdings and dicta in determining the binding effect of its own past decisions.

in modern American law, focusing on it excessively could lead to a distorted depiction of how precedent really works.

SCOPE, METHODOLOGY, AND NORMATIVE COMMITMENTS

Sometimes the scope of precedent is defined in a way that seems roughly aligned with the holding/dicta divide. In other cases, prior decisions are construed capaciously and inclusively, with deference attaching to elements beyond the narrow application of law to fact. At present, there is no user's manual to tell us which conception of precedential scope will prevail in which cases. Instead, the scope of precedent ebbs and flows in unpredictable ways.

So how *should* the scope of precedent be defined? Should the judiciary's overtures toward a broad conception of scope be cheered as facilitating guidance and stability? Or should they be lamented as an invitation to missteps and overreaching?

These are important questions, and they do not admit of a single answer. Chapter 3 showed why it is problematic to talk about the strength of precedent in the abstract. The relevant costs of retaining a flawed decision, as well as the relevant benefits of implementing a correct decision, look different depending on one's interpretive philosophy. The same is true of precedential scope. Determining the "best" way to construe precedents depends on deeper methodological and normative choices. Some theories imply that precedents should be defined narrowly. Others imply a broader conception of precedential scope. A full analysis requires attention to the role played by interpretive methodology and normative commitments.

To illustrate, let us consider several interpretive philosophies introduced in Chapter 3's discussion of precedential strength, along with a few additional examples that shed further light on the connection between methodology, normative judgments, and the scope of a prior decision's binding authority.

Common Law Constitutionalism. Notwithstanding its insistence that the meaning of the Constitution can change over time, common law constitutionalism pays considerable attention to the past. It urges the evolution of constitutional law toward just and sound results, but it recognizes judicial precedent as a source of common ground and accumulated wisdom.

Given these objectives and premises, common law constitutionalism is most compatible with a relatively broad vision of precedential scope. The common law approach relies on precedent to temper the pace of change and channel judicial discretion.[52] Defining the scope of precedents strictly – which

---

[52] David A. Strauss, *Originalism, Precedent, and Candor*, 22 CONST. COMMENT. 299, 300 (2005).

is to say, limiting a precedent's binding effect to its narrow core – would impair those functions. When a precedent's effect is limited to its targeted application of law to fact, today's judges will have extensive discretion to innovate in light of their own conclusions. For precedents to exert meaningful constraint on today's courts, they must be defined in a way that is fairly difficult to get around. This requirement suggests a broad definition of precedential scope that entails deference not only to narrow holdings, but also to elements such as doctrinal frameworks and underlying rationales. If it is too easy for judges to circumvent disfavored precedents by confining them to their facts, every day is a new day. The importance of construing precedents broadly is amplified because unlike interpretive methodologies such as originalism, common law constitutionalism makes no claim of being bound by the original meaning of the Constitution's text. Prior decisions furnish constraint by giving judges a series of reference points beyond their own intuitions about the appropriate path of constitutional law.

Common law constitutionalism also implies a broad scope of precedent through its depiction of case law as a source of collective knowledge. The theory reflects a belief in the wisdom of the ages and the limitations of individual decision-makers. It is true that common law constitutionalism depicts some values as so crucial that they must be protected, even if it means renouncing what has gone before. But generally speaking, the preference is for distilling lessons from the past, understanding what has (and has not) worked in practice, and acknowledging one's own potential for error while moving ahead gradually and deliberately.

This focus on individual limitations and collective wisdom is at odds with a strict conception of precedential scope. The wisdom of earlier judges does not manifest itself solely in narrow applications of law to fact. Rules, rationales, and doctrinal frameworks also embody the experiences and perspectives of past generations. A readiness to dismiss wide swaths of case law as hypothetical or unnecessary fits uneasily with an approach that places so much emphasis on respect for the past. The more natural practice for the common law constitutionalist is to pay close attention to the analysis contained in prior opinions, regardless of whether that analysis is categorized as holding or dicta. This does not mean deference must be given to every utterance in a prior opinion, no matter how attenuated or ill-advised. But it does mean there should be an inclination toward treating rules, frameworks, and explanations with presumptive deference even if they might fit the technical definition of dicta on some accounts.

Here again it is essential to bear in mind that deference to precedent is merely presumptive. Common law constitutionalism acknowledges that precedents may, and sometimes should, be overruled. For example, precedents ought not survive indefinitely when they impair the sound or just implementation of constitutional principles.[53] But that issue is one of precedential strength, not scope. Regardless of how powerfully a precedent is deemed to constrain, common law constitutionalism sits most comfortably alongside a capacious view of precedential scope that contemplates at least some degree of deference to a wide array of judicial propositions.

As I suggested above, adopting a broad definition of precedential scope does not entail rejecting all other safeguards against judicial overreaching. For a common law constitutionalist who supports the incremental evolution of the law, defining precedents broadly raises concerns about encouraging expansive decisions in the first instance. The worry is that if judges know precedents will be construed broadly by future courts, they will write wide-ranging opinions that settle too much, too fast. This concern underscores why rules of precedent cannot be analyzed in isolation. Common law constitutionalism works best when judges act with humility and restraint, both in interpreting old precedents and in creating new ones. Stare decisis is an important component of the judicial process, but it is far from the only one.

Originalism. While common law constitutionalism is best understood as aligned with a broad conception of precedential scope, other interpretive philosophies imply a different approach. Return to the example of originalism. An abiding focus on the Constitution's original meaning might seem to put originalism at odds with deference to precedent, at least when prior decisions ignore or misunderstand that meaning. Some originalists draw on this tension in criticizing the application of stare decisis in constitutional cases. For them, the scope of precedent makes little difference in the context of the Supreme Court's treatment of its own decisions: Regardless of whether a judicial proposition is described as holding or dicta, it should generally carry no weight beyond its persuasive force.

For other originalists, deference to precedent can be legitimate and appropriate. This is true even when the decision being reconsidered is incompatible with the original meaning of the Constitution as properly understood. For originalists who take this view of the legitimacy of stare decisis, there nevertheless may be appeal in a narrow definition of precedential scope. By construing precedents narrowly, originalists can leave some room for stare decisis while ensuring that reliance on judicial gloss does not go too far. Not every version of originalism would pursue this goal in the same way. Instead, we would expect

---

[53] *See* David A. Strauss, *Common Law Constitutional Interpretation*, 63 U. CHI. L. REV. 877, 895 (1996).

to see differences in approach based on the versions' respective normative premises. I have explained how the underlying justifications that lead a judge or scholar to embrace originalism – justifications such as popular sovereignty and consequentialism – can shape the strength of deference to which flawed precedents are entitled. Those justifications can have a similar bearing on conceptions of precedential scope.

Among those who have argued for the compatibility of originalism and judicial precedent are John McGinnis and Michael Rappaport, whose work I introduced in Chapter 2. In their view, a central reason for abiding by the Constitution's original meaning is the belief that because the Constitution was the product of supermajority agreement, it will tend to yield desirable results. The consequentialist position permits the displacement of original meaning with judicial precedent in certain situations. For example, courts may uphold mistaken precedents that have achieved widespread acceptance. In those instances, a commitment to the wisdom of supermajorities supports deferring to judicial decisions that, while inconsistent with the Constitution's original meaning, enjoy the degree of support needed for a constitutional amendment.

Through its attention to supermajority acceptance, consequentialist originalism carries ramifications not only for the strength of past decisions as precedents, but also for their scope of applicability. Rules such as "racial segregation in public schools is not allowed" and "paper money is lawful" enjoy widespread acceptance in American society. Those rules might well command the sort of supermajority support required to amend the Constitution. The implication for consequentialist originalism is that such rules may be retained even if they do not reflect the Constitution's original meaning.

Supermajority support will rarely reach other elements of judicial decisions, such as doctrinal frameworks. It is hard to imagine millions of citizens rallying around the technical argument that restrictions on independent political expenditures should be reviewed using a standard of strict scrutiny, or that categorical exceptions to First Amendment protection may emerge through historical practice but not through cost–benefit analysis. In theory, consequentialist originalism could permit deference to a doctrinal framework that swept far beyond the facts of the case that announced it. More likely, however, are scenarios in which particular applications of constitutional rules enjoy supermajority support – and thus raise the possibility of retention even if they depart from the Constitution's original meaning – while aspects such as doctrinal frameworks find no such favor.

The takeaway would seem to be that consequentialist originalism implies a narrow definition of precedential scope that focuses on specific rules rather than general frameworks. And, indeed, that will often be true. But not always.

Consequentialist originalism allows the retention of flawed precedents whose overruling would create extraordinary costs.[54] For example, if the Supreme Court were to reverse course and declare paper money unconstitutional, substantial costs would likely follow. We can imagine situations where departing from established doctrinal frameworks might likewise threaten the imposition of extraordinary costs. Take the framework for incorporating the Bill of Rights against the states, which asks whether a given right "is fundamental to our scheme of ordered liberty."[55] The Court has applied that framework in numerous cases dealing with an array of constitutional rights. The precise doctrinal test for incorporation presumably does not command anything approaching supermajority support in American society. Yet if the Court were to jettison it, there would be significant transition costs. The status of numerous constitutional rights could be cast into doubt, and judges and lawyers would need to work out a new approach to incorporation. For the consequentialist originalist, these disruptions suggest the incorporation framework might warrant preservation even if it conflicts with the Constitution's original meaning.

The incorporation example demonstrates that while consequentialist originalism will often imply a relatively narrow conception of precedential scope, in some circumstances it allows for a broader definition. In resolving issues of precedential scope under the consequentialist approach, the traditional line between holding and dicta is less important than the baseline concern with welfare maximization through supermajority wisdom. As with the example of common law constitutionalism, consequentialist originalism's underlying premises provide the basis for its treatment of precedent.

The same is true of other versions of originalism. Consider the argument that the primary reason for endorsing originalism is its success at requiring judges to decide cases based on predefined, external legal rules. The rationale is that even if other philosophies, such as pragmatism or common law constitutionalism, are plausible modes of interpretation, originalism excels at promoting the rule of law. Accepting this rule-of-law defense of originalism does not require applying the Constitution's original meaning in every case. A prominent illustration comes from the writings of Justice Scalia, who described deference to precedent as a "pragmatic *exception*" to originalism, grounded in the desire to maintain stability.[56] Justice Scalia's depiction of

---

[54] *See* JOHN O. MCGINNIS & MICHAEL B. RAPPAPORT, ORIGINALISM AND THE GOOD CONSTITUTION 186 (2013).

[55] *McDonald*, 561 U.S. at 767 (plurality op.).

[56] ANTONIN SCALIA, A MATTER OF INTERPRETATION: FEDERAL COURTS AND THE LAW (1997); *see also* ANTONIN SCALIA & BRYAN A. GARNER, READING LAW: THE INTERPRETATION OF LEGAL TEXTS 413–4 (2012).

precedent can be reframed to emphasize an underlying focus on the rule of law: While fidelity to precedent may sometimes create costs for the rule of law by supplanting democratically enacted mandates with (mistaken) judicial gloss, deference to precedent can also advance the rule of law by enhancing continuity and avoiding disruption.

Rule of law originalism suggests a fluctuating approach to precedential scope. Where the Constitution's original meaning is clear, beliefs about the connection between original meaning and the rule of law will generally counsel the narrow interpretation of flawed precedents. Hence Justice Scalia's resolution in certain contexts to abide by the Court's prior decisions, but to refrain from extending their rationale to new contexts.[57] Yet there is an exception when jettisoning a rationale or decisional framework would exact a significant toll on stability and reliance expectations. In those cases, the rule of law may be best served by construing precedents broadly and standing by them notwithstanding their flaws.

Rule of law originalism is also consistent with a relatively broad conception of precedential scope when the Constitution's original meaning is uncertain. In the face of uncertainty, precedents step in to lend predictability and precision to the law. By insisting that such precedents receive deference for their rules, rationales, and frameworks, an originalist can reinforce the notion of constitutional law as durable, impersonal, and constraining. When it comes to elevating external determinants of legal meaning over subjective intuitions, a judge who resolves disputes based on her best reading of precedent resembles a judge who resolves disputes based on her best interpretation of the Constitution's original meaning. Precedent delivers some of the same benefits as scrupulous fidelity to text and history.

Pragmatism. For a final illustration of the impact of interpretive methodology and normative commitments on the scope of precedent, consider the case of constitutional pragmatism. I have emphasized that labels like originalism and living constitutionalism, while helpful in drawing general distinctions, must not be allowed to obscure the nuance that exists within those categories. The dangers of misleading labels are even greater with respect to pragmatism, which is a term judges, lawyers, and scholars use in a host of different ways. For the sake of simplicity, I will focus on a particular version of pragmatism described by Justice Breyer. He depicts the pragmatic judge as resolving constitutional disputes with an eye toward the purposes of the relevant provision and the practical consequences of various interpretations. The goal is "an interpretation that helps the textual provision work well now to achieve its

---

[57] *See, e.g.*, General Motors Corp. v. Tracy, 519 U.S. 278, 312 (1997) (Scalia, J., concurring).

basic ... objectives." At the same time, pragmatism places a "thumb on the scale in the direction of stability" to make the law more durable and predictable.[58] Sometimes the best option for the pragmatist is to stand by things decided, even if it would have been better had those things been handled differently in the first instance.

The premises underlying pragmatism's methodology of interpretation should also inform its view of precedential scope. People and organizations make decisions based not only on what the Supreme Court decides, but also on what it says along the way. Pragmatists tend to be solicitous of reliance interests, whether reliance manifests itself in the form of public expectations or private decision-making (or both). If it would be beneficial to protect reliance expectations, those expectations should not be dismissed as inapposite merely because they attached to a judicial statement technically defined as dicta. Real-world effects, not abstract and rigid legal categories, are the core of constitutional pragmatism.

It follows that the pragmatic judge should be willing to define precedents broadly when factors such as stability and reliance are on the line. This type of thinking might well explain Justice Breyer's approach in *Parents Involved*, which I discussed above. In that case, Justice Breyer described a passage from one of the Court's previous decisions as warranting deference even as he acknowledged the passage as dicta in the formal sense. Whether classified as holding or dicta, the passage "provides, and has widely been thought to provide, authoritative legal guidance."[59] For a pragmatist like Justice Breyer, "rigid distinctions between holdings and dicta" cannot define a precedent's scope of impact in future cases. Pragmatism reflects a functional approach to the law, so it should come as little surprise that the theory would not be satisfied with trying to conceptualize a precedent's scope of applicability as "an exercise in mathematical logic."[60]

At the same time, pragmatism is consistent with the view that some judicial statements do not warrant any deference going forward. Again, the inquiry must be a practical one. If a peripheral statement in a prior Supreme Court opinion is cursory and unexplained, anyone – including constitutional pragmatists – might worry that it does not reflect the justices' serious consideration. Such statements carry a heightened risk of error. Much the same is true if the Court "hedged" its prior statement by couching it in doubts and disclaimers.[61] A qualified formulation makes it more likely that the Court

---

[58] STEPHEN BREYER, MAKING OUR DEMOCRACY WORK: A JUDGE'S VIEW 81, 153 (2010).
[59] *Parents Involved in Community Schools*, 551 U.S. at 831 (Breyer, J., dissenting).
[60] Id.
[61] *Kirtsaeng*, 133 S. Ct. at 1368.

itself did not fully commit to the implications of its statement. Even for the pragmatist, these types of judicial pronouncements will fall outside a precedent's scope of applicability. This is not because of the line between holding and dicta, but rather because of the pragmatist's attention to case-specific analysis and practical effects.

Other Normative Commitments and Constitutional Understandings. The relationship between precedential scope and interpretive philosophy is a universal phenomenon. It extends well beyond the examples discussed above. Every theory of constitutional interpretation has ramifications for the way in which precedents are defined.

The same is true of normative commitments and constitutional understandings that are not presented within the context of full-dress theories of interpretation such as common law constitutionalism or consequentialist originalism. One's devotion to certain values, and one's reading of various provisions of the Constitution, can still affect how the scope of precedent is defined. Michael Dorf, for example, defends a relatively broad view of precedent based in part on rule-of-law considerations. He argues that "[w]hen a court discards the reasoning of a prior opinion as *merely dictum*," it threatens to "relegate[] the prior decision to the position of an unjustifiable, arbitrary exercise of judicial power."[62] Lawrence Solum also highlights the link between precedent and the rule of law, though he would limit the forward-looking effects of individual decisions "to their legally salient facts." Only if a proposition emerges through a string of cases can it yield "a rule that approximates legislation."[63] Professor Solum's argument suggests a more restrictive definition of precedential scope that curbs judges' ability to articulate broad mandates in the course of a single case.

Of course, value judgments become relevant only if one believes the Constitution permits discretion in the definition of precedential scope. Not everyone does. At the center of the debate is Article III, which serves as the backdrop for the federal judiciary. Article III describes the "judicial Power" as "extend[ing]" to various classes of "Cases" and "Controversies." By connecting the judicial power with the resolution of discrete disputes, Article III arguably implies that judicial hypothesizing should not be entitled to any

---

[62] Michael C. Dorf, *Dicta and Article III*, 142 U. Pa. L. Rev. 1997, 2029–30 (1994). Professor Dorf notes a potential exception where the subsequent court "suggests an alternative basis for the outcome of the precedent case." Id. at 2030. Daniel Farber has also emphasized the rule of law in arguing against the practice of confining prior constitutional decisions "to their facts." Daniel A. Farber, *The Rule of Law and the Law of Precedents*, 90 Minn. L. Rev. 1173, 1183 (2006).

[63] Lawrence B. Solum, *The Supreme Court in Bondage: Constitutional Stare Decisis, Legal Formalism, and the Future of Unenumerated Rights*, 9 U. Pa. J. Const. L. 155, 191 (2006).

weight beyond its persuasiveness. It is possible to derive a related claim from the Constitution's more general separation of powers. When precedents are construed too broadly, the argument goes, judges may articulate wide-ranging rules and frameworks that are the rightful province of the legislature. On the other hand, Article III's distinction between inferior courts and the Supreme Court might suggest that oversight and uniformity are essential to the judicial system and the constitutional order. The implication would be that lower courts are acting lawfully (and sensibly) when they construe Supreme Court precedents broadly.

The point of briefly introducing these arguments is simply to illustrate some ways in which constitutional assumptions and understandings can inform debates over the scope of a precedent's applicability. On some views, Article III restricts the binding effect of precedents to their essential holdings, as opposed to their extraneous dicta. But even then, it is not the line between holding and dicta that is doing the work. Rather, the driving force is one's interpretation of Article III. Likewise, one might endorse the distinction between holding and dicta based on beliefs about the dangers of judicial overreaching or the heightened propensity of courts to make mistakes when they venture beyond the facts at hand. While the definition of precedential scope under such an approach might run parallel to the line between holdings and dicta as traditionally described, it would be driven by value choices and assumptions about judicial decision-making. This makes perfect sense. Speaking in terms of holding and dicta might be a useful heuristic, but the focus should remain on the underlying premises and commitments that lead a judge to conclude that certain judicial propositions warrant deference while others do not.[64]

Sometimes it is easy to figure out what a precedent stands for. When it is not, the scope of precedent depends on a host of questions about the courts, the Constitution, and the nature of judicial opinions as sources of law. To invoke the distinction between holding and dicta is not to resolve these questions, but to raise them.

---

[64] The exception would be if the holding/dicta distinction were itself entrenched and consistently enforced in the Supreme Court's cases. In that event, one possible reason for defining the scope of precedent in terms of holdings and dicta would be to respect and preserve settled law. But while the language of holdings and dicta continues to appear in the Court's opinions, there is no uniform practice of withholding deference from all judicial sentiments that range beyond the dispute at hand.

5

Precedent and Pluralism

The previous two chapters examined how constitutional philosophy affects approaches to precedent. A Supreme Court justice who adopts a general practice of deferring to precedent faces two principal questions of implementation. One is how strongly to defer. The other is how to determine when a precedent applies and when it does not. The answers to these questions depend on underlying matters of interpretive theory, normative commitment, and constitutional understanding.

Determining which precedents are vulnerable to overruling requires explaining why it is important for the law to be correct in the first place. This turns out to be complex and controversial. For some, accurate interpretation is valuable because it promotes popular sovereignty, as exercised through the people's ratification of the Constitution. For others, key considerations include morality and justice as understood in light of contemporary mores. Still others focus on consequentialist benefits and effective social policy. And the list goes on. To figure out which decisions should be stricken from the books even at the expense of continuity, we need to know both how to identify judicial mistakes and how to figure out which mistakes are in greatest need of correction.

These debates are more than theoretical; they also implicate the treatment of precedent in practice. When a justice concludes that the Supreme Court went astray in recognizing the constitutional right of corporations to advocate for political candidates, how should she assess the harm that would result from leaving the offending precedent on the books? Is it a matter of consequentialist analysis? Does it depend on the precedent's effects on popular sovereignty? Do moral judgments have some role to play? Questions like these are crucial to determining the magnitude of a constitutional mistake, yet they admit of no answer until they are connected with a deeper interpretive theory.[1]

---

[1] See Kurt T. Lash, *The Cost of Judicial Error: Stare Decisis and the Role of Normative Theory*, 89 NOTRE DAME L. REV. 2189, 2205 (2014).

If a justice's interpretive methodology emphasizes factors such as freedom from governmental oppression, a case like *Plessy v. Ferguson* (1896) will be in urgent need of overruling given its endorsement of racial segregation.[2] But a case like *Miranda v. Arizona* (1966), even if deemed incorrect in its approach to police questioning, is much more difficult to view as oppressive to individuals given its focus on providing a safeguard against official overreaching.[3] Any argument for overruling would need to invoke other considerations. Alternatively, if a justice's interpretive methodology is grounded in popular sovereignty, the denial of a constitutional right "to nondiscriminatory treatment by a private employer" might be tolerable, because the political process theoretically can provide legislative protections against employment discrimination when the courts have failed to act.[4] Yet the same denial could be problematic for theories centered on individual fairness or equal protection.

Similar questions abound. To take just a few examples:

- If a justice believes the Supreme Court incorrectly withheld constitutional protection from same-sex couples for their private relationships, what metric should she use to evaluate the harmfulness of leaving the erroneous precedent intact?[5]
- If a justice believes the states possess broad powers to impose tax-collection obligations on out-of-state sellers, how should she evaluate the harm caused by a precedent that unduly limits those powers?[6]
- If a justice believes *Roe v. Wade* (1973) was mistaken in recognizing a constitutional right to abortion, how should she weigh the ramifications of retaining *Roe* versus overruling it?[7]

To answer these questions and others like them, we need an organizing theory to tell us which effects of precedent are legally salient. That was the thesis of Chapter 3. A justice's interpretive theory is what determines whether the effects of a flawed decision are legitimate reasons for overruling it, or rather consequences that are perhaps lamentable but ultimately inapposite to the judicial process.

The same goes for a precedent's scope of applicability, as explained in Chapter 4. A justice who thinks precedents warrant presumptive deference needs to figure out when a prior decision is relevant to the case at hand.

[2] 163 U.S. 537.
[3] 384 U.S. 436.
[4] Kurt T. Lash, *Originalism, Popular Sovereignty, and Reverse Stare Decisis*, 93 VA. L. REV. 1437, 1459 (2007).
[5] *See* Lawrence v. Texas, 539 U.S. 558 (2003).
[6] *See* Quill Corp. v. North Dakota, 504 U.S. 298 (1992).
[7] *See* Planned Parenthood of Southeastern Pennsylvania v. Casey, 505 U.S. 833 (1992).

A potential starting point is the distinction between binding holdings and dispensable dicta. But the question remains *why* that distinction is appropriate for defining the scope of precedent – a question whose difficulty is exacerbated by the lack of a consistent approach at the Supreme Court. Any answer will imply a particular set of understandings about the manner in which the Constitution ought to be interpreted and implemented.

All of this would be complicated enough if the justices were in perpetual agreement about the precepts of constitutional interpretation. In such a scenario, each justice would still occasionally disagree with her peers, past and present. For example, two originalist justices might reach divergent conclusions about the original meaning of a particular provision of the Constitution. Or two pragmatic justices might disagree about whether a constitutional rule is effective in practical terms. Notwithstanding these divergences, the justices would be in basic agreement about what it means to interpret the Constitution faithfully and competently.

Overlapping interpretive and normative commitments would also facilitate a unified approach to precedent. The justices might rally around the view that a flawed precedent is most troubling when it offends popular sovereignty, or when it violates contemporary mores, or otherwise. Similarly, they might agree that the need for constraint justifies defining precedents in broad terms, or that a proper understanding of the judicial role requires limiting precedents to their essential applications of narrow rules to concrete facts. Whatever the content of their interpretive agreements, the justices would be poised to pursue a consistent vision of precedent.

OF HARMONY AND DISCORD

In reality, American constitutional practice is awash with interpretive disagreements. This is true of the federal judiciary as a whole and the Supreme Court in particular. Justice Scalia noted in 2013 that the justices were not "in agreement on the basic question of what we think we're doing when we interpret the Constitution."[8] The extent of disagreement becomes even more pronounced when we consider shifts in interpretive philosophy that occur over the years as individual justices come and go.

The modern Supreme Court does not consistently adopt any particular methodology of constitutional decision-making. Take, for instance, the originalist school of interpretation. Some justices have been clear about their

---

[8] Jennifer Senior, *In Conversation: Antonin Scalia*, N.Y. MAG. (October 6, 2013), http://nymag.com/news/features/antonin-scalia-2013-10/.

adherence to originalism, and the Court often refers to the Constitution's original meaning in the course of explaining its decisions. Occasionally, originalism even takes center stage. A prominent example is the Court's recent ruling that the Second Amendment protects an individual's right to possess firearms. There, a majority of justices joined an opinion adopting "the original understanding of the Second Amendment."[9]

Notwithstanding this endorsement of originalism, in other cases the Court resolves constitutional questions with little or no attention to original meanings. Sometimes its analysis is steeped in political theory, such as the belief that an unfettered marketplace of ideas is the lynchpin of expressive liberty. The field of campaign-finance law provides a ready illustration. When the Supreme Court ruled in *Citizens United v. FEC* (2010) that corporations cannot be barred from candidate advocacy, the majority opinion was driven by conceptual arguments about what the First Amendment "stands against": namely, "attempts to disfavor certain subjects or viewpoints."[10] The majority also invoked the Constitution's original meaning in concluding that "[t]here is simply no support for the view that the First Amendment, as originally understood, would permit the suppression of political speech by media corporations."[11] But the crux of the decision was the determination – not obviously linked to any investigation of original meanings – that "independent expenditures, including those made by corporations, do not give rise to corruption or the appearance of corruption."[12] It was left to a concurrence to conduct a deeper inquiry into the decision's consistency with the original meaning of the First Amendment.[13]

In other instances, the justices base their decisions on assessments of perceived constitutional purposes or longstanding political traditions. An example arose in 2014 when the Court interpreted the Recess Appointments Clause. A majority of justices noted that "in interpreting the Clause, we put significant weight upon historical practice" and "must hesitate to upset the compromises and working arrangements that the elected branches of Government themselves have reached."[14]

There are also cases in which contemporary moral sensibilities are prevalent, as exemplified by the Court's recognition of a constitutional right to same-sex marriage in *Obergefell v. Hodges* (2015). The majority in *Obergefell*

[9] District of Columbia v. Heller, 554 U.S. 570, 625 (2008).
[10] 558 U.S. 310, 340.
[11] Id. at 353.
[12] Id. at 357.
[13] *See* id. at 385 (Scalia, J., concurring).
[14] National Labor Relations Board v. Noel Canning, 134 S. Ct. 2550, 2559–60 (2014).

grounded its analysis in evolving constitutional norms. It noted that "[t]he history of marriage is one of both continuity and change" and added that "[t]he nature of injustice is that we may not always see it in our own times."[15] While the Court's prior "cases describing the right to marry presumed a relationship involving opposite-sex partners," they did not entrench such a view for all time. Instead, the *Obergefell* majority revised the Court's case law in order to pursue "a better informed understanding of how constitutional imperatives define a liberty that remains urgent in our own era."[16]

The point is that the Court regularly shifts between interpretive approaches without suggesting that its "different methods are reducible to one master method," much less furnishing a passkey for undertaking such a decryption.[17] I will refer to this approach as *pluralistic*, reflecting a vision of constitutional decision-making characterized by the absence of commitment to any particular interpretive theory.

To believe multiple styles of constitutional argument are legitimate is not necessarily to be a pluralist. The Court might conclude that, for example, some constitutional provisions are properly understood in light of their original meanings, while others draw on contemporary sensibilities. The Court would also need to explain the underlying normative basis of a theory that points toward original meanings in some cases and contemporary mores in others. No such explanation has been forthcoming. For better or worse, the Court has been willing to emphasize different argument styles from case to case without presenting an overarching theory grounded in a defined set of normative values. It has, in short, been pluralistic in its reasoning.

COLLECTIVE ACTION AND INDIVIDUAL CHOICE

The Supreme Court's penchant for pluralism arises in two ways. The first is via its nature as a multimember institution that decides cases by majority vote. The Court is a group of different individuals appointed by different presidents and possessing different views about the law. It operates through collective action, which means that for an interpretive theory to prevail, it must consistently win the allegiance of at least five justices. And if the theory is to have staying power, it needs continued support even as some justices leave the bench and others join.

---

[15] 135 S. Ct. 2584, 2595, 2598.
[16] Id. at 2602.
[17] Stephen M. Griffin, *Pluralism in Constitutional Interpretation*, 72 TEX. L. REV. 1753, 1757 (1994).

The need for buy-in from multiple justices decreases the likelihood that any given constitutional theory will predominate in the Court's case law, particularly over a substantial period of time. This is not to say it is impossible for five (or more) sitting justices to agree about the proper theory of constitutional interpretation. Still, given the rarity with which seats on the Court open up, it is quite the challenge to assemble five justices who share the same philosophy. When we factor in the divisiveness of American politics and the probability of shifts in the balance of political power – including the power of judicial appointment – sustained agreement over time is even more difficult to come by.

The nature of the Supreme Court as a multimember institution is not the only driver of interpretive pluralism. Pluralism can also emerge as the preferred approach of an individual justice. Debates over constitutional law include differences of opinion about whether judges should be applying interpretive theory at all. For example, Judge J. Harvie Wilkinson recently characterized leading constitutional theories as little more than "competing schools of liberal and conservative judicial activism."[18] Skepticism about interpretive theory reaches all the way to the Supreme Court. The experience of John Roberts is illustrative. During his confirmation hearings in 2005, the soon-to-be Chief Justice noted that rather than drawing on abstract theory, he favors "bottom up" judging. As he explained in a response to Senator Orrin Hatch:

> If the phrase in the Constitution says two-thirds of the Senate, everybody's a literalist when they interpret that. Other phrases in the Constitution are broader, [such as] "unreasonable searches and seizures." You can look at that wording all day and it's not going to give you much progress in deciding whether a particular search is reasonable or not. You have to begin looking at the cases and the precedents, what the Framers had in mind when they drafted that provision.
>
> So, yes, it does depend upon the nature of the case before you[,] I think.[19]

Chief Justice Roberts's testimony helps to show why the Court's interpretive pluralism is not solely the product of its status as a multimember institution. It is also the result of individual choice. Nor is Chief Justice Roberts alone in his preference for pluralism. Five years after his confirmation, Justice Kagan offered her own endorsement of a "case-by-case" approach to determining which sources and arguments are relevant in the context of a

---

[18] J. Harvie Wilkinson III, Cosmic Constitutional Theory: Why Americans Are Losing Their Inalienable Right to Self-Governance 4 (2012). For Judge Wilkinson, the "highest virtues of judging" lie in overcoming theory and being guided instead by "self-denial and restraint." Id. at 116.

[19] 109th Cong. 159 (2005).

particular dispute.[20] For case-by-case justices, interpretive pluralism is an individual phenomenon as much as an institutional one.

In defining the role of precedent, approaching disputes in a pluralistic, case-by-case manner is just as resonant as aligning oneself with a particular school of interpretation. As Adrian Vermeule points out, opting to "take each case as it comes ... constitutes an implicit choice of interpretive method and an implicit allocation of interpretive authority. It is a choice to commit interpretation to the case-specific discretion of the judges on the spot, as opposed to the discretion of judges at other times and places who might formulate general interpretive doctrine to govern the adjudicative process."[21] Irrespective of whether such pluralism is superior to the adoption of a discrete interpretive theory, the two concepts play similar roles in judicial decision-making.

Even so, there is a fundamental difference between interpretive pluralism and theory-based judging when it comes to the treatment of precedent. Pluralism denies that cases should be decided in accordance with preexisting commitments to interpretive methodologies and underlying normative justifications. That premise distinguishes pluralism from other interpretive approaches. It also presents a serious challenge when the question before the Supreme Court is whether a flawed precedent is so problematic as to warrant overruling. By design, judicial pluralism avoids ex ante prioritization of values and methodologies. Yet prioritization is necessary if the application of stare decisis depends – as I have claimed that it does – on conclusions about the harmfulness of a precedent's effects. There must be some mechanism for determining which of those effects are relevant and which are not.

THE CHALLENGES OF PLURALISM

In Chapter 2, I discussed several reasons for deferring to prior decisions. Prominent among them is the utility of precedent in enhancing the cohesiveness and impersonality of courts. At the level of the Supreme Court, a strong system of precedent encourages the justices to think and act like parts of an enduring institution.

The unifying effects of precedent are critical in a legal system characterized by interpretive pluralism. Pluralism increases the chances that substituting one justice for another will lead to the application of an entirely different interpretive methodology, particularly when the Court is closely divided. Deference to precedent can smooth out the path of the law by preserving

---

[20] 111th Cong. 81 (2010).
[21] ADRIAN VERMEULE, JUDGING UNDER UNCERTAINTY 157 (2006).

a stable core even as justices come and go. Past decisions provide common ground and separate the inclination of the individual justice from the content of the law. The aspiration is, to quote Amy Barrett, "a reasoned conversation over time between justices – and others – who subscribe to competing methodologies of constitutional interpretation."[22]

But precedent's ability to unite the Court is threatened by the prevalence of interpretive pluralism. I have argued that the importance of replacing a flawed interpretation with a correct one depends on a justice's methodological choices and normative commitments. I have made a similar claim about the definition of a precedent's scope of applicability. When the justices disagree about baseline matters of interpretation, the Court's decisions are likely to be inconsistent in their conceptions of precedent. Invocations of precedent will tend to restate interpretive disagreements instead of bridging them. In the worst-case scenario, the ideal of constitutional law as stable and enduring can give way to the notion that judicial identity and legal meaning are one and the same.

None of this is to say interpretive pluralism is, all things considered, a bad thing. Whether it would be better for US legal practice to move closer to a consensus theory of interpretation is an intricate question, and one far beyond my purview here. As a result, I make no claim about the desirability of interpretive pluralism in general. I mean only to suggest that pluralism, in both its institutional and individual varieties, makes it more difficult to fashion a workable approach to precedent that can unite judges. A theory of precedent requires a consistent way of defining decisions' scope of applicability. It also requires a stable metric for evaluating the relevant effects of a flawed decision. Pluralism complicates both pursuits. Before there can be a well-functioning doctrine of precedent, there must be a plan for responding to the challenges of pluralism.

SECOND-BEST STARE DECISIS

The Supreme Court's doctrine of stare decisis encompasses several discrete considerations, albeit considerations that are applied loosely and flexibly. While the justices continue to disagree over the proper treatment of precedent in individual cases, both the doctrinal structure and the animating tension

---

[22] Amy Coney Barrett, *Precedent and Jurisprudential Disagreement*, 91 TEX. L. REV. 1711, 1737 (2013); *see also* Frederick Schauer, *Precedent*, 39 STAN. L. REV. 571, 600 (1987) ("Using a system of precedent to standardize decisions subordinates dissimilarity among decisionmakers, both in appearance and in practice.").

between legal continuity and legal correctness are established features of the Court's jurisprudence.

Neither reciting the governing rules nor acknowledging the choice between continuity and correctness is sufficient to achieve consistency. The threshold problem is that the value of getting the law right is a controversial proposition. The difficulty is particularly acute within the realm of constitutional law. Specifying the value of correct interpretation carries profound implications for the treatment of precedent, because it determines what is at stake in tolerating an interpretive error.

One response is to view stare decisis through a particular methodological lens by examining how a justice should treat precedent if she is an originalist, or a common law constitutionalist, or a pragmatist, and so on. This type of analysis is invaluable for understanding how precedent operates within various methodological schools. It helps judges and commentators who are considering a particular methodology to evaluate its assumptions and implications. It also informs arguments for why one methodology is superior to others.

In the pages ahead, I am going to defend a different approach to precedent, one that is designed for a Supreme Court populated by justices who often disagree with each other on matters of interpretive philosophy. The objective is to tailor the doctrine of stare decisis to a world in which constitutional interpretation is rife with methodological and theoretical disagreements.

Those disagreements characterize what I call the *second-best world* of constitutional law. The second-best world stands in contrast to an idealized state of affairs in which the justices largely agree on the appropriate ends and means of constitutional interpretation. Whether or not interpretive pluralism is healthier than widespread interpretive agreement as a general matter, pluralism creates unique challenges for the treatment of precedent. From the standpoint of developing a workable and coherent doctrine of stare decisis, a world of pluralism is a second-best world.

While the theory of the second best has been described and employed in various ways in the economic and legal literature, the conception I will draw upon envisions the theory as a means of optimizing the performance of an imperfect system. Its central insight is straightforward: If a system suffers from one flaw, it might make sense to intentionally introduce another imperfection in response to the first. Once we exit the ideal world, we cannot take for granted that the proper approach is to approximate the ideal as closely as possible. The question is how best to proceed in the actual world where we find ourselves. The answer may include steps that would, if viewed in isolation, seem like deviations from the ideal state of affairs.

Second-best analysis offers important lessons for the doctrine of stare decisis. I have argued that the prevalence of interpretive pluralism creates challenges for the treatment of precedent that would not exist under conditions of widespread agreement over constitutional philosophy. We might imagine two possible responses. One option is to leave the existing doctrine unchanged while hoping pluralism will not be too much of a drag on its effectiveness. That approach is consistent with the current status of precedent at the Supreme Court. The Court's discussions of stare decisis are sophisticated in many respects, but they do not account for the ways in which interpretive philosophy influences attitudes toward precedent.

The other option for responding to pluralism, and the one that I will defend, is grounded in the theory of the second best. It resists the idea that stare decisis should operate the same way in a system marked by interpretive pluralism as it would in a system of interpretive harmony. Instead, stare decisis ought to take a different shape in response to pluralism's prevalence. For example, considerations that would be relevant to the durability of precedent under ideal conditions might be excluded from the calculus when pluralism is the order of the day. This suggestion may seem counterintuitive, because it entails countering one flaw in the system by consciously introducing another. But that is the essence of second-best thinking: When part of a system deviates from its ideal state, sometimes the most promising path forward requires making other adjustments instead of acting as if the initial flaw doesn't exist.

Second-best analysis of interpretive theory is nothing new. Leading constitutional scholars have examined the interplay between second-best analysis and legal interpretation, and I will draw on their work in thinking specifically about a second-best theory of judicial precedent. The central issue I will engage is how the Supreme Court's doctrine of stare decisis could be revised to operate more effectively against a backdrop of pluralism.

The second-best theory of stare decisis uses compensating adjustments to allow precedent to serve its central purposes. Without a second-best accommodation, applications of precedent tend to reflect deeper methodological and normative commitments. In many cases these commitments remain submerged, but occasionally they bubble up to the surface. In 2003, the Supreme Court concluded that retaining a precedent that failed to protect same-sex relationships would "demean[] the lives of homosexual persons."[23] Years later, the Court warned that withholding constitutional protection from corporate electioneering would validate a "brooding governmental power" at odds with

---

[23] *Lawrence*, 539 U.S. at 575.

"confidence and stability in civic discourse."[24] The same case produced a concurrence that chronicled various problems the Court has alleviated through its willingness to depart from precedent.[25] Included on the list was the Court's most heralded reversal-of-course – its repudiation of racial segregation in *Brown v. Board of Education* (1954)[26] – which is so widely lauded precisely because the justices sought to eradicate a catastrophic harm. These examples demonstrate how arguments for overruling are grounded in conclusions about a given precedent's conceptual and normative flaws. Those conclusions, in turn, reflect choices about the types of effects that are relevant to a precedent's retention or dismissal.

Under conditions of interpretive harmony, determining the relevance of legal harms would pose little problem for the doctrine of stare decisis. Given their agreement about interpretive theory, the justices would possess a uniform metric for evaluating precedents' effects. Every justice would deem precedents harmful based on some prespecified and universal criterion, be it morality, popular sovereignty, welfare maximization, or otherwise. The justices might not always reach the same conclusions, but they would speak the same language.

In the real world of interpretive pluralism, the calculus changes. The proliferation of competing methodologies makes it more difficult to reach agreement about the legal relevance of various harms. The prospect of agreement is slimmer still when the Supreme Court is viewed as an enduring institution whose composition changes over time. By tethering a decision's continued vitality to the perceived gravity of its offenses – a perception that will vary from justice to justice – the prevailing approach to stare decisis robs precedents of independent value beyond their attractiveness on the merits. The same phenomena of interpretive pluralism and "reasonable disagreement"[27] that threaten the durability of particular decisions end up destabilizing stare decisis itself.

The foregoing discussion relates to the degree of deference a precedent commands. Problems of pluralism also affect the inquiry into precedents' scope of applicability. Though precedential scope is often described in terms of binding holdings and dispensable dicta, we have seen that the situation on the ground is more complex. Relevant questions include whether a precedent should receive deference for its articulated doctrinal framework, what to make of judicial asides, and how future justices should treat an opinion's

---

[24] *Citizens United*, 558 U.S. at 349.
[25] *See id.* at 377 (Roberts, C. J., concurring).
[26] 347 U.S. 483.
[27] *See* RICHARD H. FALLON, JR., IMPLEMENTING THE CONSTITUTION 103 (2001) ("Stare decisis . . . furnishes a functionally crucial response to the phenomenon of reasonable disagreement.").

expression of its rationale. The answers depend on underlying assumptions about the competence, institutional role, and constitutional authority of the courts. Establishing a consistent account of precedential scope requires doctrinal accommodations that can overcome interpretive disputes.

Before we can pursue a doctrine of precedent that makes good on its promise of uniting judges across time and enhancing the impersonality of constitutional law, there must be a reconceptualization to account for the pervasiveness of interpretive disagreement. Our second-best world of interpretive pluralism requires a second-best doctrine of stare decisis.

Under the second-best approach, precedent becomes a tool of unification rather than division. It represents a shared commitment to respecting the Court's institutional past. This commitment sometimes calls upon the Court to uphold a precedent notwithstanding its deleterious (in the view of today's justices) effects. Such deference carries a cost; the conscious perpetuation of error should not occur lightly. But the question is not whether stare decisis has a price. It is whether the price is worth paying. I will contend that the virtues of deference often justify the tolerance of error, so long as stare decisis is applied in a manner that is consistent, impersonal, and – to the greatest extent possible – independent of disputes over interpretive philosophy. Indeed, quotidian disputes over constitutional methodology are a leading reason why stare decisis is so important. Without deference, a change in the composition of the Court is a change in the fabric of the law. The driving objective of second-best stare decisis is the separation of precedent from interpretive theory in a way that transcends the identities of individual judges.

TOWARD A SECOND-BEST APPROACH

The ensuing chapters develop the theory of second-best stare decisis. Consistent with my emphasis on the value of continuity, I seek to preserve the existing doctrine of stare decisis where possible. Yet the second-best approach identifies revisions and accommodations designed to insulate stare decisis from disputes over interpretive philosophy.

On the issue of precedential strength, second-best analysis yields two potential strategies for addressing the challenges of pluralism. The first solution, which I explain in Chapter 6, focuses on reconstructing the doctrine of stare decisis around considerations that can operate independently of interpretive philosophy. Familiar considerations such as procedural workability, factual accuracy, and reliance expectations can be redefined to reduce their dependence on constitutional theory, making them suitable for application by judges across the methodological spectrum. At the same time, some factors that might be relevant under conditions of interpretive harmony – including jurisprudential coherence, flagrancy of error, and a precedent's perceived harmfulness – cannot function against the backdrop of pluralism. Second-best stare decisis generally excludes those factors from the examination of a precedent's fitness for retention.

In developing my account of second-best stare decisis, I begin by assuming that a majority (at least) of Supreme Court justices continues to support stare decisis as a general matter. This assumption is based on the justices' statements in case after case about the centrality of precedent and the virtues of deference. The justices commonly describe stare decisis as a mechanism for "maintaining public faith in the judiciary as a source of impersonal and reasoned judgments."[28] They depict the doctrine as integral to "the very concept of the rule of law underlying our own Constitution," which "requires such continuity over time that a respect for precedent is, by definition, indispensable."[29] They recognize precedent as promoting "the evenhanded, predictable, and consistent development of legal principles," while at the same time "foster[ing] reliance on judicial decisions" and "contribut[ing] to the actual and perceived integrity of the judicial process."[30] Deference to precedent "permits society to presume that bedrock principles are founded in the law rather than in the proclivities of individuals," an effect that "contributes to the integrity of our constitutional system of government."[31] Ultimately, "[f]idelity to precedent" is "vital to the proper exercise of the judicial function."[32] It is nothing less than a "foundation stone of the rule of law."[33] As these statements illustrate, the doctrine of stare decisis enjoys strong support at the Supreme Court. The controversy surrounds its application to particular cases.

Later in Chapter 6, I relax the assumption of a Court that remains committed to stare decisis. My inquiry shifts to why an individual justice should accept second-best stare decisis without any guarantee that her present and future judicial colleagues will follow suit. I defend the second-best theory as a valuable tool for promoting continuity, impersonality, and coordinated action, and I explain why an individual justice's support for it should not depend on the behavior of her peers or successors.

As an alternative to the doctrinal approach to precedential strength, Chapter 7 describes a structural response to interpretive pluralism that

[28] *Moragne v. States Marine Lines, Inc.*, 398 U.S. 375, 403 (1970).
[29] *Casey*, 505 U.S. at 854.
[30] *Payne v. Tennessee*, 501 U.S. 808, 827 (1991).
[31] *Vasquez v. Hillery*, 474 U.S. 254, 265 (1986).
[32] *Citizens United*, 558 U.S. at 377 (Roberts, C. J., concurring).
[33] *Michigan v. Bay Mills Indian Community*, 134 S. Ct. 2024, 2036 (2014).

requires overrulings to receive support from a supermajority of justices. The structural response increases the likelihood that overrulings will rest on factors that bridge methodological divides; the greater the number of votes required to achieve a particular result, the better the chances that some votes must come from justices who disagree with one another on matters of interpretive theory. Unlike the doctrinal version of second-best stare decisis, the structural alternative does not promote judicial impersonality on the individual level by encouraging a justice to subordinate her views to those of her predecessors. I will emphasize this distinction in depicting the doctrinal approach to precedential strength as superior to its structural cousin. Nevertheless, the simplicity of the supermajority requirement makes it worthy of consideration by those who see value in legal continuity but who have reservations about the efficacy or wisdom of altering the content of stare decisis doctrine.

Second-best stare decisis also suggests a revised approach to defining a precedent's scope of applicability, as I explain in Chapter 8. Existing practice supports the principle that rules announced by the Supreme Court warrant deference in future cases. Much the same is true of the principle that judicial asides and hypotheticals do *not* warrant deference. Given their widespread acceptance, these norms can guide determinations of precedential scope in the second-best world. As for statements of rationale contained in Supreme Court decisions, second-best stare decisis counsels an intermediate position that treats such statements as worthy of deference only to the extent they illuminate a precedent's rule of decision.

Stepping back, my basic claim is that for stare decisis to do what the justices have said it should do, the existing doctrine must be reconsidered. Most importantly, analysis of the strength and scope of precedent must be separated from debates about interpretive philosophy, even if those debates would be relevant to the treatment of precedent under ideal conditions. Instead of linking precedent to competing interpretive theories, the second-best approach seeks to infuse stare decisis with independent content that holds steady regardless of a justice's methodological and normative inclinations.

When a justice defers to her predecessors despite reservations about the merits of their decisions, she reinforces the generality of constitutional norms. Fidelity to precedent can "transform[] the Court from an ever-changing collection of individual judges to an institution capable of building a continuing body of law."[34] It also underscores the distinction between the judiciary and

---

[34] Daniel A. Farber, *The Rule of Law and the Law of Precedents*, 90 MINN. L. REV. 1173, 1183 (2006).

the political branches, promoting a vision in which changing the law and changing the judge are very different things.

Lest there be any doubt, I wish to emphasize that despite seeking to bridge methodological divides, my theory of second-best stare decisis is itself unmistakably normative. It privileges the impersonality and continuity of law, which I view as values that are accepted by judges across the philosophical spectrum. My project is not to develop a value-free account of stare decisis, but rather to develop an account whose normative baselines can draw together judges who might otherwise be inclined to disagree.

Disagreements over interpretive theory are here to stay. Outright disavowals of theory also appear to be sturdy components of the constitutional landscape. But stare decisis need not be undermined by such phenomena. Untangled from debates over interpretive theory, second-best stare decisis embodies a fundamental commitment to continuity and impersonality – a commitment to the rule of law rather than the rule of men and women. It contributes to the perception and reality of a Supreme Court that speaks "for the Constitution itself rather than simply for five or more lawyers in black robes."[35]

---

[35] Earl M. Maltz, *Some Thoughts on the Death of Stare Decisis in Constitutional Law*, 1980 WIS. L. REV. 467, 484.

6

Precedential Strength in Doctrinal Perspective

This chapter considers the implications of second-best stare decisis for determining the strength of precedent. The first step is to examine how the Supreme Court's existing doctrine of stare decisis operates in a world of interpretive pluralism. From there, I suggest a series of doctrinal revisions to overcome the challenges of pluralism. I seek to preserve and refine components of the existing doctrine that provide meaningful guidance in a second-best world of pluralism, while limiting or excluding components whose content depends on methodological and normative commitments that vary from judge to judge. Notwithstanding other benefits that can arise from a system of precedent-based judging – benefits such as predictability, efficiency, and the protection of expectations – the core of second-best stare decisis is impersonality and continuity. Precedent allows the law to transcend the moment.

Second-best stare decisis leaves individual justices at liberty to apply their preferred methods of interpretation in cases of first impression and in diagnosing whether a precedent was erroneous. But it revises the Court's rules of precedent to pursue a doctrine that works across methodological lines. In doing so, it facilitates coordinated action among justices who are inclined to view the world differently.

This latter feature most clearly separates a commitment to second-best stare decisis from a commitment to interpretive methodologies such as originalism or living constitutionalism. Fostering agreement around a particular interpretive methodology is a tall order in our pluralistic legal culture. It requires some justices to take the dramatic step of disavowing their constitutional philosophies. By contrast, asking an originalist or living constitutionalist to recognize a meaningful role for precedent does not require her to abandon her interpretive philosophy wholesale. Second-best stare decisis reflects a shared sacrifice, because it calls upon every justice to give presumptive respect to some decisions – and, by implication, to the methodologies and values that yielded them – that she views as flawed. As I have noted, to prioritize impersonality and continuity is to make a normative choice, and one that should be evaluated as such. Nevertheless, the endorsement of second-best stare decisis is less dramatic, and less jarring, than the displacement of one interpretive methodology by another.

THE DOCTRINE OF STARE DECISIS

Stare decisis is founded on the principle that today's judges do not write on a clean slate. That same principle applies to the doctrine of stare decisis itself. Precedent is an integral component of American legal practice. Its importance reaches back to the founding, and beyond. The resonance of stare decisis is apparent in Alexander Hamilton's characterization of precedent as a safeguard against the exercise of "arbitrary discretion in the courts."[1] It is equally evident in James Madison's view that the Constitution's ambiguities would be "liquidated" over time through judicial and political decisions.[2]

Within the Supreme Court's case law, stare decisis has moved beyond abstract principles to yield a discrete set of relevant considerations. When a new justice takes her place on the bench, she is greeted by a preexisting doctrine of stare decisis, just as she encounters preexisting doctrines on scores of other topics. The Court has described several factors as relevant to the analysis. The most prominent account comes from *Planned Parenthood of Southeastern Pennsylvania v. Casey* (1992), where the Court discussed its decision in *Roe v. Wade* (1973) regarding the constitutional status of abortion rights. In surveying the components of stare decisis doctrine, the *Casey* majority identified the following factors:

> So in this case we may enquire whether *Roe*'s central rule has been found unworkable; whether the rule's limitation on state power could be removed without serious inequity to those who have relied upon it or significant damage to the stability of the society governed by it; whether the law's growth in the intervening years has left *Roe*'s central rule a doctrinal anachronism

---

[1] THE FEDERALIST NO. 78 (Alexander Hamilton).
[2] See, e.g., THE FEDERALIST NO. 37 (James Madison) ("All new laws, though penned with the greatest technical skill, and passed on the fullest and most mature deliberation, are considered as more or less obscure and equivocal, until their meaning be liquidated and ascertained by a series of particular discussions and adjudications."); Caleb Nelson, *Stare Decisis and Demonstrably Erroneous Precedents*, 87 VA. L. REV. 1, 10–4 (2001) (explaining and contextualizing Madison's position); cf. THE FEDERALIST NO. 78 (A. Hamilton) (noting that in the face of inconsistent laws, "it is the province of the courts to liquidate and fix their meaning and operation").

discounted by society; and whether *Roe*'s premises of fact have so far changed in the ensuing two decades as to render its central holding somehow irrelevant or unjustifiable in dealing with the issue it addressed.[3]

In developing a second-best approach to precedent, it will be useful to begin with the factors included in *Casey*'s influential account. For ease of exposition, I have reordered them and described them as procedural workability, factual accuracy, jurisprudential coherence, and reliance and disruption. After discussing the suitability of each factor in our second-best world, I turn to other questions that shape the Supreme Court's applications of stare decisis. Among the most important of those are whether the perceived severity of a precedent's error should affect its retention, and how to account for a precedent's negative consequences.

PROCEDURAL WORKABILITY

The inquiry into workability responds to the "mischievous consequences to litigants and courts" that can result from a vague or byzantine rule of decision.[4] The rationale for paying attention to workability is intuitive. Precedents that have created "uncertainty and arbitrariness of adjudication" warrant reconsideration.[5] Those precedents impose costs that all judges can recognize as undesirable.

The characterization of a decision as workable or unworkable sometimes seems to track views about the decision's soundness on the merits.[6] This correlation might suggest the diagnosis of workability cannot be separated from a justice's interpretive and normative preferences. And, in fact, there is little doubt that when workability is defined too broadly, methodological and normative commitments can creep into the analysis. At base, however, a decision's workability is independent of disputes over interpretive philosophy. The workability

---

[3] 505 U.S. at 855; *see also* Montejo v. Louisiana, 556 U.S. 778, 792–3 (2009); Leegin Creative Leather Products, Inc. v. PSKS, Inc., 551 U.S. 877, 923–9 (2007) (Breyer, J., dissenting); Barry Friedman, *The Wages of Stealth Overruling (with Particular Attention to* Miranda v. Arizona*)*, 99 GEO. L. J. 1, 26 (2010); Michael Stokes Paulsen, *Does the Supreme Court's Current Doctrine of Stare Decisis Require Adherence to the Supreme Court's Current Doctrine of Stare Decisis?*, 86 N.C. L. REV. 1165, 1173–8 (2008).

[4] Swift & Co. v. Wickham, 382 U.S. 111, 116 (1965).

[5] Johnson v. United States, 135 S. Ct. 2551, 2562 (2015); *see also* Thomas R. Lee, *Stare Decisis in Economic Perspective: An Economic Analysis of the Supreme Court's Doctrine of Precedent*, 78 N.C. L. REV. 643, 670 (2000).

[6] *Compare* Dickerson v. United States, 530 U.S. 428, 444 (2000) (defending the relative workability of the *Miranda* rule), *with* id. at 463 (Scalia, J., dissenting) (disputing *Miranda*'s "supposed workability").

analysis is amenable to principled application regardless of a particular justice's interpretive predilections. It simply requires a reconceptualization.

The critical step is rejecting the premise that a precedent becomes unworkable because a justice disagrees with its rationale or is troubled by its results. Saying a precedent is poorly reasoned or has wrought moral or political harms is not an argument from workability. It is an argument about the precedent's interpretive approach and substantive effects.

The proper reasons for paying attention to a decision's workability are procedural in nature. They deal with whether courts, litigants, and other stakeholders have been able to understand and apply a rule without undue difficulty. A rule of decision that is hopelessly convoluted or exceedingly vague renders a precedent unworkable regardless of its rationale and substantive effects. Likewise, a rule of decision that is unmistakably clear must be acknowledged as procedurally workable even if its results have been disastrous.

I will discuss the treatment of substantive effects in greater depth below. For now, the focus is distinguishing those effects from considerations of procedural workability, the latter of which possess independent force irrespective of a justice's interpretive methodology. Whether a precedent has been clear enough for courts to understand and apply does not depend on whether a particular justice is an originalist, a pragmatist, or a common law constitutionalist. That makes procedural workability an appropriate consideration for the doctrine of stare decisis in our second-best world of interpretive pluralism.

This is not to say the justices will always agree. There are different degrees of workability, and disputes will surely arise about whether a particular precedent is, notwithstanding some procedural flaws, capable of furnishing adequate guidance to the bench and bar. Second-best stare decisis is compatible with that reality. The second-best approach is not quixotic. It does not seek to eliminate disagreements in judgment. The goal is to facilitate reasoned deliberation in a common grammar that transcends interpretive disputes. Second-best stare decisis can tolerate competing conclusions in the context of an individual case. What it rejects are criteria that have no independent content unless they are situated within a particular methodological framework. Because the creation of workable decisions – and the revision or eradication of unworkable ones – has value across a range of methodological perspectives, procedural workability stands as a legitimate component of second-best stare decisis.

FACTUAL ACCURACY

Judicial decisions contain factual premises, and those premises can be wrong. The error may have existed from the beginning, as when the Supreme Court repeats a mistaken statement by a litigant regarding federal policy.[7] Or a premise may have disintegrated over time, as when technological developments undermine the Court's prior characterization of certain forms of media.[8] In either situation, factual accuracy is compromised.

As with their treatment of workability, courts occasionally conflate diagnoses of factual error with assessments of a precedent's legal reasoning. Consider the Supreme Court's discussion of factual mistakes in *Casey*. The Court concluded there had been no factual developments that undermined the "central holding" of *Roe* regarding viability as the critical point for determining the government's power to prohibit nontherapeutic abortions.[9] In explaining its conclusion, the Court invoked two precedents that it characterized as resting on factual mistakes. The first case was *Lochner v. New York* (1905), which *Casey* described as reflecting inaccurate assumptions about "the capacity of a relatively unregulated market to satisfy minimal levels of human welfare."[10] The second case was *Plessy v. Ferguson* (1896), which *Casey* described as overlooking the pernicious stigmatization of racial segregation.[11]

Such an understanding of what constitutes a factual premise is too capacious. One can accept that both *Lochner* and *Plessy* deserved to be overruled while still recognizing that their respective errors ranged beyond their factual premises. The dispositive change from *Plessy* to *Brown v. Board of Education* (1954),[12] and from *Lochner* to *West Coast Hotel Co. v. Parrish* (1937),[13] was not empirical reality. It was the opinions and values through which reality is perceived and understood. Opinions and values are vital, but they do not possess the objectivity of facts.

The *Casey* approach is not the only way to identify which of a judicial decision's components are factual. Factual content can be understood more narrowly as driven by empirical observations that do not depend on methodological or normative commitments. A useful example comes from the field of broadcast regulation. The Supreme Court ruled in *FCC v. Pacifica Foundation* (1978) that broadcasters are subject to punishment for disseminating indecent speech. Among the reasons for this conclusion were broadcast media's pervasiveness and accessibility to children.[14]

---

[7] The example is discussed in Allison Orr Larsen, *Factual Precedents*, 162 U. Pa. L. Rev. 59, 63–4 (2013).
[8] FCC v. Fox Television Stations, Inc., 556 U.S. 502, 533 (2009) (Thomas, J., concurring).
[9] *Casey*, 505 U.S. at 860.
[10] Id. at 861–2.
[11] See id. at 863.
[12] 347 U.S. 483.
[13] 300 U.S. 379.
[14] See 438 U.S. 726, 748–51.

Pacifica was controversial from the outset, and it remains so today. Challenges have made their way to the Supreme Court twice in recent years. Both times, the Court disposed of the cases without overruling or reaffirming *Pacifica*. But Justice Thomas and Justice Ginsburg penned separate opinions criticizing the *Pacifica* approach. Justice Ginsburg was brief in her remarks, arguing that *Pacifica* was mistaken from the beginning and had become worse in light of changing technologies.[15] Justice Thomas offered more elaboration along similar lines. He characterized *Pacifica* and a predecessor case, *Red Lion Broadcasting Co. v. FCC* (1969), as a "deep intrusion into the First Amendment rights of broadcasters." He also described technological advances as undermining the idea that broadcasting is uniquely pervasive and therefore more susceptible to regulation.[16]

Whatever the merits of these criticisms, the question for purposes of stare decisis is what happens if a majority of the Court follows the lead of Justices Thomas and Ginsburg and concludes that *Pacifica* is wrong. *Pacifica* is a prime example of a case whose factual premises have eroded. It is no longer true to say broadcasting is unique in its pervasiveness or accessibility to children. Because those characteristics were important components of *Pacifica*'s rationale, the case is properly viewed as subject to reconsideration. The presumptive deference owed to *Pacifica* has been rebutted by the disintegration of its factual predicates. That does not necessarily mean *Pacifica* should be overruled. There may be other reasons for preserving it (for instance, based on the reliance it has engendered) or possibilities for reconceptualizing it (for instance, by focusing on the government's authority to license broadcasters). Even so, flawed factual premises warrant a fresh look at the decision.

Another example comes from the field of taxation. The Supreme Court addressed the tax obligations of mail-order sellers in *Quill Corp. v. North Dakota* (1992).[17] The case dealt with a state's authority to impose tax-collection obligations on sellers who maintained no physical presence within the state. Viewed through the lens of precedent, the proper outcome seemed clear enough. The Court's prior opinion in *National Bellas Hess, Inc. v. Department of Revenue* (1967) had sided with sellers in comparable circumstances.[18] But in the years since *Bellas Hess* was decided, developments in related areas of constitutional law had arguably rendered it a doctrinal outlier. The question in *Quill* was whether the Court should reaffirm *Bellas Hess* despite doubts about

---

[15] FCC v. Fox Television Stations, Inc., 132 S. Ct. 2307, 2321 (2012) (Ginsburg, J., concurring in the judgment).
[16] *Fox Television Stations*, 556 U.S. at 531–4 (Thomas, J., concurring).
[17] 504 U.S. 298.
[18] 386 U.S. 753.

its soundness by contemporary standards or overrule the case to enhance the internal consistency of constitutional law.

The Court chose the former course. It reaffirmed that the Commerce Clause forbids a state from imposing tax-collection obligations on mail-order sellers who lack a physical presence in the state. Along with defending *Bellas Hess*'s application of the Commerce Clause as suited to its particular context, the Court noted the importance of reliance expectations. It explained that mail-order sellers had expended significant resources based on the Court's previous decision and that altering the rules could threaten "the basic framework of a sizable industry."[19]

Today's retail world is different from the one the Court encountered in *Quill*. As Justice Kennedy recently noted, the years since *Quill*'s issuance have witnessed "dramatic technological and social changes," which arguably give many out-of-state sellers "a sufficiently 'substantial nexus'" to justify imposing tax-collection obligations upon them.[20] According to Justice Kennedy, developments in e-commerce have changed what it means for a business to be "present" in a state.

Like the innovations in communications technology since *Pacifica*, the technological developments in online retailing since *Quill* are the types of bona fide factual changes that can rebut the presumption of deference to precedent even in a second-best world of interpretive pluralism. The Court's prior opinions considered the degree to which sellers can connect with a given state notwithstanding the lack of any bricks-and-mortar presence. The proliferation of Internet retail has changed that calculus considerably. Some justices might nevertheless conclude out-of-state sellers should remain exempt from tax obligations. But for justices who reject that conclusion, developments in the retail industry brought about by technological advances are sufficient to justify the reconsideration of precedent. Like the broadcast media, interstate retailers operate in an environment that has undergone significant changes. The evolution of the retail environment is a sensible reason for reconsidering precedent, and one that is not bound up with any particular methodology of interpretation. That makes it an appropriate consideration within a system of second-best stare decisis.

Again, it does not necessarily follow that *Pacifica* and *Quill* should be overruled. Whether an overruling is warranted depends on other factors as well. We will reach these additional factors in due course. My present aim is to illustrate how the concept of factual inaccuracy can be pared down to its objective core.

---

[19] *Quill*, 504 U.S. at 317.
[20] Direct Marketing Association v. Brohl, 135 S. Ct. 1124, 1135 (2015) (Kennedy, J., concurring).

A streamlined conception of what constitutes a factual premise facilitates deliberation across methodological lines. An incorrect factual premise is an incorrect factual premise, regardless of a justice's interpretive philosophy.

JURISPRUDENTIAL COHERENCE

Under existing law, precedents lose their force if they become "mere survivor[s] of obsolete constitutional thinking."[21] The operative question, to recall the Supreme Court's language in *Casey*, is "whether the law's growth in the intervening years" has left a precedent as "a doctrinal anachronism discounted by society."[22]

In theory, jurisprudential coherence is another consideration that can be separated from methodological disagreements. The consistency of one precedent with another does not depend on any particular interpretive philosophy. It reflects the belief that sound judging aspires to consistent decisions, which is a commitment shared by justices across the methodological spectrum. But while decisions will sometimes be glaringly incompatible, in other cases the inquiry into jurisprudential coherence runs parallel with debates over a precedent's soundness. Was the Supreme Court's case law before 2010 inconsistent in failing to protect corporate electioneering, notwithstanding the strong protection given to political speech more generally? Or did the case law properly recognize the unique dynamics of corporate advocacy in elections? Is the Court's brightline rule regarding the tax liability of out-of-state retailers an anachronistic holdover from an absolutist era, or a specialized application that makes sense within the broader doctrinal scheme? How did the Court's more recent cases involving abortion rights and equal protection affect the durability of an earlier decision to uphold the constitutionality of a criminal prohibition against same-sex relationships? Without an objective baseline, there is too great a risk of these questions being answered by reference to interpretive commitments that vary from justice to justice, robbing stare decisis of its ability to serve as a bridge between methodologies.

The problem is exacerbated by inconsistency in defining precedents' scope of applicability. If we lack a clear sense of what a precedent stands for, we cannot determine its compatibility with other cases. But even a uniform definition of precedential scope would leave a great deal of ambiguity in the assessment of jurisprudential coherence. When the Court was deliberating about *Citizens United v. FEC* (2010), there was no doubt that its precedents permitted

---

[21] *Casey*, 505 U.S. at 857; *see also* MICHAEL J. GERHARDT, THE POWER OF PRECEDENT 31 (2008).
[22] *Casey*, 505 U.S. at 855.

restrictions on corporate electioneering. The question was whether other cases, while not directly applicable, pointed in a different direction. Likewise, when the Court reconsidered the constitutionality of prohibitions against same-sex relationships in *Lawrence v. Texas* (2003), *Bowers v. Hardwick* (1986) was the governing precedent. That did not resolve the issue of jurisprudential coherence; the Court also needed to evaluate the impact of other decisions that illuminated broader principles in its case law despite not being squarely on point.

If definitions of precedential scope do not settle debates about jurisprudential coherence, other considerations must be doing the work. To be sure, a justice can consider a series of cases, extract their general themes, and ask whether a given precedent deviates from them. The issue will always be whether outliers are justified on their own terms. There might be good reasons for treating corporate electioneering differently from electioneering by individuals, or for recognizing special rules for the tax treatment of out-of-state retailers. Or there might not. These determinations are complicated and contestable.

The best explanation for why *Citizens United* treated the Court's precedents on corporate electioneering as anomalous (and wrong) rather than context-sensitive (and right) is the majority's conclusion that the prior decisions were antithetical to core First Amendment values. The same is true of *Lawrence*. The majority's characterization of *Bowers* as a doctrinal anachronism was connected to the conclusion that *Bowers* permitted states to "demean" the "existence" of consenting adults and to "control their destiny by making their private sexual conduct a crime," as underscored by the statement that *Bowers* "was not correct when it was decided."[23] The foregoing depictions are emblematic of a more general phenomenon in the Court's case law. They are steeped in methodological and normative commitments, which second-best stare decisis seeks to avoid.

As I have noted, factors such as procedural workability and factual accuracy can also intermingle with interpretive philosophy. But those factors are more susceptible to a paring down that separates them from methodological and normative commitments. The inquiry into jurisprudential coherence admits of no such narrowing, at least in practical terms. Its wide-ranging nature impedes its decoupling from interpretive and normative debates. Notwithstanding its potential relevance in a world of interpretive agreement, the inquiry into jurisprudential coherence must be excluded from second-best stare decisis.

[23] 539 U.S. 558, 578.

RELIANCE AND DISRUPTION

Procedural unworkability, factual inaccuracy, and jurisprudential incoherence are potential reasons for rejecting a flawed precedent. On the other side of the scale is the impact of an overruling on reliance expectations. The Supreme Court has expressed reluctance about overruling precedents that command significant reliance.[24]

While disputes over the extent of reliance are significant and unavoidable, they need not collapse into debates about interpretive philosophy. All else being equal, the disruption of reliance interests is undesirable, impairing the value of prior behaviors and requiring the modification and revision of plans. Sometimes, of course, the disruption of reliance is warranted notwithstanding the attendant costs. Yet that does not change the nature of the costs themselves.

Reliance interests have a sweep that exceeds methodological bounds. A precedent reasoned on originalist grounds may generate reliance, as may a precedent reasoned on living constitutionalist grounds, or pragmatic grounds, or any other grounds one might imagine. This breadth brings its own kind of neutrality. To say reliance interests ought to matter is not to make a choice that privileges one interpretive philosophy at the expense of others. The reliance a precedent has commanded is a reason for upholding it regardless of the precedent's rule of decision, much as a precedent's procedural unworkability is a reason for revisiting it no matter its substance. Neutrality is important to the enterprise of second-best stare decisis, which is constantly seeking to transcend interpretive divides. Indeed, the neutrality of reliance expectations might help to explain their prominent status in the modern doctrine, which itself provides further reason for preserving reliance as part of the stare decisis calculus going forward.

Resolving to consider reliance expectations as part of the stare decisis inquiry is not the end of the analysis. There is also the further matter of determining which types of reliance are relevant. The Supreme Court's case law suggests that disruption is most problematic in situations involving investment-backed expectations and rights in property and contract.[25] Nevertheless, the rationale for protecting reliance can apply to noneconomic liberties as well. Whatever the nature of the underlying right, when stakeholders have taken tangible

---

[24] For recent expressions of this point, see Michigan v. Bay Mills Indian Community, 134 S. Ct. 2024, 2036 (2014); Harris v. Quinn, 134 S. Ct. 2618, 2652 (2014) (Kagan, J., dissenting). *Cf.* Walton v. Arizona, 497 U.S. 639, 673 (1990) (Scalia, J., concurring in part and concurring in the judgment). *See also* Henry P. Monaghan, *Taking Supreme Court Opinions Seriously*, 39 Md. L. Rev. 1, 7 (1979) ("History has its claims, at least where settled expectations of the body politic have clustered around constitutional doctrine.").

[25] *Casey*, 505 U.S. at 855–6; *Quill*, 504 U.S. at 317.

steps or made concrete plans in reliance on Supreme Court pronouncements, the disappointment of their expectations is pertinent.

Reliance by governmental officials such as legislators presents a more complicated issue. Some Supreme Court decisions treat governmental reliance as a legitimate part of the stare decisis calculus.[26] A potential counterpoint is *Citizens United*, which overruled a precedent that had commanded considerable reliance from Congress and state legislatures. But the *Citizens United* majority did not declare legislative reliance to be inapposite; rather, it described that factor as "not . . . compelling."[27] In light of the Court's other opinions giving regard to legislative reliance, it would be curious if the *Citizens United* majority meant to renounce its past practice without acknowledging what it was doing. The "not . . . compelling" language is better understood to mean that within the context of corporate electioneering, legislative reliance was not sufficiently weighty to save a flawed precedent.

By treating government reliance as meaningful, courts express respect for good-faith efforts by coordinate branches to comply with judicial edicts. Protecting legislative reliance also acknowledges the reality that it is private citizens who bear the costs of sending politicians back to the drawing board when judges change the rules of the game. These considerations support the inclusion of governmental reliance in the stare decisis calculus even in the second-best world of interpretive pluralism.

The same cannot be said for reliance by society at large. Broad notions of societal reliance on precedent have played a role in major constitutional cases. In *Casey*, the Court recognized the interests of "people who have ordered their thinking and living around" the continued vitality of *Roe*.[28] Similarly, when it reaffirmed *Miranda v. Arizona* (1966), the Court cited the status of the *Miranda* warnings as "part of our national culture."[29] *Roe* and *Miranda* are exceptional in their salience and profile, creating questions about whether the Court's invocations of societal reliance should extend to other areas of constitutional law. And unlike assertions of private and legislative reliance, appeals to societal reliance do not depend on the concrete expectations of stakeholders whom an overruling will affect most directly. The form of analysis is necessarily more abstract.

The objectives served by protecting societal reliance are promoted to a considerable extent by the very existence of a meaningful doctrine of stare decisis.

[26] Randall v. Sorrell, 548 U.S. 230, 244 (2006) (Breyer, J.); Harris v. United States, 536 U.S. 545, 567–8 (2002), *overruled in* Alleyne v. United States, 133 S. Ct. 2151 (2013); Hilton v. South Carolina Public Railways Commission, 502 U.S. 197, 202 (1991).
[27] Citizens United v. FEC, 558 U.S. 310, 365.
[28] *Casey*, 505 U.S. at 856.
[29] *Dickerson*, 530 U.S. at 428.

Societal reliance is distinct from private and legislative reliance because it captures the myriad effects that overruling a well-known precedent can have on various communities, including people who have not taken tangible action based on the precedent. To illustrate, return to the example of *Miranda*. The overruling of that case – and the corresponding reinvention of the rules of engagement for criminal suspects – could matter immensely to perceptions of the law's continuity and impersonality, even for those who will never hear their *Miranda* rights read to them. This does not mean *Miranda* is impervious to reconsideration. But it does mean an overruling would affect more than the people most directly affected by its rule.

The best response is to demand a special justification for overruling a precedent, whether *Miranda* or any other decision, that goes beyond disagreement with the precedent's reasoning. A general practice of deference to precedent is a way of respecting societal reliance on the universe of Supreme Court pronouncements. Such a practice reduces the need for undertaking difficult and controversial inquiries into societal reliance within the context of specific disputes.

Societal reliance might well be a sensible consideration for a doctrine of stare decisis fashioned under conditions of abiding interpretive agreement. In our second-best world, a doctrine of stare decisis must make compromises in order to appeal to a wide cross-section of judges. Societal reliance does not enjoy the same grounding in existing case law as do more direct forms of reliance by private citizens and government officials. It rests on a different set of conceptual underpinnings. What is more, societal reliance can receive indirect protection from a doctrine of stare decisis that demands a special justification for overruling precedent. On balance, these arguments lead me to conclude that societal reliance must be excluded from second-best stare decisis. Though private reliance and governmental reliance raise their fair share of challenges in application, they are better established and more amenable to consistent analysis than reliance by society at large. Expectations still matter in the second-best world, but societal reliance must find its protection in the presumptive respect all precedents receive.

FLAWED REASONING AND FLAGRANCY OF ERROR

Beyond the *Casey* factors, another consideration that frequently finds its way into discussions of stare decisis is the reasoning of the precedent under review. The presence of error is not a sufficient ground for overruling a precedent. As the Supreme Court wrote in *Casey*, "a decision to overrule should rest on some special reason over and above the belief that a prior case was wrongly decided."[30] Nevertheless, the justices sometimes include the soundness of a precedent's reasoning among the relevant considerations in deciding whether to preserve it.[31]

A way to resolve this apparent tension is to draw distinctions among precedents based on the flagrancy of their errors. On this account, the fact that a precedent is wrong – or "badly reasoned," if you prefer – is not a justification for overruling it. By comparison, when a precedent is not simply mistaken but clearly or manifestly so, the extent of its error becomes an adequate basis for doing away with it. Caleb Nelson has provided a powerful defense of this position on both theoretical and historical grounds. He contends that withholding deference from manifestly erroneous precedents may be a desirable alternative to embracing a "*general* presumption against overruling past decisions."[32]

Within the contours of a single interpretive school, classifying dubious precedents based on the flagrancy of their error is both practicable and useful. If, for example, a justice thinks constitutional rules should be assessed pragmatically based on their costs and benefits, it is natural that the justice will distinguish between precedents whose costs *slightly* outweigh their benefits and precedents whose costs *greatly* outweigh their benefits. In this scenario, the latter category includes cases of manifest error, whereas the former category includes cases of ordinary error that do not themselves furnish sufficient justification for overruling. A similar analysis applies to other interpretive methodologies. If one accepts the validity of originalism, it is prudent to distinguish between precedents that reflect *probable* misreadings of the Constitution's original meaning and those that reflect *blatant* misreadings. Again, such a distinction facilitates the sorting of precedents into the categories of manifest error and ordinary error. That categorization informs the determination of which mistakes the Court should live with and which it should rectify.

In our pluralistic world, the prospect of distinguishing precedents based on their degree of error becomes more complicated.[33] To illustrate, simply combine the examples discussed in the previous paragraph. If Justice A believes that pragmatism is the proper method of interpreting the Constitution, how is

---

[30] *Casey*, 505 U.S. at 864; *see also Harris*, 134 S. Ct. at 2652 (Kagan, J., dissenting) ("The special justifications needed to reverse an opinion must go beyond demonstrations (much less assertions) that it was wrong; that is the very point of *stare decisis*."); Nelson, *Stare Decisis and Demonstrably Erroneous Precedents*, *supra* note 2, at 8.

[31] *See, e.g., Citizens United*, 558 U.S. at 362–3; *Montejo*, 556 U.S. at 793; *Payne*, 501 U.S. at 827.

[32] Nelson, *Stare Decisis and Demonstrably Erroneous Precedents*, *supra* note 2, at 4.

[33] Professor Nelson notes this issue, recognizing the risk that "current judges may be committed to an entirely different interpretive method than their predecessors, and they may be too quick to decide that their predecessors' method was illegitimate." *Id.* at 67.

she to determine whether a precedent that is reasoned on originalist grounds reflects an ordinary error or a manifest error? And if Justice B adheres to originalism, how is she to distinguish between ordinary error and manifest error within precedents that are couched in pragmatic terms?[34]

A potential solution, which is based on *interpretive fidelity* to one's preferred philosophy, is to treat as manifestly erroneous all precedents that reflect a methodology different from one's own. An originalist justice would characterize all nonoriginalist interpretations as manifestly erroneous and, thus, subject to overruling. A nonoriginalist justice would take the same view of precedents decided on originalist grounds. And so the divide between ordinary error and manifest error would collapse into disagreements over interpretive philosophy. The problem with this approach is that it sacrifices the ability of stare decisis to unite justices who adhere to divergent theories of constitutional interpretation. Interpretive philosophy determines flagrancy of error, and flagrancy of error determines susceptibility to overruling. If precedents are only as strong as the interpretive commitments of five Supreme Court justices, the continuity and impersonality of constitutional law is impaired.

Rather than treating all precedents that arise from rival interpretive schools as egregiously wrong, the justices might show *interpretive empathy* by placing themselves within the decisional mindset a prior decision reflects. An originalist justice would not treat flawed decisions as manifestly erroneous simply because they were reasoned on pragmatic grounds. Instead, she would evaluate those decisions against a backdrop assumption of pragmatism's validity. Nor would a pragmatic justice treat all originalist precedents as manifestly erroneous. Instead, she would assess the flagrancy of error from the standpoint of an originalist. This practice would preserve a distinction between the adoption of a given interpretive philosophy and the declaration of manifest error.

But interpretive empathy presents difficulties of its own. Assuming that the justices have the time and capacity to deploy divergent methodologies from case to case, interpretive empathy requires them to embrace, at least hypothetically, an interpretive philosophy they might view as imprudent or illegitimate. An originalist justice is required to channel a competing methodology that is incompatible with the tenets of originalism. The same goes for the pragmatist or common law constitutionalist, who must imagine himself as a

---

[34] *See* Jill E. Fisch, *The Implications of Transition Theory for Stare Decisis*, 13 J. CONTEMP. LEGAL ISSUES 93, 101 (2003) (arguing that the outcome of a Supreme Court case "may reflect a variety of policy, methodological and political choices, but is unlikely to demonstrate that the minority view is objectively without merit").

momentary originalist regardless of any doubts he may harbor about the originalist enterprise.

Additional problems arise with respect to precedents that do not fit neatly into one interpretive box. Supreme Court decisions often describe different types of arguments as pointing toward the same result.[35] That practice can render it impracticable for a later justice to adopt the methodological mindset of the Court that issued the precedent: There may be no way to determine what, exactly, that mindset was.

In light of the difficulties associated with interpretive fidelity and interpretive empathy, the flagrancy of a precedent's error fits uneasily with the doctrine of stare decisis in a pluralistic legal culture. The egregiousness of a precedent's error coheres with the doctrine of stare decisis only in a world of interpretive agreement. Second-best stare decisis must look elsewhere for its content.

It is possible, if unlikely, that a Supreme Court opinion may cross into the realm of illegitimacy, for instance because it was written by a justice who expressly ignored the relevant enactments and ruled based on personal affinity or a flip of the coin. Such decisions, of course, are entitled to no deference whatsoever. Beyond that category of extreme cases, second-best stare decisis focuses on factors apart from theory-dependent conclusions about the soundness of a decision's reasoning.

SUBSTANTIVE EFFECTS

The importance of getting a case right will naturally be informed by the effect of getting it wrong.[36] Does it follow that precedents with undesirable consequences should have a limited shelf life?

I submit that the answer is no. The assessment of a precedent's harmfulness depends on conclusions about legal relevance, which themselves depend on theories of constitutional interpretation. Substantive assessments, as well as the methodological and normative commitments they reflect, are therefore unsuitable for a world of interpretive disagreement. Second-best stare decisis responds by excluding substantive effects from the overruling calculus in the ordinary course. In selecting the best interpretation of a disputed constitutional

---

[35] See Richard H. Fallon, Jr., A Constructivist Coherence Theory of Constitutional Interpretation, 100 HARV. L. REV. 1189, 1192–3 (1987).

[36] Cf. Henry Paul Monaghan, Stare Decisis and Constitutional Adjudication, 88 COLUM. L. REV. 723, 760 (1988) ("The most difficult question in identifying the harmful effects due to a wrongly decided controlling precedent is whether this criterion can be rendered sufficiently principled so that it is not simply a euphemism describing decisions that a Court majority very much dislikes.").

provision, the justices will continue to disagree about the types of benefits and harms that are legally relevant. Second-best stare decisis has no objection to that practice. It simply prevents such disagreements from reemerging when the justices turn to the distinct question of whether a flawed precedent should be retained or jettisoned.

Treating substantive effects as inapposite reflects a compromise that cuts across methodological and ideological lines.[37] Justices who would otherwise be inclined to view a precedent's injustice or inefficacy as a reason for overruling must set those factors aside. Likewise, justices who emphasize values such as popular sovereignty will need to mediate their view that precedents are in greater need of overruling when they impede democratic self-government; the primacy of popular sovereignty is not a value that extends across interpretive methodologies. These are just a few illustrations of a general point: Determining which types of effects are legally relevant is theory-dependent by definition, making it unsuitable for a doctrine of stare decisis designed to bridge interpretive disputes. Conclusions about the salient effects of flawed decisions can serve as the basis for declaring a precedent to be erroneous (or for resolving a case of first impression), but they are generally excluded from the inquiry into a precedent's retention. Rather than drawing on the substantive value of interpreting the Constitution correctly, second-best stare decisis revolves around factors whose application can be cordoned off from disputes over interpretive theory.

Disregard of substantive effects characterizes the ordinary course of second-best stare decisis. But the ordinary course is not the only course. There is a category of exceptional situations in which a precedent's substantive effects may play a legitimate role in the second-best analysis. Cases may occasionally arise in which a justice perceives an overwhelming justification for renouncing a precedent due to its substantive effects. The common law constitutionalist might view a precedent as not merely unfair, but profoundly immoral. The pragmatist might view a precedent as not merely ill-advised, but disastrous in its practical implications. The popular sovereignty originalist might view a precedent as not merely anti-democratic, but an intolerable affront to the authority of the people. And so on.

Despite its general exclusion of substantive effects, second-best stare decisis acknowledges the legitimacy of substantive considerations in these

---

[37] John McGinnis and Michael Rappaport make a similar point in their consequentialist defense of originalism: "[A] constitution in a pluralistic society should rest to some extent on a compromise among people's views of the good in that society." JOHN O. MCGINNIS & MICHAEL B. RAPPAPORT, ORIGINALISM AND THE GOOD CONSTITUTION 5 (2013).

exceptional cases. Fidelity to precedent is not absolute. It is a presumption, subject to override when certain criteria are met. In most cases, those criteria should exclude a precedent's substantive effects in order to prevent stare decisis from being mired in debates over interpretive philosophy. Yet second-best stare decisis can recognize exceptional cases in which substantive effects are relevant without jeopardizing the larger project of accommodating the treatment of precedent to a pluralistic world.

The key is to ensure that attention to substantive effects remains the exception rather than the rule. Invoking substantive considerations to justify an overruling triggers a corresponding obligation to imagine what the consequences would be if one's judicial colleagues were to behave in the same way with respect to precedents they view as severely problematic. This type of aggregated analysis sharply limits the category of cases in which substantive considerations are relevant.

For example, even under the second-best approach, a justice could leave open the possibility that considerations of morality can be relevant to the durability of precedent. But she would reserve those considerations for extreme cases rather than allowing them to permeate the doctrine of stare decisis in every constitutional dispute. A different justice might determine that precedents posing a substantial threat to popular sovereignty – perhaps by inhibiting the free elections necessary for meaningful self-government – should be overturned based on their substantive effects. Still other justices might conclude the effects of constitutional mistakes are most severe when the Court has overstepped its proper role by intervening in a divisive political or social debate. Whichever of these (or other) conceptual lenses a particular justice employs, second-best stare decisis forecloses the broader conclusion that all erroneous precedents are subject to reconsideration based on their substantive effects. While that latter approach may be sensible in a world of interpretive agreement, it fails under conditions of interpretive pluralism.

Acknowledging the relevance of substantive effects in extraordinary cases also makes second-best stare decisis more plausible in practical terms. Sitting and future justices might well balk at upholding what they view as the worst of the worst precedents. The substantive-effects exception responds by acting as a safety valve. It provides space for correcting the Court's most harmful (however that concept is defined) mistakes without creating pressure to distort the ordinary tools of stare decisis analysis. So long as substance-based overrulings are limited to rare and exceptional situations, they do not threaten the enterprise of second-best stare decisis. On the contrary, the doctrine operates as it should: by creating a strong presumption that yields when countervailing considerations are truly compelling.

SECOND-BEST STARE DECISIS BEYOND THE CORE FACTORS

I began by discussing the implications of second-best analysis for the rules of stare decisis as described in *Casey*, which represents the Supreme Court's most prominent account of the doctrine. I also applied the second-best approach to two other factors – the soundness of a precedent's reasoning and the harmfulness of its substantive effects – that often emerge in disputes over the durability of precedent. Taken together, these considerations are properly understood as the core of the Court's modern approach to stare decisis. Still, other considerations also crop up from time to time in the Court's discussions of precedent. I will briefly discuss three of those factors as further examples of how second-best analysis applies to the doctrine of stare decisis.

Age. Older precedents sometimes receive heightened deference in light of their vintage. Their staying power over the years may have shown them to be sound. Older precedents have also had more time to generate reliance by stakeholders. It follows, the argument goes, that older precedents should receive more respect than newer ones, the latter of which can be corrected "before state and federal laws and practices have been adjusted to embody" them.[38]

The role of a precedent's age is complicated by Supreme Court opinions privileging newer opinions over older ones. This often occurs in connection with the inquiry into jurisprudential coherence, which I discussed above. When the Court depicts prior decisions as having been undermined by more recent ones, the consequence is to elevate the new over the old. To similar effect is Justice Ginsburg's statement about the importance of being faithful to "later, more enlightened decisions" while revising or discarding decisions that have become "outworn."[39] The principle that newer opinions can "undermin[e]" the "doctrinal underpinnings" of older ones means that in some cases, recent decisions take priority.[40]

The overruling of recent decisions can also be troubling from the standpoint of judicial impersonality. Recall Justice Marshall's dissent in *Payne v. Tennessee* (1991), in which he criticized the majority for overruling recent precedents even though "[n]either the law nor the facts," but "[o]nly the personnel of this

---

[38] South Carolina v. Gathers, 490 U.S. 805, 824 (1989) (Scalia, J., dissenting); Mitchell v. Helms, 530 U.S. 793, 835–6 (2000) (plurality op.); *see also, e.g., Montejo*, 556 U.S. at 792; STEPHEN BREYER, MAKING OUR DEMOCRACY WORK: A JUDGE'S VIEW 152 (2010).

[39] John R. Sand & Gravel Co. v. United States, 552 U.S. 130, 144 (2008) (Ginsburg, J., dissenting); *Lawrence*, 539 U.S. at 573–6.

[40] *See, e.g., Dickerson*, 530 U.S. at 443.

Court," had changed.[41] Abrupt overrulings following changes in the Court's composition can blur the line between the meaning of the Constitution and the identity of the individuals who occupy the bench. They reinforce both the perception and reality that constitutional change occurs primarily through the judicial appointment process rather than the Article V amendment process. As Justice Stevens once observed, "Citizens must have confidence that the rules on which they rely in ordering their affairs . . . are rules of law and not merely the opinions of a small group of men who temporarily occupy high office."[42]

The problem is not that a precedent's vintage is unsuitable for consideration under a second-best approach. Vintage is the type of objective, independent factor that lends itself to application by justices across the methodological spectrum. The problem is the Court has not consistently treated earlier precedents as more venerable than later ones, nor has it offered a convincing account of why overrulings are more problematic when precedents are old. The better approach is to focus directly on issues such as a precedent's reliance implications without filtering the analysis through the foggy lens of a precedent's age.

Dissent and Criticism. A case's divisiveness can affect its staying power. Deference is reduced when a precedent was "decided by the narrowest of margins, over spirited dissents challenging [its] basic underpinnings."[43] Along similar lines, the justices sometimes ask whether a precedent has drawn criticism from the bench and scholarly community, which can affect the extent to which the precedent has generated reliance expectations among stakeholders.[44] The inverse occurred in *Casey*, where the lead opinion described the criticism faced by *Roe* as a reason for standing by that decision.[45] But the *Casey* Court made clear that its rationale reflected the exceptional degree of public interest in *Roe*. In the ordinary course, it is more common to find criticism as cutting *against* deference rather than in its favor.

In defending this practice, we might posit that divided opinions are more likely to occur in difficult cases. Such cases, in turn, are relatively likely to result in unsound decisions. There is also a reliance angle: All else being equal, perhaps stakeholders are (or should be) less likely to rely on decisions that are hard-fought and closely divided. By definition, those decisions were the fewest votes away from overruling. And if several justices felt strongly

---

[41] *Payne*, 501 U.S. at 844 (Marshall, J., dissenting).
[42] Florida Department of Health & Rehabilitative Services v. Florida Nursing Home Association, 450 U.S. 147, 154 (1981) (Stevens, J., concurring).
[43] *Payne*, 501 U.S. at 828–9 (majority op.).
[44] See, e.g., *Citizens United*, 558 U.S. at 380 (Roberts, C. J., concurring).
[45] See *Casey*, 505 U.S. at 867.

enough about an issue to dissent in dramatic fashion, they may be more likely to persist in their disagreement as they try to win a majority through persuasion or attrition.

There is another side to the story. It is possible that the majority opinion in a divisive case is particularly likely to be *soundly* reasoned, precisely because the competing arguments received such extensive attention. The Supreme Court took this position in *Patterson v. McLean Credit Union* (1989), where part of its justification for refusing to overrule a statutory precedent owed to the fact that "[t]he arguments about whether [the precedent] was decided correctly in light of the language and history of the statute were examined and discussed with great care in our decision." The dissenting view was considered and understood, but it "did not prevail," and the Court saw no reason to reopen the debate.[46] Justice Marshall made a similar point in his *Payne* dissent, which criticized the majority for departing from precedent based on arguments the Court had recently rejected.[47] Understood in this way, contentious decisions represent the antithesis of the lightly considered statements the Court has described as unworthy of deference due to the superficial deliberation they appear to have received.[48]

On balance, neither the presence of a spirited dissent nor the persistence of criticism is a dependable proxy for a decision's likelihood of error on the merits. Moreover, if dissents and criticism are meant as proxies for a decision's effect on reliance expectations, it is better to evaluate reliance directly. That leaves little reason for infusing dissent and criticism with independent force in the stare decisis analysis.

Nature of Decisional Rule. I noted in Chapter 1 that the Supreme Court continues to maintain a distinction between its statutory and constitutional precedents, with the former receiving a higher degree of deference. The Court also gives heightened deference to decisions in fields such as property and contract law, on the rationale that those decisions often have the greatest impact on reliance expectations. By contrast, rules of evidence and procedure receive diminished deference. Those types of rules do "not affect the way in which parties order their affairs," and their revision does "not upset settled expectations on anyone's part."[49]

Inquiry into the nature of a decisional rule is compatible with the principles of second-best stare decisis. Whatever their methodological and normative inclinations, the justices will often be able to agree about whether a rule is

---

[46] Patterson v. McLean Credit Union, 491 U.S. 164, 171 (1989).
[47] See *Payne*, 501 U.S. at 846 (Marshall, J., dissenting).
[48] See, e.g., McCutcheon v. FEC, 134 S. Ct. 1434, 1446 (2014) (plurality op.).
[49] Pearson v. Callahan, 555 U.S. 223, 233 (2009).

substantive or procedural. The more difficult question is whether the nature of decisional rule reveals anything meaningful about the deference owed to a precedent.

It is possible that the nature of a decisional rule correlates with reliance expectations and, thus, with the disruption an overruling would entail. But that is not always the case. Take *Hohn v. United States* (1998). There, the Supreme Court considered whether it had jurisdiction to review denials of certificates of appealability, which petitioners in federal habeas corpus proceedings need in order to appeal from an adverse decision. The Court found itself to possess the requisite jurisdiction, but it acknowledged that its conclusion conflicted with a precedent issued some fifty years prior. Explaining its decision to overrule the precedent, the Court cited its practice of giving reduced deference to procedural rules. In dissent, Justice Scalia agreed that "procedural rules do not *ordinarily* engender detrimental reliance." Yet he disagreed with the majority because the case at hand was not ordinary. Even if the relevant precedent had not affected primary conduct by private citizens, Congress had presumably paid attention to it. Irrespective of its procedural nature, the precedent warranted preservation in light of the "reliance of Congress upon an unrepudiated decision central to the procedural scheme it was creating."[50]

Whatever the proper result in *Hohn*, the colloquy between majority and dissent shows why the nature of a precedent's decisional rule is not always an accurate proxy for reliance and disruption. Sometimes procedural and evidentiary rules do not engender reliance, and sometimes they do. In light of that variability, the better course is the direct analysis of reliance interests. Again, this is not because the nature of a decisional rule is out of bounds for second-best stare decisis. The fact that a particular feature of a case has independent content apart from debates over interpretive methodology is necessary for its inclusion in the second-best analysis, but it is not sufficient. The feature must also tell us something meaningful about when precedents should be retained and when they should be overruled.

IMPLEMENTING THE SECOND-BEST DOCTRINE

By now we have encountered a host of factors that influence the durability of precedent. Without excluding the possibility that other relevant considerations might exist, we are well positioned to summarize the operation of second-best stare decisis as compared to the Supreme Court's existing doctrine.

---

[50] Hohn v. United States, 524 U.S. 236, 259–61 (1998) (Scalia, J., dissenting).

Second-best stare decisis begins with inquiries into a decision's procedural workability and the accuracy of its factual premises. These factors can justify overruling a flawed precedent. They inform, in other words, the importance of getting the law *right*. On the other side of the scale is the disruption of reliance expectations that an overruling is likely to cause. The prospect of disruption affects the value of allowing the law to remain *settled*.

The pivotal difference between the Court's existing account of stare decisis and this second-best approach is the latter's introduction of doctrinal revisions designed to alleviate the problems posed by interpretive disagreement. Under second-best stare decisis, a decision that fails on a metric like procedural workability or factual accuracy loses its presumptive claim to deference. In the vernacular of the Court, procedural and factual failures are special justifications that warrant reconsidering the precedent. The inquiry then turns to whether, notwithstanding the presence of a sufficient justification for overruling, the precedent should be retained for the sake of protecting reliance expectations.

I have also suggested the compatibility of second-best stare decisis with a narrow exception that allows the overruling of cases whose substantive effects are – from the standpoint of an individual justice applying her own interpretive methodology – too detrimental to tolerate. That exception permits the consideration of a precedent's substantive effects in extraordinary cases. At the same time, it underscores that substantive effects are irrelevant to second-best stare decisis in the ordinary course.

Outside of exceptional cases in which substantive effects justify an overruling, the question is how to structure the consideration of procedural workability, factual accuracy, and reliance. One approach is to view a decision's procedural unworkability or factual mistakes as creating a presumption that it should be overruled. Only if the precedent has commanded substantial reliance from private citizens or government actors would it be retained. Courts would still need to work out the details of issues such as when a procedural shortcoming rises to the level of unworkability and whether any factual mistake, as opposed to only a material mistake, is sufficient to justify an overruling. They would also need to articulate principles for determining when the reliance a precedent has commanded is extensive enough to preserve it. But our concern here is with the general framework, which would ask the justices to examine the relevant factors as a progression. A finding of unworkability or a factual mistake would trigger the presumption of overruling. A finding of substantial reliance would rebut the presumption and require the precedent's retention. Those inquiries would proceed sequentially and independently.

Alternatively, second-best stare decisis might give the Court more flexibility to evaluate competing values in comparative terms. After analyzing workability, accuracy, and reliance, a justice could reach a final determination of whether, all things considered, the precedent should be retained. Structured in this way, second-best stare decisis would channel judicial discretion toward the appropriate factors without dictating how those factors are arranged and compared. Ultimately, such an approach would require the weighing of incommensurable values.[51] Though it creates obvious challenges, comparing incommensurables is a familiar feature of legal practice. The justices weigh unfettered expression against safety and security. They consider equal protection alongside educational diversity. They assess the virtues of open economic markets against the backdrop of state sovereignty. The list goes on and on.

To be effective, second-best stare decisis need not avoid any comparison of incommensurables. It need only keep those comparisons distinct from disputes over interpretive methodology. Different justices will sometimes reach different conclusions about whether a precedent is so unworkable as to relinquish its claim to deference, or so factually flawed as to justify an overruling notwithstanding the attendant disruption. There will always be a need for judgment. Under the second-best approach, the terms of the debate are uniform, and they transcend methodological disputes.

On balance, I view the latter, more flexible approach as preferable to a rigid sequencing. To borrow a distinction from David Strauss, the driving objective of second-best stare decisis is not to furnish an algorithm for the overruling of precedent. It is to defend a "set of attitudes" about precedent and the nature of the Supreme Court's role in interpreting the Constitution.[52] If the doctrine of stare decisis is to achieve the lofty goals the Court has set for it, it must find a way to unite justices of varying interpretive sympathies. Hence the need to emphasize considerations that operate independently of interpretive philosophy while curtailing the relevance of considerations that assume different shapes depending on one's methodological and normative commitments.

There will, of course, be disagreements over the application of second-best stare decisis. Those disagreements will sometimes reflect divergent judgments about issues such as the relative values of factual accuracy and undisturbed reliance. Second-best stare decisis makes no effort to squeeze out all the normativity from judging. What it pursues is a common set of metrics that are suitable from a range of interpretive perspectives. Second-best stare decisis entails shared dedication to the principle that disagreement is not reason enough to

---

[51] See Cass R. Sunstein, *Incommensurability and Valuation in Law*, 92 MICH. L. REV. 779, 796 (1994); Fallon, *A Constructivist Coherence Theory of Constitutional Interpretation*, supra note 35, at 1239.
[52] DAVID A. STRAUSS, THE LIVING CONSTITUTION 40 (2010).

discard a precedent. The theory also limits the extent to which one's commitment to methodologies such as originalism or living constitutionalism dictates one's approach to precedent. Instead, the terms of the debate are settled in advance and defined in a way that is inclusive rather than rivalrous. Stare decisis becomes a doctrine like any other. The justices will still disagree, but they will disagree in the right way.

PRECEDENT AND THE INDIVIDUAL JUSTICE

A theory of adjudication that would be desirable if endorsed by a majority of Supreme Court justices might lose its resonance if endorsed by only a single justice. The ultimate question is not how the Court as an entity should proceed. It is what "decision procedure should a nine-member body employ to reach the best decisions *they* can over an array of cases highlighting experiential and political differences among the nine decisionmakers?"[53] The point is relevant to second-best stare decisis, for it raises the question whether an individual justice should compromise her vision of optimal legal interpretation absent assurances that her colleagues (and successors) will follow suit.

There is no guarantee that a Supreme Court justice's application of second-best stare decisis will convince her colleagues to take the same path. Nor is there any guarantee that the adoption of second-best stare decisis in a majority opinion will entrench that approach in perpetuity. Nevertheless, justices who apply second-best stare decisis can help to establish its prevalence going forward. And even if a justice finds herself paying greater attention to precedent than her colleagues do, she can still make a valuable contribution in her own right. Adopting the second-best approach is about tempering one's interpretive philosophy for the sake of behaving like a member of an impersonal and enduring institution. To be sure, the benefits of stare decisis are greatest when a majority of justices endorse it. But a single justice who casts her lot with stare decisis can promote the ideals of continuity and impersonality. The act of compromising one's interpretive predilections underscores the separation between judge and law, as well as the ideal that legal rules are general norms to which courts commit themselves across the span of time. A vote for second-best stare decisis represents a contribution to the rule of law irrespective of the

---

[53] Frederick Schauer, *Statutory Construction and the Coordinating Function of Plain Meaning*, 1990 SUP. CT. REV. 231, 255; *see also* ADRIAN VERMEULE, THE SYSTEM OF THE CONSTITUTION 137 (2011) ("Even if all judges should adopt a given theory, it does not follow that any one should, because others may not.").

conduct of one's judicial peers.[54] For a single justice, a vote to uphold precedent in a particular case is a means of strengthening a doctrine that provides value to the constitutional system more broadly.

Consider three scenarios that a precedent-friendly Supreme Court justice might confront. In the first scenario, most of her colleagues have decided to overrule an applicable precedent. A few justices have resisted that conclusion, but not on stare decisis grounds; they simply think the majority is mistaken on the merits. Our justice believes the majority has the better of the argument, but she would preserve the applicable precedent for reasons of stare decisis. In this situation, our justice could choose to abandon stare decisis by adding her voice to the chorus of justices in the majority. Yet that approach is unlikely to affect the impact of the Court's opinion, which already enjoys majority support. Our justice thus gives up relatively little by writing a dissent on grounds of stare decisis.

In making this choice, the justice does not alter the outcome of the case at hand. But she does promote the principle that justices are willing to stand by precedents despite their personal misgivings. If our justice believes it advances the rule of law when judges subordinate – and are seen as subordinating – their individual views for the sake of keeping faith with their court's institutional history, she makes a contribution by deferring to precedent even if her colleagues do not follow her lead. Likewise, if our justice believes deference to precedent is a useful second-best principle for facilitating coordinated action, her dissenting opinion may enhance the viability of stare decisis in future cases by keeping it on the Court's agenda. In all events, her choice to dissent carries little cost given that her vote did not affect the outcome of the case.[55]

In the second scenario, most of the Court's members believe the precedent under consideration is correct. Our justice disagrees with that conclusion on the merits, but she thinks stare decisis requires upholding the precedent. Our justice could eschew considerations of stare decisis and write a dissent, but her choice would not change the outcome of the case. On the other hand,

---

[54] Cf. ADRIAN VERMEULE, JUDGING UNDER UNCERTAINTY 146 (2006) (noting that "[s]o long as the relevant theory does not require or assume a critical mass or threshold of judicial coordination – so long as individual judges may make a strictly divisible or marginal contribution to the aims specified by the theory – then the infeasibility of sustained judicial coordination poses no problem").

[55] The Supreme Court occasionally states that closely divided decisions are entitled to reduced deference going forward. On that logic, an opinion supported by six votes may receive marginally greater deference in future cases than an opinion supported by five votes. I criticized this practice as unjustified earlier in the chapter. Even if the practice persists, it is difficult to foresee a situation in which five justices are prepared to overrule a decision but refrain from doing so because it received six votes rather than five, or seven rather than six, and so on.

our justice could concur in the majority's result, issuing a separate opinion to explain that her vote is based on stare decisis. Again, this course of action contributes to the vitality of stare decisis going forward while imposing little cost.

Finally, imagine a scenario in which our justice's colleagues are evenly split. She is the "swing" vote, with the power to control the outcome of the case. There is an applicable precedent on the books, but none of her colleagues gives it much import. Instead, they reach their decisions purely on the merits. Now our justice has the opportunity to infuse the doctrine of stare decisis with considerable salience. She can explain that regardless of her views on the merits, she believes proper application of stare decisis requires abiding by the applicable precedent even if it is incorrect. In this way, our justice demonstrates that stare decisis affects not just rationales but results. She succeeds in bringing about the proper outcome (from the perspective of stare decisis) in the case at hand. In doing so, she also strengthens the general practice of precedent-following on the Court. Whatever happens in the years ahead, she will have demonstrated that stare decisis transcends interpretive and normative commitments.

These scenarios do not exhaust the possibilities. Some cases might lead to a wider array of positions among smaller factions of justices. But in the common scenarios I have described, the best course for our justice will be to apply second-best stare decisis regardless of what her colleagues choose to do.[56] Our justice can treat precedent with presumptive deference without worrying about her colleagues' votes. And if her colleagues ultimately adopt the same mindset as her, we have the framework for a meaningful doctrine of stare decisis in Supreme Court decision-making.

A general practice of precedent-following might also arise from the justices' belief that if they wish for their preferred precedents to stand the test of time, they must be willing to abide by some decisions with which they disagree. Adrian Vermeule explains how judges who are involved in repeated interactions might be inclined to defer to precedent to encourage reciprocation from their colleagues.[57] Michael Gerhardt makes a related point in depicting the justices as recognizing that by showing disdain for disfavored precedents, they put their preferred precedents on shakier ground.[58]

To the extent justices think in such strategic terms, the likelihood increases of creating a meaningful doctrine of stare decisis as a mechanism for protecting

---

[56] I hasten to reiterate that applying second-best stare decisis does not always mean abiding by precedent; there are situations in which precedent should yield.
[57] See VERMEULE, THE SYSTEM OF THE CONSTITUTION, *supra* note 53, at 142.
[58] See GERHARDT, THE POWER OF PRECEDENT, *supra* note 21, at 79.

the good (from the perspective of an individual justice) at the cost of enduring some bad. Even if the justices disregard these strategic considerations – either because they find the prospect of retaliation to be unsuitable to the Court's work, or because they regard the Court's future as sufficiently unpredictable that credible threats of retaliation are undermined – there remains the argument I developed above: A vote in favor of stare decisis, even by a single justice, strengthens the doctrine going forward, enhancing its ability to generate benefits such as impersonality, stability, and the facilitation of coordinated action.

As the foregoing discussion suggests, while tomorrow's justices always possess the power to depart from particular precedents or even to abandon the doctrine of stare decisis entirely, today's justices can make such developments less likely. A justice who operates within a practice of consistent deference to precedent faces an "argumentative burden" in justifying her choice to overrule.[59] She must explain why she perceives a suitable reason for departing from precedent, or why she thinks no such reason is required despite her predecessors' claims to the contrary. If she doubts her ability to make these arguments in a persuasive manner, she may be inclined to defer to a precedent even if she questions its soundness. That result would only come to pass in a system within which deference to precedent is the customary practice. By respecting precedent today, a justice makes it more likely that precedent will command respect tomorrow.

There is also the question of whether precedent-friendly justices should be wary of "ratchet" effects that threaten to chip away at their preferred vision of constitutional law.[60] The concern is that if some justices are more inclined than others to defer to precedent, and if that distinction tracks differences in interpretive approach, over time the law may move toward the view preferred by those who eschew stare decisis. Foreseeing this possibility, justices who would otherwise defer to precedent might consider voting to overrule most or all decisions that reflect an interpretive methodology different from their own.

Such a choice would, I think, be unwise. While it may be possible to make educated guesses about how one justice's treatment of precedent is likely to be received by her colleagues in the immediate future, the long-term effects on the Court's case law are difficult to predict. To begin, it is not necessarily correct to view judicial philosophies as static. A commitment to precedent by proponents of one philosophy might have dynamic effects in encouraging

---

[59] Cf. Frederick Schauer, Precedent, 39 STAN. L. REV. 571, 580 (1987).
[60] Lawrence B. Solum, The Supreme Court in Bondage: Constitutional Stare Decisis, Legal Formalism, and the Future of Unenumerated Rights, 9 U. PA. J. CONST. L. 155, 193 (2006).

proponents of other philosophies to become more receptive to decisions with which they disagree, leading to the establishment of a meaningful doctrine of stare decisis across interpretive schools.

There is also the possibility that stare decisis might create short-term costs but long-term gains for its adherents. An originalist justice who upholds a nonoriginalist decision might make a marginal contribution to the salience of nonoriginalist constitutional rules. But perhaps the originalist justice who stands by precedent will contribute to a perception of originalism as linked with constancy and impersonality as well as principled fidelity to text and history in cases of first impression, eventually increasing the prominence of the originalist school and leading to the appointment of more originalist justices. The likelihood would increase that cases of first impression would henceforth be decided according to originalist principles, and that originalist precedents would be insulated from overruling. Of course, this turn of events is uncertain. But so is the alternative account in which receptivity to precedent undercuts the impact of originalism going forward.

Nor is it clear that a justice's commitment to stare decisis will privilege one interpretive methodology at the expense of others. Even if future justices are inclined to overrule precedents that conflict with their preferred constitutional theories, there is no reason to think such justices will disproportionately come from a particular methodological school. It is plausible that the Court could vacillate between periods in which originalist justices regularly overruled nonoriginalist precedents, and periods in which living constitutionalist justices regularly overruled originalist precedents. The aggregate effect would be a certain amount of overruling, but it would not be a ratchet that steadily entrenched one theory while undermining others. The ratchet concern would arise only if frequent overruling were correlated with the prevalence of a particular interpretive philosophy. That need not be the case. Indeed, as I have argued, there is ample room in theories as diverse as originalism and living constitutionalism for meaningful deference to precedent.

By deferring to a flawed precedent, today's justice might act in a way that some of her colleagues would not. She might also sacrifice the power to right a constitutional wrong. The extent of the sacrifice is reduced by the fact that second-best stare decisis preserves the justice's ability to rectify the worst of the worst constitutional errors, even at the cost of continuity. But the more important point is that the power to rectify perceived constitutional mistakes is fleeting in a world without stare decisis. Such power lasts only until the Court's balance of power shifts, at which time a new majority is in a position to dispense with contrary precedents. Fidelity to precedent, by contrast, promotes coordinated action among differently minded jurists regardless of what happens in the years ahead. By helping to establish second-best stare decisis as an influential doctrine, even a single justice can make it harder for future justices to depart from precedent – and, as a result, less likely that they will try.

Concerns about judicial disregard for precedent do not only face forward. They also encourage today's Court to look backward for times when prior justices gave precedent less than its due. Consider, for example, those who believe that the Warren Court was unfaithful to the Court's prior teachings on criminal procedure[61] or that the Rehnquist Court contravened established case law on federalism. A Supreme Court justice who possesses such a belief faces a choice. She may abide by the existing precedents, unfaithful as they may have been to older cases. Or she may engage in her own overruling with the goal of restoring the legal rules that were improperly supplanted.

There is support in the Supreme Court's case law for the conclusion that an opinion borne of inadequate respect for its ancestors deserves the same irreverent treatment from its heirs. Hence the Court's willingness to overrule opinions that "deviated sharply from our established . . . jurisprudence"[62] or that represented a doctrinal "aberration."[63] Yet second-best stare decisis suggests the better course is to stand by existing precedents regardless of what came before. The crucial moment is the present one. The choice facing today's justice is whether to vote in favor of reaffirming or overruling. That choice should occur within the framework of second-best stare decisis, which avoids theory-laden determinations of whether a precedent was faithful to the cases that preceded it.

As I have noted, second-best stare decisis has a normative core; it prioritizes values such as impersonality and continuity, and in doing so it implicitly gives less salience to other values. Yet despite its normative foundations, the theory is not aligned with any particular interpretive methodology. It will counsel against overruling some precedents that are disfavored by originalists, but it will do the same with respect to precedents that are disfavored by living constitutionalists. A commitment to stare decisis is not a commitment to originalism, living constitutionalism, or any other theory. It is a commitment to the abiding continuity of constitutional law, even as individual justices come and go.

---

[61] VERMEULE, THE SYSTEM OF THE CONSTITUTION, *supra* note 53, at 144.
[62] Seminole Tribe of Florida v. Florida, 517 U.S. 44, 64 (1996).
[63] *Citizens United*, 558 U.S. at 355.

ALTERNATIVES TO SECOND-BEST STARE DECISIS

Stare decisis is not the only option for a Supreme Court concerned about the role of precedent in a pluralistic system. Scholars have put forth a variety of thoughtful alternatives that warrant consideration.

Begin with the work of Adrian Vermeule. Professor Vermeule's approach to adjudication emphasizes factors such as institutional competence and empirical understandings. Within the realm of constitutional interpretation, Professor Vermeule contends that courts "should adopt an unassuming and unambitious posture" by deferring to interpretations by the political branches unless "no reasonable basis for interpretive dispute exists" because a constitutional provision is clear. Professor Vermeule thus joins company with James Bradley Thayer, who depicted judicial review as a safeguard against legislation that is plainly unconstitutional while preserving ample room for the political branches to operate in situations of constitutional uncertainty.[64] Yet Professor Vermeule's theory is perhaps most notable for its rigorous attention to institutional limitations and empirical realities. He argues, for example, that the agency costs and risks of error associated with judicial review are often understated. He also contends that the decision costs and instability that come with ambitious judicial review are definite, while the benefits of such review are speculative. Arguments such as these lead Professor Vermeule to defend a far more limited judicial role than currently prevails at the Supreme Court.[65]

My aim is not to evaluate Professor Vermeule's arguments with respect to cases of first impression, though that is surely an issue of vast importance. Rather, I am interested in the implications of Professor Vermeule's theory for cases in which there is a controlling precedent on the books. In that scenario a justice faces a choice between two types of deference: deference to Supreme Court precedent and deference to the political branches. There are benefits to both approaches. On the one hand, deferring to judicial precedent promotes continuity and coordinated action. On the other hand, Professor Vermeule raises serious questions about the wisdom of judicial forays beyond the Constitution's text. If the problems associated with aggressive judicial review are hefty enough, there may be an argument for deferring to the political branches even at the cost of overruling precedent.

It is notable, though, that some of the problems Professor Vermeule highlights are alleviated by a strong practice of precedent-following. For example,

---

[64] James B. Thayer, *The Origin and Scope of the American Doctrine of Constitutional Law*, 7 HARV. L. REV. 129, 144 (1893).

[65] *See* VERMEULE, JUDGING UNDER UNCERTAINTY, *supra* note 54, at 230–1.

deferring to precedent can avoid disruption and limit transition costs. And while second-best stare decisis requires the exercise of judgment, the same is true of political deference. Within a system of judicial review, the Supreme Court cannot defer to all political actions. It must scrutinize those actions to determine whether they violate the Constitution. For Professor Vermeule, this inquiry ends with the Constitution's text.[66] But the justices frequently disagree over whether the Constitution's text does, in fact, provide a clear answer to a disputed question. Recent illustrations have arisen in cases involving redistricting procedures, recess appointments, and the right to bear arms, among others. Those disagreements reduce the ability of political deference to unite judges of varying interpretive predilections. By contrast, second-best stare decisis avoids the need to determine whether precedents are inconsistent with the Constitution's text. This does not necessarily mean stare decisis is superior to political deference, as the former entails difficult inquiries into considerations such as the reliance a precedent has engendered. Still, it shows that choosing between the approaches on grounds of administrability is more complicated than it may initially appear.

Keeping with the theme of coordinated action, let us turn to the theory of constitutional implementation advanced by Richard Fallon. Professor Fallon disputes the notion that various types of constitutional arguments constantly compete for theoretical primacy. In his view, considerations such as constitutional text and theory are relevant, but so are judicial precedents and value judgments. What is more, the various considerations commonly reinforce each other. Mindful of this interdependence, Professor Fallon defends an approach of "constructivist coherence" that validates several styles of constitutional argument rather than emphasizing some at the expense of others.[67]

Professor Fallon's theory contemplates a meaningful doctrine of stare decisis. Precedent acts as a source of common ground for judges and justices, and a prior decision's emergence from the deliberative judicial process generally indicates its reasonableness.[68] Second-best stare decisis is fully in accord. Yet it resists the argument that considerations such as value judgments should customarily inform the overruling calculus. To reduce the possibility that debates over stare decisis will rehash underlying disagreements about interpretive methodology, second-best stare decisis limits the role of substantive effects to exceptional cases in which they are (in light of a particular justice's methodological and normative commitments) intolerable. Beyond those exceptional

---

[66] Id. at 230.
[67] See generally Fallon, A Constructivist Coherence Theory of Constitutional Interpretation, supra note 35.
[68] RICHARD H. FALLON, JR., IMPLEMENTING THE CONSTITUTION 103 (2001).

situations, second-best stare decisis preserves the distinction between the durability of precedent and the normative choices that explain a justice's adherence to a given interpretive philosophy.

The role of substantive effects also separates second-best stare decisis from common law constitutionalism of the sort defended by David Strauss. Second-best stare decisis and common law constitutionalism are aligned in their devotion to precedent as a valuable source of common ground. But common law constitutionalism reflects the belief that certain types of substantive effects – for example, considerations of morality – are integral to the evolution of precedent.[69] Second-best stare decisis takes no such position; it seeks to appeal to justices irrespective of their views about the legal relevance of moral judgments. So while common law constitutionalism allows substantive considerations to play a leading role in the decision to overrule, second-best stare decisis avoids those considerations in all but the rarest cases. The hope is that regardless of their views about the relevance of factors such as moral judgments, Supreme Court justices will accept second-best stare decisis in light of the theory's methodological neutrality.

Finally, consider the argument that the best response to interpretive pluralism is scrupulous fidelity to the Constitution's original meaning. In analyzing this type of claim, Professor Vermeule depicts the version of originalism associated with (among others) Justice Scalia as a second-best theory "in which an interpretive approach should be chosen so as to offset some predictable error or skew in judicial decisionmaking"– for example, the tendency to read one's own values into the law.[70] Building from this position, one might conclude that in a world of interpretive disagreement, the original meaning of the Constitution's text is a useful source of common ground that should appeal to judges of various interpretive stripes.

Once again, I make no attempt to assess this claim as it relates to cases of first impression. But where there are relevant precedents on the books, I wish to suggest that stare decisis may have greater utility as a second-best theory than does fidelity to the Constitution's original meaning. The consultation of judicial precedents will often provide a more robust and accessible set of rules than will direct appeal to whichever sources of original meaning one deems most relevant.[71] A justice knows where to look for precedents and what to do

---

[69] David A. Strauss, *Common Law Constitutional Interpretation*, 63 U. CHI. L. REV. 877, 895 (1996).
[70] VERMEULE, JUDGING UNDER UNCERTAINTY, *supra* note 54, at 245.
[71] Thomas W. Merrill, *Originalism, Stare Decisis and the Promotion of Judicial Restraint*, 22 CONST. COMMENT. 271, 279–80 (2005).

when she finds them. The same is not always true with respect to consultation of historical materials, whose availability, import, and relative hierarchy can raise tricky questions. If one believes fidelity to original meanings is generally appropriate based on an underlying commitment to values such as popular sovereignty or consequentialism, that is a good reason to undertake inquiries into original meanings. When the question shifts to whether stare decisis or originalism provides a more effective basis for facilitating coordinated action, the relative ease of access to, and familiarity with, judicial decisions looms large.

These reflections on alternative approaches to interpretive pluralism are preliminary by design. I make no claim to having exhausted the implications of adopting second-best stare decisis as opposed to other potential responses to pluralism. My goal has been to introduce second-best stare decisis as a means of fostering continuity, impersonality, and coordinated action in a world marked by pluralism. To generate these benefits, the doctrine of stare decisis must offer enough independent content to prevent it from becoming an echo chamber for controversial assertions about which theory of constitutional interpretation is best. Furnishing that content is the central enterprise of second-best stare decisis.

7

Precedential Strength in Structural Perspective

The previous chapter developed a set of proposals to make the doctrine of stare decisis more suitable for operation in a second-best world of interpretive disagreement. This chapter briefly considers an alternative approach focused on the structure of Supreme Court decision-making: a requirement of supermajority agreement before a precedent can be overruled.

SUPERMAJORITY STARE DECISIS

Requiring a supermajority vote to overrule precedent is a simple mechanism for responding to the complications created by interpretive pluralism. Rather than revising the doctrine of stare decisis for the second-best world, the supermajority approach permits the consideration of any factor – from procedural workability to factual accuracy to all manner of substantive effects – that an individual Supreme Court justice deems relevant to a precedent's retention. By increasing the number of justices whose votes are needed to jettison a precedent, the supermajority requirement raises the probability that the Court's collective decision to overrule must bridge methodological divides.[1]

In a pluralistic legal environment, it will often be difficult to cobble together a supermajority to overrule unless a precedent is unacceptable from multiple perspectives. Depending on the composition of the Court, building even a five-justice majority may require considerable compromise. As the requisite number of votes rises to six or seven, it becomes decreasingly likely that a majority coalition could overrule a precedent without drawing together adherents of competing methodological schools. Preserving precedents absent

---

[1] I assume for purposes of argument that there is no constitutional prohibition against the Supreme Court's changing its voting rules in order to, say, require a supermajority before overruling a precedent.

supermajoritarian disapproval is a way of reducing the impact of interpretive disagreement (at any given moment) and vacillation (across time).

Supermajority stare decisis resembles an approach laid out by Jacob Gersen and Adrian Vermeule in their examination of the *Chevron* doctrine of administrative law.[2] They emphasize the conceptual problems that arise when "individual decision-makers are charged with internalizing a legal norm of deference that is conceptually ill defined and that cuts against both their individual judgments of what is best and their biases and prejudices."[3] Instead of asking individual judges to defer to administrative agencies, Professors Gersen and Vermeule contend that agency interpretations should be upheld unless a supermajority of the reviewing court believes them to be incorrect. Through this modification of ordinary voting rules, deference becomes "an emergent property of the aggregate vote, rather than of individual decisions."[4] While their focus is administrative law, Professors Gersen and Vermeule briefly extend their claims to the operation of stare decisis, where a supermajority requirement could "avoid[] the inevitable uncertainty involved in lumpy linguistic formulations like 'strong' and 'super-strong' deference accorded to prior judicial decisions."[5]

The structural version of second-best stare decisis adopts a similar rule while emphasizing a different rationale: the need to overcome methodological pluralism. Under the supermajority approach to stare decisis, each justice makes her own decision about the durability of precedent. Though the justices' votes are aggregated, their analyses are personal and distinctive. As with the doctrinal version of second-best stare decisis, the likely effect of a supermajority voting rule is a reduction in the number of overrulings. But that result, while consistent with the justices' descriptions of stare decisis as the rule rather than the exception, is less important than the creation of a framework that increases the conceptual distance between the durability of precedents and the prevalence of various interpretive methodologies.

IMPLEMENTATION

There are two ways the Supreme Court might implement supermajority stare decisis. First, it could adopt the supermajority requirement through its case law and internal practices. Second, it could formally amend its operating rules. Templates exist for both approaches. The "Rule of Four" regarding

---

[2] *See* Chevron U.S.A. Inc. v. Natural Resources Defense Council, Inc., 467 U.S. 837 (1984).
[3] Jacob E. Gersen & Adrian Vermeule, Chevron *as a Voting Rule*, 116 YALE L. J. 676, 685 (2007).
[4] Id.
[5] Id. at 706 n.60.

the votes necessary for certiorari does not appear in the Court's formal rules. Similarly, the *Marks* principle, which governs the binding effect of fractured Supreme Court decisions, arose from the Court's case law.[6] By contrast, the Court's official rules describe the factors that are relevant to certiorari, albeit not in much detail.[7]

Though both options are defensible, the better course for implementing the supermajority voting requirement is a revision to the Court's rules. After the rules were updated, the procedure for overruling would be set forth clearly in an accessible and integrated document. Following the change, there would be little chance that a five-justice majority might depart from the supermajority requirement within the confines of a significant or controversial case.[8] The supermajority requirement would remain in place unless and until the Court formally removed it, reflecting the stability and predictability that stare decisis seeks to provide.

MOVING TOWARD MINIMALISM

In evaluating supermajority stare decisis, it is important to consider its potential impact on the content of judicial opinions. If enough justices were sympathetic to a particular methodological school, the Supreme Court could explain its reasons for overruling disfavored precedents in significant depth notwithstanding the requirement of supermajority agreement. In periods of pluralism, however, there may be no single theory that encompasses the various reasons why different justices voted to overrule. As a result, we would expect the Court's majority opinions to exhibit a minimalist account of stare decisis. That phenomenon is already a possibility under an approach that requires five votes to overrule. Increasing the requisite number to six or seven would make it more likely that opinions of the Court would need to be minimalist in their reasoning.

The minimalist account would allow joint decisions regarding the durability of precedent without the need for intricate theories about what makes a precedent susceptible to overruling. The problems posed by interpretive pluralism would not stand in the way of pronouncements on the fate of precedent. As Cass Sunstein has explained, minimalism responds to interpretive

---

[6] Marks v. United States, 430 U.S. 188, 193 (1977).
[7] *See* Sup. Ct. Rule 10.
[8] *Cf.* Neil Duxbury, The Nature and Authority of Precedent 129 (2008) (noting that "by issuing something akin to a legal press release" that announced a change in its approach to stare decisis in 1966, the UK House of Lords ensured that "any future composition of the House would be making a massive climb-down were it to change the status of its precedents again").

pluralism by shifting the focus to "concrete outcomes" that are acceptable to judges of varying interpretive stripes. Minimalism's endgame is the construction of "[i]ncompletely theorized agreements."[9] Judges may not agree "all the way down,"[10] but they can act collectively based on the beliefs they *do* share. Through the fashioning of incompletely theorized agreements, judges also evince a healthy "reluctance to challenge the basic commitments of one's fellow citizens when it is not necessary to do so."[11]

The introduction of a supermajority requirement for overruling could be expected to amplify the role of incompletely theorized agreements in Supreme Court decision-making. Increasing the number of justices whose votes are required to overrule leads to a corresponding increase in the chances that some justices within the overruling coalition will disagree on matters of interpretive methodology. Rather than declaring an impasse, the justices could take a minimalist approach by joining an opinion that renounces the applicable precedent without furnishing a detailed rationale.

COMPARING THE DOCTRINAL AND STRUCTURAL APPROACHES

Notwithstanding their shared attention to the challenges of interpretive pluralism, the doctrinal and structural versions of second-best stare decisis differ dramatically. The doctrinal approach developed in Chapter 6 draws on the distinction between considerations that can operate independently of interpretive methodology and considerations that cannot. The structural alternative avoids the need for such distinctions by increasing the number of justices whose votes are required to overrule.

The supermajority requirement operates as if the overruling of precedent is essentially a matter of judicial will – of "having the votes." Each justice may take into account whatever factors she wishes and defer to her successors as much or as little as she likes. Deference to the past occurs through the aggregation of multiple justices' behaviors, not necessarily through the choices of justices as individuals.

The doctrinal approach works differently. It asks each justice to subordinate her personal views in order to keep faith with the Court's institutional identity. While the structural approach has the advantage of simplicity, the doctrinal approach is geared toward promoting impersonality at the level of

---

[9] Cass R. Sunstein, One Case at a Time: Judicial Minimalism on the Supreme Court 13–4, 57 (1999).
[10] Stephen W. Hawking, A Brief History of Time 1 (1988).
[11] Sunstein, One Case at a Time, *supra* note 9, at 50–1.

the individual.[12] If justices invoke stare decisis to defend precedents they like but withhold deference from precedents they disapprove – even if they do so under a regime that requires supermajority support for overrulings – stare decisis relinquishes much of its ability to promote the Court's operation as a unified institution rather than an accumulation of individual actors. Given the centrality of impersonality to the nature of stare decisis as the Supreme Court has described it, this sacrifice is problematic. Indeed, in my view the structural solution is inferior to the doctrinal version of second-best stare decisis set forth in Chapter 6 precisely because the former fails to promote impersonality at the level of the individual jurist. Nevertheless, for those who have concerns about the doctrinal approach, the structural variant warrants consideration as an alternative response to interpretive pluralism.[13]

---

[12] For other potential arguments against adopting a supermajority requirement for the overruling of precedent, see MICHAEL J. GERHARDT, THE POWER OF PRECEDENT 105–6 (2008).

[13] It is possible to combine the doctrinal and structural approaches by requiring a supermajority vote while excluding certain factors from the stare decisis calculus. Such an approach would sacrifice the simplicity of the pure structural approach. Still, it could be attractive if one were to conclude that, even after incorporating the doctrinal revisions to stare decisis that I have proposed, the incidence of overruling remained too frequent. Under that scenario, integration of the supermajority requirement would preserve the doctrinal revisions of second-best stare decisis while reducing the likelihood that any particular precedent would be overruled. Given my focus on doctrinal design rather than specific outcomes, I take no position on the desirability of such an approach.

8

Compromise, Common Ground, and Precedential Scope

Chapters 6 and 7 examined the strength of precedential constraint against a backdrop of interpretive disagreement. The strength of precedent informs the choice between deferring to a flawed decision and overruling it.

Overruling only becomes necessary once a precedent is deemed to apply to the facts at hand. Even the most entrenched precedents are effectively nonconstraining if future courts can easily circumvent them. That creates a need for clear and consistent rules to determine when precedents apply to a newly arising dispute and when they do not. Without such rules, precedents lose much of their force regardless of how resistant they are to overruling.

As we saw in Chapter 4, the Supreme Court often characterizes precedents' scope of applicability as arising not only from their results, but also from their articulated rules and supporting rules and reasons. At the same time, the Court continues to reiterate the classic distinction between holdings and dicta. I have contended that this approach to precedential scope is uneven. For example, despite its tendency to defer to rules and reasons in addition to results, the Court occasionally treats supporting rationales as dispensable. It has also suggested that certain types of dicta can, through factors such as their indicia of deliberation, become worthy of deference.

The initial step in improving the rules of precedential scope is to smooth out these inconsistencies. But there must also be another step. The implications of precedential scope depend on underlying theoretical commitments and constitutional understandings. The proliferation of competing interpretive theories reduces the likelihood of widespread agreement about how precedents are defined. The odds are slimmer still when the Court is viewed as an institution continuing over time, such that even the momentary emergence of consensus might give way to a different perspective at some later date.

This chapter proposes a second-best approach to precedential scope designed to enhance the consistency and coherence of stare decisis notwithstanding the reality of interpretive pluralism. Drawing on the Court's existing jurisprudence, I suggest several principles for defining a precedent's impact on future cases. The goal is to promote respect for the Court's status as an enduring institution while rebuffing any suggestion that each and every utterance contained in a judicial opinion warrants deference going forward.

DOCTRINAL RULES AND FRAMEWORKS

The inquiry into scope begins with considering whether a Supreme Court opinion sets a precedent for a *rule* of decision or rather a *specific application* of law to concrete facts. There appears to be general agreement among the justices about the Court's authority to articulate rules infused with binding force. The justices commonly formulate rules that are manifestly designed to guide future decisions in the lower courts and the Supreme Court itself, and those rules receive deference in due course. The rules may be relatively targeted, like a mandate to apply strict scrutiny to content-based restrictions on speech. Or they may take the shape of broader doctrinal frameworks, such as the protocol for determining whether various protections in the Bill of Rights are enforceable against the states. Either way, deference is treated as attaching to the Court's rules of decision.

The explanation for this practice is clear enough. Withholding deference from judicial rules makes it harder to develop and maintain a systematic legal framework. As Larry Alexander puts it, "Every rule, by virtue of being a rule, decides issues that are broader than the particular facts of the cases in which they are announced."[1] Second-best stare decisis recognizes this fact by beginning from the premise that a decision's scope of applicability includes its articulated rule (if there is such a rule) as well as its fact-specific result. The articulated rule may be fairly basic, or it may take the form of a multifactor doctrinal framework. Whether they are simple or elaborate, second-best stare decisis defines the scope of precedent broadly enough to encompass the Supreme Court's rules of decision.

RATIONALES

The implications of second-best stare decisis are more complicated with respect to judicial rationales, by which I mean the reasons offered to support decisions. The Supreme Court has noted that a "well-established rationale upon which the Court based the results of its earlier decisions" generally

---

[1] Larry Alexander, *Constrained by Precedent*, 63 SOUTHERN CAL. L. REV. 1, 25 (1989).

receives deference in future cases.[2] At other times, however, the Court distinguishes between a precedent's rule and its "descriptive" components, with deference attaching to the former but not the latter.[3] A consistent doctrine requires choosing between these two approaches, lest variation in the definition of precedent end up diluting the force of stare decisis.

Treating rationales as authoritative is a way of respecting the statements of prior justices. It also makes case law a source of more robust guidance for litigants, courts, and other stakeholders. These features suggest the importance of interpreting decisional rationales objectively rather than subjectively. It is not the prior justices' private intentions that matter, but rather the words they used to explain themselves within the confines of a publicly released opinion. Those words are what guide stakeholders' understandings of legal rules. Moreover, paying attention to the objective expressions that make up a judicial opinion reflects a recognition that the justices can affect the law only by working through the formal channels that govern the operations of the Court as an institution.

In addition to evincing respect for prior decisions and enhancing the guidance that each opinion provides, construing decisions broadly gives greater power to justices who are establishing precedents in the first instance. That effect may be disconcerting if one interprets Article III as placing strict limits on the ability of judges to establish binding precedents, or if one thinks decisions are more likely to be sound in their logic and accurate in their inferences when they hew closely to the facts at hand. Second-best stare decisis responds by trying to find a solution with wide appeal. It suggests an accommodation that seeks buy-in from justices of diverse methodological predilections. As it relates to the status of decisional rationales, the second-best approach is founded on compromise and shared sacrifice. Rationales need not receive deference irrespective of how widely they range, but neither should they be treated as dispensable. Instead, rationales should receive deference to the extent they illuminate the content of the applicable legal rule. The justification for paying attention to a supporting rationale is not its intrinsic worth. It is the rationale's function in clarifying the articulated rule – a rule that, in light of modern Supreme Court practice, has a well-established claim to respect.

To illustrate, consider the First Amendment implications of "true threats," which the Supreme Court has addressed in cases such as *Virginia v. Black* (2003). *Black* called upon the Court to determine when the burning of a cross

---

[2] Seminole Tribe of Florida v. Florida, 517 U.S. 44, 66–7 (1996).
[3] United States v. Stevens, 559 U.S. 460, 471 (2010).

is protected by the Constitution, and when it falls into the category of unprotected threats. Along the way, the Court explained that unprotected threats "encompass those statements where the speaker means to communicate a serious expression of an intent to commit an act of unlawful violence to a particular individual or group of individuals."[4]

As lower courts attempted to apply *Black*, one area of uncertainty was whether a statement is an unprotected threat only if the speaker intended to put the hearer in fear, or whether it is enough that "a reasonable speaker would foresee the statement would be interpreted as a threat."[5] There is, in other words, ambiguity regarding the content and implications of the rule announced in *Black*. To resolve this uncertainty under second-best stare decisis, a future jurist would look to *Black*'s supporting rationale in attempting to shed light on its rule of decision. For example, *Black* stated that a prohibition against threats "'protect[s] individuals from the fear of violence' and 'from the disruption that fear engenders.'"[6] That statement is an expression of the Supreme Court's reasoning, not part of its rule of decision. Even so, the second-best approach allows consideration of the statement to help identify the applicable rule. The quoted language may be understood as providing some (though certainly not dispositive) support for reading *Black* to mean statements can be subject to restriction and punishment even if the speaker did not intend to instill fear in the hearer, at least if it was quite obvious that such fear would result. Understood in this way, the Court's rationale helps to inform the interpretation of its rule, and the rule and rationale work together to define the precedent's scope of applicability to future disputes.

For an example that is problematic from the standpoint of second-best stare decisis, consider *United States v. Stevens* (2010).[7] In *Stevens*, which I discussed in Chapter 4, the Court invalidated a federal statute dealing with depictions of animal cruelty. In reaching its conclusion, the Court withheld deference from its prior statements that speech is unprotected for First Amendment purposes if it falls into a category of expression whose costs far exceed its benefits – a principle the government argued should apply to the depictions of cruelty prohibited by the statute at issue. The Court rejected the government's argument and drew a firm distinction between rules of decision and descriptions of reasoning. The trouble with this distinction is that the Court's prior invocations

---

[4] 538 U.S. 343, 359.
[5] United States v. Elonis, 730 F.3d 321, 323 (3rd Cir. 2013), *rev'd*, 135 S. Ct. 2001 (2015). The Supreme Court resolved *Elonis* on statutory grounds without elaborating on the constitutional line between protected speech and unprotected threats.
[6] *Black*, 538 U.S. at 360 (quoting R.A.V. v. City of St. Paul, 505 U.S. 377, 388 (1992)).
[7] *Stevens*, 559 U.S. at 460.

of cost–benefit analysis shed considerable light on what appeared to be its rule for identifying exceptions to First Amendment protection. As Chapter 4 explained, prior to *Stevens* there was a powerful argument that one test for whether a category of speech fell beyond the Constitution's purview involved a systematic comparison of its costs and benefits. When it refused to credit the rationale of its prior cases, the *Stevens* Court arguably changed the governing rule as it was best understood in light of the existing case law. This does not necessarily mean *Stevens* was incorrect on its own terms; *Stevens* may be sound from the perspective of one who has interpretive, normative, or structural concerns about infusing decisional rationales with binding force. But under second-best stare decisis, the Court's prior endorsements of cost–benefit analysis warranted presumptive respect. Those endorsements helped to explain the Court's rule of decision in its prior cases, and they were therefore entitled to deference.

Another problematic treatment of decisional rationales occurred in *United States v. Alvarez* (2012), also discussed in Chapter 4. The case dealt with a prohibition against false claims of military commendation. At several points in the decades before *Alvarez*, the Supreme Court had declared that false statements do not possess inherent First Amendment value. Rather, the idea seemed to be that such statements are protected in order to provide breathing room for truthful speech. In *Alvarez*, a plurality withheld deference from the Court's past teachings about the constitutional value of falsity. The plurality distinguished the prior cases as dealing with particular subcategories of false speech such as defamation and fraud, which lead to direct and tangible harms.[8]

Alvarez effectively rejected the logic of the Court's earlier discussions of falsity. The operative rule shifted from one in which false speech is constitutionally unprotected to one in which false speech is protected unless the government has a very good reason for restricting it. The *Alvarez* decision did not simply distinguish the Court's prior cases. It recast their reasoning.

It may be that *Alvarez* actually improved the law of free speech. The same goes for *Stevens*. But regardless of whether those decisions were right or wrong on the merits, second-best stare decisis would have required the Court to recognize in each case that it was considering a departure from precedent. At that point, the Court would have asked whether an overruling was warranted in light of factors such as procedural workability, factual accuracy, and reliance interests.

---

[8] 132 S. Ct. 2537.

The obligation to defer to decisional rationales leaves open the possibility of distinguishing cases that do not apply to the dispute at hand. Distinguishing is a tried and true part of American constitutional jurisprudence, and it remains entirely proper under the theory of second-best stare decisis. Newly arising facts sometimes call for the recognition of distinctions. Those distinctions must occur within a broader system of deference to rules and reasons. Construing precedents broadly leaves less room for distinguishing than would exist if precedents were understood as "small units, full of rarely duplicated particulars."[9] Yet even on the account of precedential scope I have defended, distinguishing remains legitimate and appropriate so long as it leaves prior decisions intact. As Michael Dorf has put it, the later Court's charge is not to adopt a "rigidly literalist interpretation" of an opinion's "statement of reasons." It is to acknowledge meaningful differences without "undermin[ing] the original principle" that the opinion established or applied.[10]

One can imagine any number of situations in which the act of distinguishing leaves the rationales of prior decisions intact. Cases involving the Fourth Amendment allow for distinctions in light of new technologies, such as smart phones, that dramatically alter the nature of interactions between police officers and private citizens. Constitutional rules governing the criminal sentencing of adults allow for adaptation as applied to juvenile offenders. And so on. The point of second-best stare decisis is not to ignore meaningful differences, but to ensure that earlier judges' rules and rationales are preserved. If that is not possible, distinguishing is off the table, and the question becomes whether to reaffirm or overrule.

In a pair of recent articles, Richard Re has sought to carve out something like a middle ground between overruling and distinguishing. He defends the practice of narrowing disfavored precedents by interpreting them as more limited in scope than their best reading might suggest.[11] Professor Re contends that narrowing can be less disruptive than overruling, and that it can avoid (or at least delay) the need for more dramatic clashes with precedent. His analysis is insightful, and he is quite right to note that narrowing need not imply deception or bad faith. Yet I nevertheless remain skeptical of the conclusion that there is a place for narrowing within the Supreme Court's constitutional jurisprudence, at least if narrowing may be grounded in nothing more than disagreement with a precedent on the merits. It is true that narrowing is likely

---

[9] Frederick Schauer, *Precedent*, 39 STAN. L. REV. 571, 602 (1987); *see also* id. at 594–5.
[10] Michael C. Dorf, *Dicta and Article III*, 142 U. PA. L. REV. 1997, 2058–9 (1994); *see also* id. at 2057.
[11] Richard M. Re, *Narrowing Precedent in the Supreme Court*, 114 COLUM. L. REV. 1861, 1863 (2014).

to be less disruptive than overruling. It likewise is true that narrowing can be a milder affront to prior courts than outright repudiation. But the smallest degree of disruption, as well as the greatest respect for precedent, comes from standing by settled law without overruling *or* narrowing it.

If every precedent is understood as a bundle of applications, it arguably should take a greater showing to overrule all of them than to overrule only some of them. To borrow the Supreme Court's terminology, it should take a somewhat less "special" justification to trim a precedent – which is to say, to overrule it in part – than to jettison it altogether. I see nothing wrong with this type of calibration in theory. And as Professor Re suggests, when the Court has reservations about a particular precedent, it might sometimes be sensible to overrule narrowly rather than broadly by preserving as much of the existing rule as is suitable. My point is that even a partial overruling is, at base, a deviation from the Court's institutional past. As such, it requires a justification that goes beyond disagreement on the merits. And for stare decisis to promote continuity and impersonality, the justification should operate independently of doctrinal considerations whose content is bound up with interpretive and normative commitments that vary from judge to judge. The willingness to tolerate a flawed precedent contributes to a steady, overarching rule of law. Sometimes that means resisting the urge to repudiate, or even to narrow, disfavored precedents. For all its costs, this resistance is worthwhile if it allows the Court to operate as a unified institution rather than a fluctuating assemblage of individual voters.

ALTERNATIVE HOLDINGS

Sometimes a single decision contains more than one statement of rule or rationale. Take the example of a police officer who is sued for violating a person's constitutional rights. The Supreme Court might conclude that no constitutional right was violated. It might add that even if there had been a constitutional violation, the right in question was not so clearly established as to overcome the police officer's qualified immunity from liability.[12] Either of those conclusions would be sufficient to sustain the Court's decision. The question is whether *both* conclusions should receive deference going forward.

A legal conclusion that is unnecessary to resolve a case might nevertheless reflect a well-considered articulation of the Court's analysis and approach. Aspirations of impersonality and respect for one's predecessors counsel against treating such conclusions as dispensable simply because they did not affect

---

[12] *Cf.* Pearson v. Callahan, 555 U.S. 223, 236 (2009).

the bottom line of the decisions that contained them. Considerations of stability and predictability support the same result: The Court can lend precision and predictability to the law, and provide guidance for future judges, by continuing to elucidate a legal issue even when it might have elected to stop its analysis at some earlier point. Alternative holdings accordingly are entitled to deference under second-best stare decisis, just as they are as a matter of general federal practice.[13]

ASIDES AND HYPOTHETICALS

Next come judicial observations that do "not explain why the court's judgment goes in favor of the winner."[14] While I noted some important exceptions in Chapter 4, the Supreme Court's tendency is to treat such statements as dispensable dicta.

As was true of the status of decisional rules, the Court's general approach to judicial asides provides a baseline for second-best stare decisis. Some interpretive theories depict unnecessary asides as overstepping judicial authority or creating a heightened risk of erroneous pronouncements. Other theories accept that judicial asides can exert binding force so long as they are clear, well considered, and thoroughly explained. The justifications for the latter position are that asides can furnish guidance, promote uniformity, encourage reliance, and constrain future judges.

To facilitate the consistent definition of precedents' scope of applicability, a choice must be made between the two approaches. Tethering a precedent's zone of impact – in other words, what the precedent *means* – to competing philosophical predilections runs counter to the aspirations of impersonality and continuity that animate second-best stare decisis. Without a consistent definition of scope, a precedent's meaning is unknowable until it is situated within a particular interpretive methodology. Just as second-best stare decisis resists interpretive vacillation as a driver of overrulings, it resists interpretive vacillation as the determinant of what a given decision stands for.

---

[13] *See, e.g.*, Union Pacific Railroad Co. v. Mason City & Fort Dodge Railroad Co., 199 U.S. 160, 166 (1905) ("[W]here there are two grounds, upon either of which the judgment of the trial court can be rested, and the appellate court sustains both, the ruling on neither is *obiter*, but each is the judgment of the court, and of equal validity with the other."); 18 MOORE'S FEDERAL PRACTICE § 134.03 ("When there are alternative holdings, each alternative should be given stare decisis effect."); Richard M. Re, *Should* Chevron *Have Two Steps?*, 89 IND. L. J. 605, 627–8 (2014) (referring to "courts' long-recognized authority to issue holdings in the alternative").

[14] Pierre N. Leval, *Judging Under the Constitution: Dicta About Dicta*, 81 N.Y.U. L. REV. 1249, 1256 (2006).

As a conceptual matter, it is a live debate whether extraneous statements warrant deference. The issue is less controversial as a matter of Supreme Court practice. Notwithstanding occasional exceptions, the Court generally withholds deference from gratuitous or counterfactual statements. The entrenchment of that practice supports its inclusion as a principle of second-best stare decisis. In theory, second-best stare decisis could accommodate an approach that gives deference to extraneous statements just as well as it could accommodate the converse principle. The tiebreaker, so to speak, is the body of existing case law. Absent any reason for disrupting settled practice, second-best stare decisis places a thumb on the scale for the status quo, reflecting a broader pursuit of a stable and continuous legal order. Future courts may certainly choose to treat prior opinions' asides and hypothetical statements as illuminating and persuasive. In terms of constraining effect, however, those statements are beyond a precedent's scope of applicability. Ultimately, the best course is to validate the approach more in line with the Supreme Court's prevailing practice. Asides and hypotheticals do not warrant formal deference beyond their persuasive appeal.

When this treatment of asides and hypotheticals is combined with full deference to decisional rules and qualified deference to statements of rationale, we arrive at an intermediate definition of precedential scope, representing a compromise between theories that would construe precedents narrowly and theories that would construe them broadly. The resulting arrangement may not be ideal from the standpoint of any interpretive theory. But it is a workable solution that promotes the consistent treatment of precedent across cases while respecting existing practices. This spirit of continuity, common ground, and compromise coheres with the ideal of the Supreme Court as a unified institution that maintains its character and identity across generations.

INTERPRETIVE METHODOLOGIES

So far I have addressed the implications of interpretive methodology for the strength of a precedent's constraint and the scope of its applicability. I have not yet discussed whether interpretive methodologies are themselves entitled to deference. On the one hand, a consistent interpretive methodology could create benefits for a legal regime by enhancing stability and predictability. On the other hand, the ability to declare the presumptive decisional protocol for every subsequent constitutional dispute would be an enormous power for any group of Supreme Court justices to exercise.

There is also a practical objection to treating interpretive methodologies as entitled to deference in future cases. Stare decisis does not get off the ground unless it can appeal to justices across the methodological spectrum. Each justice is asked to sacrifice some of her decisional autonomy in order to serve the goals of the Court as an institution. This is a lot to ask, though I have contended that the request is justified by the benefits of continuity and impersonality. Though it is reasonable to urge a justice to subordinate her personal views within the context of particular cases, it is unreasonable (and unrealistic) to request that she adopt, for all intents and purposes, an interpretive methodology that is not her own. The notion that a justice must adhere to an overarching interpretive philosophy merely because it prevailed at the time of her appointment runs contrary to the spirit of compromise and coordination inherent in second-best stare decisis. Asking a justice to interpret all constitutional provisions using a methodology of which she disapproves – be it originalism, living constitutionalism, or otherwise – is asking too much. It requires extraordinary sacrifice without a sufficient return. No justice would make such a pledge, and no justice should.[15]

A related question is whether an interpretive methodology might warrant deference in the context of a particular legal provision. For example, when the Supreme Court interpreted the Second Amendment as protecting certain individual rights to gun ownership, its opinion was largely (though not exclusively) originalist in its reasoning.[16] Does it follow that in future cases the Court must presumptively use an originalist methodology whenever it faces questions about the Second Amendment's contours and applications? I think the answer is no. Second-best stare decisis seeks to transcend interpretive disputes, not entrench the methodological choices of previous courts. To allow a current majority to declare that all future cases involving the Second Amendment (or the First Amendment, or any other constitutional provision) must presumptively be addressed using a particular methodology creates too great an imposition on justices for whom that methodology is problematic.

An individual justice, consulting her own interpretive commitments and beliefs about the virtues of avoiding disruption, might conclude that the best course is to abide by a methodology that she would otherwise reject.[17] Such an analysis is perfectly legitimate, though obviously debatable. If, by contrast, the justice decides that such adherence is not warranted, second-best stare decisis makes no attempt to convince her otherwise. Supreme Court justices are empowered to establish rules, frameworks, and rationales that revolve around

---

[15] For another perspective on the prospect of deferring to interpretive methodologies, see generally Chad M. Oldfather, *Methodological Stare Decisis and Constitutional Interpretation*, in PRECEDENT IN THE UNITED STATES SUPREME COURT (Christopher J. Peters, 2013).
[16] *See* District of Columbia v. Heller, 554 U.S. 570 (2008).
[17] *See* Alexander, *Constrained by Precedent, supra* note 1, at 5–6.

the case at hand. Allowing them to entrench the selection of general interpretive methodologies would disrupt the proper balance between past and present.

WHAT ABOUT CHEVRON?

Notwithstanding my focus on constitutional precedent, it is worth pausing to consider a significant aspect of statutory interpretation that straddles the line between doctrinal framework and interpretive methodology. I am speaking of the *Chevron* doctrine of administrative law, which is named after a 1984 case involving environmental regulation but whose ramifications extend across a range of issues and industries. The *Chevron* doctrine provides that administrative agencies' interpretations of certain types of statutes must be upheld so long as they are reasonable. This is true even if the reviewing court does not believe the agency's interpretation is the best one.[18]

Chevron creates several puzzles for the doctrine of stare decisis. These include whether an agency's discretion to adopt any reasonable interpretation exists even after a court has construed the statute, and whether agencies may alter their own interpretations – for example, following the election of a new president. The puzzle I wish to consider involves the status of the *Chevron* doctrine itself. Does the Supreme Court's practice of deferring to reasonable administrative interpretations warrant presumptive deference via the doctrine of stare decisis? This question has taken on greater import in recent years as Justice Thomas (along with some prominent commentators) has reinvigorated debate about whether the *Chevron* rule is defensible on the merits.[19] He has also raised the possibility that the Court's "agency deference regimes" might not be "entitled to *stare decisis* effect."[20]

As a descriptive matter, the Supreme Court continues to treat the *Chevron* doctrine as settled law. The Court commonly applies the doctrine to new facts and contexts, and it does so without rationalizing the doctrine from the ground up or defending it as a matter of first principles. Less attention has been paid to whether the *Chevron* approach warrants deference in excess of its persuasiveness.

---

[18] Chevron U.S.A. Inc. v. Natural Resources Defense Council, Inc., 467 U.S. 837 (1984).
[19] *See* Michigan v. Environmental Protection Agency, 135 S. Ct. 2699, 2712 (2015) (Thomas, J., concurring); *see also, e.g.,* PHILIP HAMBURGER, IS ADMINISTRATIVE LAW UNLAWFUL? (2014). For a contrasting view, see ADRIAN VERMEULE, LAW'S ABNEGATION (2016).
[20] *See* Perez v. Mortgage Bankers Association, 135 S. Ct. 1199, 1214 n.1 (2015) (Thomas, J., concurring in the judgment).

From the perspective of second-best stare decisis, treating the *Chevron* doctrine as entitled to deference would push the bounds of precedential scope too far. *Chevron* commits substantial discretion to administrative agencies and brings about a corresponding contraction of the interpretive domain of judges. There are arguments for grounding this approach in considerations such as expertise, congressional expectation, and judicial uniformity. But notwithstanding its potential benefits, *Chevron* works like an interpretive methodology that applies across a large chunk of statutory cases. I have argued that it is too much to ask a Supreme Court justice to embrace originalism, or common law constitutionalism, or pragmatism, or any other –*ism* on grounds of stare decisis. While deference to precedent properly encompasses results, rules, and frameworks, it stops short of requiring adherence to broader interpretive philosophies. In much the same way, it would be improper to ask a justice to accept a particular method of resolving countless statutory disputes going forward. A justice might well conclude *Chevron* was correct when it was decided and remains correct today. Or she might conclude, based on her individual interpretive philosophy, that considerations such as the reliance that *Chevron* has commanded justify its retention notwithstanding any shakiness on the merits.[21] Second-best stare decisis objects to none of this. It merely suggests that if the justice concludes otherwise, she ought not feel compelled to continue applying *Chevron* based on an institutional commitment to stare decisis.

Were five or more justices to begin departing from *Chevron*, a remaining issue would be what to do about prior decisions that had been resolved under the *Chevron* regime. The Court has invoked *Chevron* in validating numerous administrative interpretations. Whatever the fate of *Chevron* in the years ahead, those decisions will continue to warrant deference unless they are overruled. The decisions are not methodological frameworks like the *Chevron* doctrine itself. They are concrete applications in specific contexts with tangible results, and the justifications for stare decisis extend to them in full measure.[22] Conceivably, this opens up the possibility that preexisting applications of *Chevron* could receive presumptive deference even as the Court resolves other statutory disputes without invoking the *Chevron* apparatus. That is perfectly fine. In a pluralistic world, differences in interpretive methodology are commonplace.

None of this is to say *Chevron* is wrong (or right). What I have tried to demonstrate are the problems with asking justices to forsake their preferred methodologies not simply within a particular domain of interpretation, but

[21] See Alexander, *Constrained by Precedent*, *supra* note 1, at 5–6.
[22] By contrast, were an administrative agency to deviate from its prior interpretation of a statute, a judicial decision deferring to the agency's prior approach would relinquish its stare decisis effect.

across a huge swath of future cases. Whether the justices would be well served to coalesce around the *Chevron* approach for reasons apart from stare decisis is another matter entirely.

REVISITING THE STRUCTURAL SOLUTION

In examining second-best approaches to precedential strength, I began (in Chapter 6) with a doctrinal proposal before considering (in Chapter 7) a structural one. The structural option provides that no precedent may be jettisoned unless a supermajority of justices votes to overrule it. Given that I have now sketched a doctrinal approach to revising the definition of precedential scope, it is natural to ask whether there ought to be a corresponding structural alternative. The goal would be to leverage supermajority voting requirements in order to insulate determinations of precedential scope from methodological rifts and cycles.

With respect to precedential strength, I suggested that the structural proposal is inferior to the doctrinal proposal for reasons involving the value of impersonality. Similar reasons explain the superiority of a doctrinal approach to precedential scope. Indeed, I think a structural approach to scope would be deeply problematic. The first question would be where to put the presumption. Should precedents be construed narrowly absent a supermajority vote to the contrary, or should they be construed broadly unless a supermajority says otherwise? There is no comparable problem in the context of precedential strength, because the Supreme Court's case law makes clear that the presumption must be in favor of fidelity to precedent.

Beyond that uncertainty, a supermajority approach to scope would imply that a precedent's meaning is a contingent fact. In difficult cases, the question of what a precedent stands for could not be confidently answered until a supermajority had spoken. This conception of precedent stands in tension with the notion of stare decisis as promoting the continuity of law. Declaring that a precedent may be overruled in light of countervailing considerations exacts some toll on stability and impersonality. But the toll is far greater if there is contingency at the very heart of what a precedent *means*. Notwithstanding its potential benefits in the context of precedential strength, the supermajority approach is ill suited to defining a precedent's scope of applicability.

PRECEDENTIAL SCOPE BEYOND THE SUPREME COURT

I noted at the outset that my primary concern would be the operation of precedent at the US Supreme Court. At the same time, I suggested that much of my analysis would have some relevance to the role of precedent in the lower federal courts and the state courts. In concluding my discussion of precedential scope, I wish to make a few points about those latter contexts.

Begin with the lower federal courts. Decisions of a federal court of appeals are binding on district courts within the relevant circuit. They also exert horizontal force on future appellate panels, which are required to follow circuit law. Generally, only an en banc court of appeals may overrule a panel decision, though some circuits have developed procedural alternatives to streamline the process.[23]

These horizontal and vertical implications of circuit precedents are similar to the implications of precedents issued by the Supreme Court. The similarity may suggest that questions of precedential scope should be resolved identically in the two domains. But to assume such equivalence would be premature. There are possible distinctions between circuit court precedents and Supreme Court precedents. For one thing, it is at least conceivable that intermediate appellate courts may tend to make more interpretive errors than the Supreme Court. This is not due to any lesser competence, but rather to the fact that the Supreme Court ordinarily gets to benefit from a circuit court's reasoning in reaching its own decision, while the converse is not true. A reduced risk of error might also result from the Supreme Court's relatively light docket and the substantial attention its cases receive from countless stakeholders who provide diverse perspectives in the form of amicus curiae briefs. Because increased risks of error can dilute the net benefits of precedential constraint, there is a potential argument that circuit court decisions should be construed more narrowly than Supreme Court decisions in both vertical and horizontal operation.

The same conclusion might follow from the Supreme Court's unique position atop the judicial hierarchy. If one adopts a view of the Supreme Court as the federal judiciary's manager, perhaps the Court should possess broad powers to issue binding guidance, even in the form of generalized and wide-ranging statements. That argument does not carry the same resonance with respect to federal circuit courts, which have smaller areas of oversight and more cases through which they can explicate the law.

Despite these differences, the benefits of uniformity, consistency, and stability that can arise from deference to Supreme Court precedent remain salient in the context of circuit precedent. And a system that adopts distinct approaches for defining Supreme Court and circuit precedents might prove troublesome to administer, bolstering the argument for a unified model of precedential scope.

[23] See Chapter 1.

There are related questions about whether Supreme Court precedents should play the same role in the lower courts as they do in the Supreme Court itself. For example, we could imagine a scenario in which the Supreme Court construes its precedents according to the principles of second-best stare decisis, while the lower courts interpret Supreme Court precedents more broadly. The rationale would be that the virtues of uniformity and the need for guidance justify a capacious view of vertical precedent, while the dangers of entrenching mistakes warrant a more restrictive approach when the Supreme Court is reconsidering its own pronouncements. Whether such a dichotomy would make sense depends on a host of factors, including structural understandings about the role of the lower federal courts and their relationship with the Supreme Court.

For now, I leave off with this general map of the conceptual terrain. In constructing a system of precedent, the initial step should be to examine the implications of constraint at each level of the judicial hierarchy. Only upon completing that project can we determine whether the benefits of a uniform approach outweigh the costs of disregarding court-specific considerations.

The similarities between the Supreme Court and the circuit courts do not necessarily extend to the relationship between the federal and state judiciaries. It is well established that state courts are constrained by Supreme Court decisions on federal and constitutional matters. According to the justices, that constraint serves to "preserve the integrity of federal law."[24] But there are obvious differences between state courts and federal courts that may affect the operation of precedent. The first is their constitutional status. As Evan Caminker has explained, "though the Supremacy Clause declares that 'the Judges in every State shall be bound' by federal law, neither that Clause nor any other demands that state courts defer to a particular actor's interpretation of federal law."[25] And even if one thinks state courts have a duty to follow Supreme Court decisions, a question remains as to how those decisions should be defined.

The simplest response – that the scope of precedent should be the same in the state courts as it is in the lower federal courts – carries the advantages of clarity and efficiency.[26] Still, it is debatable whether the calculus should be identical once considerations of federalism enter the picture. In declining to

---

[24] Michigan v. Long, 463 U.S. 1032, 1041 (1983); see also, e.g., James v. City of Boise, 136 S. Ct. 685, 686 (2016) (per curiam).

[25] Evan H. Caminker, Why Must Inferior Courts Obey Superior Court Precedents?, 46 STAN. L. REV. 817, 837 (1994) (footnote omitted) (quoting US CONST. art. VI, cl. 2); see also Nelson Lund, Stare Decisis and Originalism: Judicial Disengagement from the Supreme Court's Errors, 19 GEO. MASON L. REV. 1029, 1039 (2012).

[26] See JAMES E. PFANDER, ONE SUPREME COURT: SUPREMACY, INFERIORITY, AND THE JUDICIAL POWER OF THE UNITED STATES 23 (2009).

review decisions that include an adequate and independent ground in state law, the Supreme Court has emphasized the importance of "[r]espect for the independence of state courts."[27] The sovereignty of the states might justify a greater sphere of discretion for state court judges in their treatment of Supreme Court precedent. That is, even if one views the principles of second-best stare decisis as suitable for the Supreme Court (and perhaps the lower federal courts), one might nevertheless support a narrower scope of Supreme Court precedent within the state courts for reasons of federalism.

My present goal is not to pass judgment upon arguments such as these, but simply to illustrate how federal-state relations may inform the operation of Supreme Court precedents in the state courts. The more general takeaway is familiar by now: The analysis of precedential scope must always be attuned to institutional context.

---

[27] *Long*, 463 U.S. at 1040.

9

Implications and Transitions

The previous three chapters discussed options for revising the treatment of precedential strength and precedential scope in a legal system characterized by interpretive pluralism. I described my overarching approach in terms of second-best stare decisis. Here, I continue to explore the ramifications of second-best stare decisis by discussing its interplay with prominent interpretive methodologies such as living constitutionalism and originalism. I also consider how the American legal system might manage the transition from the existing doctrine of stare decisis to a second-best theory along the lines I have proposed.

STARE DECISIS AND THE LIVING CONSTITUTION

Let us begin with the implications of second-best stare decisis for interpretive methodologies that promote constitutional change via avenues other than formal amendment. Living constitutionalist theories customarily pay substantial attention to the Constitution's text, but they depart from originalist theories by emphasizing the need for constitutional law to keep pace with a changing society.

We have seen that some approaches within the living constitutionalist school leave significant room for stare decisis. A good example is David Strauss's theory of common law constitutionalism. For Professor Strauss, precedent is the centerpiece of constitutional law. Though constitutional text retains an important role, judicial precedent serves as the primary source of guidance and common ground for judges and the citizenry at large.[1]

Richard Fallon likewise devotes considerable attention to precedent in describing a vision of constitutional "implementation" through which the

---

[1] Professor Strauss's theory is discussed in Chapter 3.

Supreme Court identifies the Constitution's meaning and makes choices about how best to put that meaning into practice. The formation of legal doctrine is crucial for implementing the Constitution in a world characterized by reasonable disagreements and the need for coordinated action. Pluralism, Professor Fallon explains, sometimes requires judges to "subordinate their personal views of how the Constitution would ideally be understood and implemented."[2] That subordination creates space for deference to precedent, which can serve as "a reasonable accommodation of competing considerations."[3]

Cass Sunstein likewise defends the process of constitutional evolution while emphasizing the relevance of reasonable disagreement and interpretive pluralism. He generally supports minimalist decision-making through the forging of "incompletely theorized agreements."[4] The basic argument is that judges should affirmatively seek out areas of agreement, and just as affirmatively avoid debates over deeply held theoretical and normative commitments. Professor Sunstein's account provides an interesting counterpoint to the pursuit of overlapping consensus described in the political philosophy of John Rawls.[5] Both scholars place a premium on seeking common ground without unnecessarily challenging others in their deeply held beliefs. But while the Rawlsian version of overlapping consensus pursues common ground on foundational questions, incompletely theorized agreements reflect the view that "people can often agree on particulars, including shallow principles, when they disagree about or are uncertain on abstractions."[6] Hence Professor Sunstein's championing of minimalism, whereby judges avoid "abstract theories" that foster discord and instead seek to build from their agreement on particulars such as the "concrete outcomes" of cases.[7]

Like Professors Strauss and Fallon, Professor Sunstein relies on judicial precedent as a source of common ground. For him, precedent facilitates judicial agreement by providing a backdrop for comparisons, analogies, and extensions while effectively taking some arguments off the table.[8] In this way, pursuit of incompletely theorized agreements goes hand in hand with deference to precedent. Arguments from precedent can be understood as a species of incompletely theorized agreement that allow differently minded judges to work together.

[2] RICHARD H. FALLON, JR., IMPLEMENTING THE CONSTITUTION 11 (2001).
[3] Id. at 103.
[4] For an introduction to Professor Sunstein's theory, see Chapter 7.
[5] See generally JOHN RAWLS, POLITICAL LIBERALISM (1993).
[6] CASS R. SUNSTEIN, ONE CASE AT A TIME: JUDICIAL MINIMALISM ON THE SUPREME COURT 250 (1999).
[7] Id.
[8] See id. at 43.

Each of these versions of living constitutionalism coheres with second-best stare decisis in significant respects. Second-best stare decisis promotes continuity and impersonality, notwithstanding the challenges of pluralism, by striving to bridge diverse interpretive methodologies. Common law constitutionalism, constitutional implementation, and minimalism each share this goal to varying degrees. There is, however, a major difference. As explained in Chapter 6, second-best stare decisis excludes the consideration of a precedent's substantive effects in all but the most exceptional situations. While living constitutionalism may permit the overruling of a precedent based on normative disapproval of its results, second-best stare decisis usually does not. The second-best approach rejects normative judgments about a precedent's substantive effects in the ordinary course, allowing them to enter into the analysis only when a justice perceives them as so extraordinarily problematic as to be intolerable. This approach is not without its costs; it means second-best stare decisis sometimes demands the retention of precedents that a justice views as immoral and unfair. Nevertheless, I have argued that the approach is justified by the need to prevent applications of stare decisis from collapsing into theory-dependent disputes over whether precedents are good or bad as viewed through a particular methodological and normative lens. The result is to make second-best stare decisis more resistant than living constitutionalism to judge-led revision of legal rules.

To illustrate, imagine a Supreme Court justice who believes the Constitution protects a certain liberty that carries great importance in light of modern thinking about morality and justice. For our purposes, identifying the liberty in question is unnecessary, and potentially distracting; the point is that our justice is confident that the Constitution should be interpreted as protecting it to keep pace with contemporary mores. Imagine, too, that our justice is faced with a longstanding precedent that denies the constitutional status of the relevant liberty. Notwithstanding our justice's disapproval of the precedent, second-best stare decisis generally would require its retention absent a finding of procedural unworkability or factual inaccuracy. Without such a justification, the precedent would remain binding despite what our justice deems to be its moral failings. An exception would arise only if the precedent's substantive effects were so extraordinarily problematic as to be intolerable (from the perspective of our justice's individual interpretive philosophy). It is thus conceivable that in instances of, say, abject immorality, a living constitutionalist might have grounds for overruling a precedent irrespective of factors such as workability and factual accuracy. That, however, is the rare exception. In the lion's share of cases, a precedent's harmful results – whether their undesirability flows from problems of morality or otherwise – cannot justify its overruling under the second-best approach. Nor does second-best stare decisis permit the circumvention of this rule through the strategic avoidance of disfavored opinions. By predefining the rules that govern precedents' scope of applicability, second-best stare decisis ensures that flawed decisions have constraining effect.

As this example demonstrates, fidelity to precedent can represent a serious sacrifice from the standpoint of living constitutionalism. That sacrifice is unavoidable if stare decisis is to play its role in the system of constitutional adjudication. For precedent to unify the Supreme Court over time and reduce the importance of individual preferences and interpretive vacillations, the doctrine of stare decisis must transcend methodological boundaries. The results will not be perfect from the perspective of living constitutionalists – or, as I will explain below, from the perspective of originalists, or adherents of any other methodological school. That, in a way, is the point. As a response to interpretive pluralism, second-best stare decisis entails revisions, compromises, and deviations from optimal theories of interpretation. The theory asks individual justices to mediate their methodological and normative commitments to promote the ideal of a continuous and impersonal Court.

Second-best stare decisis also requires an accommodation from living constitutionalism in the definition of precedential scope. The extent of accommodation depends on the version of living constitutionalism under consideration. For example, a common law constitutionalist might be in agreement with second-best stare decisis when it comes to treating decisional rationales as presumptively binding. Those rationales often encompass the accumulated wisdom that common law constitutionalism emphasizes. Likewise, defining the scope of precedent to include rationales is a way of furnishing more common ground for the justices to work with in advancing the project of incremental, case-by-case adjudication.

But other versions of living constitutionalism suggest a different approach to precedential scope. To see how, return to the minimalist theory described by Professor Sunstein. Minimalism generally promotes a relatively narrow conception of precedent in order to facilitate agreement about the narrow particulars of cases.[9] That tendency will sometimes put minimalism at odds with second-best stare decisis, the latter of which defines precedents more broadly in order to reflect the Supreme Court's prevailing practices and to provide greater constraint on future decision-makers. Of course, I have argued that even the minimalist justice is well served to overcome her individual qualms by recognizing that a workable doctrine of stare decisis is grounded

[9] *See* Cass R. Sunstein, *Foreword: Leaving Things Undecided*, 110 HARV. L. REV. 4, 20 (1996).

in compromise. While this is (I submit) a justifiable sacrifice, it is a sacrifice nonetheless, and it ought to be acknowledged as such in thinking through the implications of second-best stare decisis.

STARE DECISIS AND ORIGINAL MEANING

Just as it does with respect to living constitutionalists, second-best stare decisis requests some accommodations from originalists as it pursues a system of precedent that works in a pluralistic world.

In examining the implications of second-best stare decisis for various versions of originalism, it will be useful to draw a threshold distinction between cases in which the Constitution's original meaning is murky and those in which it is clear. That distinction picks up a theme introduced in Chapter 2, which surveyed various arguments for how deference to precedent might be understood as consistent with the Constitution's text, structure, and context. Among the possibilities I raised is that the role of judicial precedent might be informed by the need for constraint as courts grapple with constitutional uncertainties. I also considered arguments that certain principles of stare decisis arise from the text of Article III or from the common law background against which the Constitution was enacted. Moving beyond these threshold questions of legitimacy, my present aim is to analyze what the application of second-best stare decisis would mean for various versions of originalism in practice.

When Original Meanings are Murky. Sometimes the Constitution does not furnish a clear answer to a disputed question. How often such cases arise depends in part on where one sets the bar for constitutional clarity. But even those who set the bar relatively low are likely to encounter cases in which the evidence of original meaning is less than convincing, or in which the Constitution's "majestic generalities" do not obviously cash out as specific outcomes.[10] Second-best stare decisis suggests that in such situations, Supreme Court justices ought to defer to precedent unless there are procedural or factual flaws that justify reconsideration. Where the Constitution's original meaning is too uncertain to steer the Court toward a specific outcome, precedent takes the wheel.

In these areas of constitutional uncertainty, second-best stare decisis acts like a fallback rule to stabilize the law and limit judicial discretion. For certain

---

[10] Arizona State Legislature v. Arizona Independent Redistricting Commission, 135 S. Ct. 2652, 2689 (2015) (Roberts, C. J., dissenting) (quoting West Virginia Board of Education v. Barnette, 319 U.S. 624, 639 (1943)).

versions of originalism, this result should be welcome. Some proponents of originalism emphasize principles of constraint and stability. They contend that the original meaning of the Constitution's text is better than competing methodologies at requiring judges to decide cases based on a predefined, external source of legal rules. Relative to other methodologies of interpretation, the argument goes, originalism is "more compatible with the nature and purpose of a Constitution in a democratic system."[11] When it comes to privileging external determinants of legal meaning over subjective judgments, a Supreme Court justice who resolves a dispute based on her best reading of precedent closely resembles a justice who resolves it based on her best interpretation of the Constitution's original meaning; both justices are constrained by publicly available sources of legal norms.

By reducing the frequency of judge-made changes to the law, deference to precedent also promotes legal continuity. This is another respect in which the argument for second-best stare decisis shares a plank with prominent arguments for originalism. Originalism embraces a vision of constitutional law as resistant to changes other than those which proceed through the amendment process set forth in Article V. Second-best stare decisis reflects a comparable sensibility by endorsing a presumption of fidelity to precedent. The presumption is particularly important when the Constitution's original meaning is uncertain, because it allows precedent to stave off judicial vacillation by serving as the law's stable core.

A fallback rule of stare decisis thus delivers many of the same rule-of-law benefits as scrupulous fidelity to text and history. Different justices occasionally will reach different conclusions regarding the implications of precedent, just as they occasionally will adopt different interpretations of the historical record. Nevertheless, the study of precedents, like the study of original meanings, requires the justices to move beyond their individual intuitions in order to apply predefined, publicly accessible legal rules. The effect is to leverage the disciplining power of precedent within an originalist framework. The choice between constraint by original meaning and constraint by judicial precedents is not a choice at all; it is a matter of "and" rather than "or."

The use of precedent as a fallback is also consistent with theories like consequentialist originalism. The consequentialist approach, as we have seen, combines a focus on maximizing welfare with an assumption that rules adopted by supermajorities are likely to deliver desirable results.[12] Where the

[11] Antonin Scalia, *Originalism: The Lesser Evil*, 57 U. Cin. L. Rev. 849, 862 (1989).
[12] *See* John O. McGinnis & Michael B. Rappaport, Originalism and the Good Constitution 19–21 (2013). I introduced the theory of consequentialist originalism in Chapter 3.

Constitution's original meaning is unclear, deference to precedent is justifiable in consequentialist terms if it tends to produce greater benefits than alternative approaches to the resolution of constitutional disputes. For those who see significant value in judicial constraint and legal stability, there is a good argument that this condition holds true. The consequentialist payoff arises from the enhancement of predictability, continuity, and uniformity that precedent furnishes by supplementing textual ambiguity with durable judicial interpretations. It also reflects the value of cultivating impersonal legal norms that resist alteration as new justices take their seats on the bench. And when a precedent has engendered substantial reliance, the consequentialist argument for preserving it becomes even stronger. Retaining a precedent whose overruling would threaten significant disruption – say, by undermining the lawfulness of paper money or toppling the Social Security system – is a means of controlling transition costs to serve the greater good. Ultimately, then, falling back on precedent can advance the consequentialist project of maximizing welfare without disturbing the baseline assumption that supermajorities tend to make sound choices.

The implications of second-best stare decisis may be more controversial for versions of originalism that are grounded in considerations of popular sovereignty. I introduced popular sovereignty originalism in Chapter 3 by noting its depiction of the written Constitution as the most resonant expression of the will of the people. We might surmise that the popular sovereignty account would have no problem with deferring to precedent in cases of constitutional uncertainty, because in those cases the people's will cannot confidently be discerned. But the analysis needs to go a step further. If the Supreme Court's reaffirmance of precedent ends up invalidating actions by the legislative or executive branches, there may be an affront to popular sovereignty notwithstanding the absence of clear direction from the Constitution's text and original meaning.[13] When they rebuff the political branches without a clear constitutional basis for doing so, courts arguably lack democratic authorization to exercise the power of judicial review. Fidelity to precedent accordingly might be criticized for elevating the judiciary above the people.

The severity of this problem is reduced by the fact that judicial precedent, like enacted constitutional text, is binding only to the extent that today's generation allows it to be. It is true that the judiciary exacts some cost on popular sovereignty when it improperly recognizes constitutional rights whose elimination would require a constitutional amendment. The amendment process is too costly and cumbersome to fully mitigate judicial errors. Still, just as the

[13] See KEITH E. WHITTINGTON, CONSTITUTIONAL INTERPRETATION 54 (1999).

people hold the power to amend the Constitution's text, they hold the power to overturn mistaken judicial interpretations using the very same amendment process.

Perhaps the possibility of a popular override is not enough. Perhaps maximizing respect for popular sovereignty demands either adhering to the Constitution's original meaning or, where the original meaning is uncertain, deferring to the actions of political government. That position leaves no room for abiding by precedent in zones of constitutional uncertainty if the result is to strike down legislative or executive action. But not every constitutional lawyer who privileges popular sovereignty must pursue it unflinchingly and at the expense of all other values. One might conclude instead that respect for popular sovereignty demands only that judges apply the Constitution's original meaning when it is clear. Judicial fidelity to clear constitutional meaning safeguards the people's ability to control their government by allowing them to override any official action – be it political or judicial – via the amendment process. The corollary is that when the Constitution's original meaning is uncertain, judges may legitimately defer to precedent without relinquishing or compromising their devotion to the ultimate sovereignty of the people.

My point in raising this argument is not to suggest that popular sovereignty *requires* deference to precedent in situations of constitutional uncertainty. My claim is simply this: For those who see greater value in fostering doctrinal consistency and systemic stability than in upholding legislative and executive actions when their compatibility with the Constitution's original meaning is unclear, a fallback rule of deference to precedent can stand alongside a defense of originalism that is founded on considerations of popular sovereignty. The prospect of peaceful coexistence reduces the extent to which second-best stare decisis challenges the premises of popular sovereignty originalism.

Finally, precedent may play a significant role within versions of originalism that embrace the practice of *constitutional construction*. Several scholars have pressed the argument that constitutional adjudication is most profitably viewed as consisting of two steps: interpretation and construction. Interpretation revolves around the determination of semantic meanings and linguistic facts. Construction refers to the process of turning those meanings and facts into legal rules.[14] Principles of construction are of special interest when the Constitution's semantic meaning is unclear and a court must draw on something other than constitutional text to resolve the case before it.

---

[14] *See, e.g.*, Lawrence B. Solum, *The Interpretation-Construction Distinction*, 27 CONST. COMMENT. 95, 103–4 (2010).

That "something" can be precedent. When a Supreme Court justice harbors doubts about the Constitution's original meaning, she can defer to prior cases, thereby redirecting the forces of legal change toward other channels. The justifications for this practice are the familiar considerations of continuity and impersonality that I have emphasized throughout the book. To be sure, there are other ways to guide the process of construction. In the face of constitutional uncertainty, the justices might choose to uphold the actions of the political branches. Or they might take the opposite approach by protecting individual liberty absent a clear basis in the Constitution to support the government's action. Or they might build out constitutional doctrine to ensure consistency with the prevailing practices, challenges, and mores of modern society.[15] One need not deny any of these possibilities in order to acknowledge that second-best stare decisis is itself a plausible principle of constitutional construction. Faced with a situation of constitutional uncertainty, a justice who prizes impersonality and continuity might well conclude the best course is to defer to what her predecessors have done. And she might be bolstered in this conclusion by her recognition of the challenges of interpretive pluralism, which obstruct agreement by differently minded justices about the methodological and normative commitments that should drive constitutional interpretation. Given that we can expect different justices to possess different views about which values – deference to political majorities, protection of individual liberty, and so forth – should drive the enterprise of constitutional construction, there is something to be said for a second-best approach that simply emphasizes respect for what has gone before. In its commitment to impersonality, its fostering of coordinated action, and its promotion of a continuous and stable body of law, second-best stare decisis has much to recommend it as a principle of construction in situations of constitutional uncertainty.

When Original Meanings are Clear. Second-best stare decisis becomes more controversial when a justice determines that a precedent departed from the Constitution's original meaning. For the originalist justice, the cost of standing by precedent rises dramatically when the alternative is fidelity to the Constitution's clear meaning as originally understood. It is no longer a matter of deferring to precedent when the inquiry into original meanings leaves multiple options on the table. Now the justice is faced with abiding by a decision she views as incorrect from the standpoint of her interpretive philosophy.

Many proponents of originalism accept that original meanings, even when they are relatively clear, should sometimes yield to judicial precedent. Justice

---

[15] These are (drastic) oversimplifications of proposals advanced by Keith Whittington, Randy Barnett, and Jack Balkin, respectively.

Scalia took this position in noting the importance of reliance and stability.[16] Consequentialist originalists also raise the possibility of standing by an erroneous precedent, as when its overruling would create substantial costs.[17] Likewise, Kurt Lash has argued from the perspective of popular sovereignty originalism that "in a case where the costs of reversal are at their highest and the costs to popular sovereignty of upholding the case are at their lowest, a justice may adhere to stare decisis without completely undermining democratic legitimacy."[18]

The compatibility of originalism with second-best stare decisis is another matter. In some cases there will be no conflict. For example, second-best stare decisis allows for the preservation of precedents whose overruling would be extremely disruptive – a view that is shared by some versions of originalism. Yet important differences remain. As we have seen, even if a precedent conflicts with the Constitution's original meaning, and even if that precedent impairs popular sovereignty by improperly recognizing a constitutional liberty, second-best stare decisis would generally prevent its overruling absent some procedural or factual flaw. Second-best stare decisis also departs from consequentialist originalism by deferring to erroneous precedents even when their overruling would not entail significant disruption. These illustrations reflect the broader point that second-best stare decisis protects certain precedents which would otherwise be rejected on originalist grounds.

The gap between originalism and second-best stare decisis shrinks to some degree due to the latter's exception for precedents whose substantive effects are extraordinary and intolerable. Still, the substantive-effects exception is narrow by design. That means cases will arise in which second-best stare decisis asks the originalist justice to tolerate a precedent she would otherwise renounce. Again, this sacrifice must be acknowledged, though I have argued that it is necessary for stare decisis to work properly in a world of interpretive pluralism.

By embracing second-best stare decisis, originalists would not imply that originalism is somehow flawed or in need of mitigation. Rather, they would mediate their theoretical commitments in order to accommodate the reality of

---

[16] See ANTONIN SCALIA, A MATTER OF INTERPRETATION: FEDERAL COURTS AND THE LAW 139–40 (1998).
[17] MCGINNIS & RAPPAPORT, ORIGINALISM AND THE GOOD CONSTITUTION, supra note 12, at 179.
[18] See Kurt T. Lash, Originalism, Popular Sovereignty, and Reverse Stare Decisis, 93 VA. L. REV. 1437, 1474 (2007); id. at 1479 (stating that "[i]n theory . . . a majoritarian consensus may develop in regard to a matter originally removed from the political process"); but cf. id. at 1476 (cautioning that "it would be inappropriate to expand the reach of prior erroneous [constitutional] precedents to situations that have not received long-term bipartisan acceptance").

interpretive pluralism. One can believe strongly in the appeal of originalism while recognizing that others might plausibly reach a different conclusion; originalism can be both correct and subject to reasonable debate. It is that phenomenon of reasonable disagreement that triggers the need for a second-best approach to stare decisis.

Originalism and Precedential Scope. I have been discussing the ramifications of second-best stare decisis for an originalist justice who is faced with an applicable, but flawed, precedent. The question in that situation is whether to stand by or overrule the precedent – a question of the precedent's strength. As usual, we must round out the analysis by inquiring into the distinct issue of precedential scope.

Given their emphasis on the original meaning of the Constitution, some originalists will harbor doubts about aspects of the second-best approach to scope. To illustrate, return to the example of false speech, whose restriction the Supreme Court formerly permitted on the rationale that falsity has no constitutional value. I argued (in Chapter 8) that second-best stare decisis would treat such a rationale as entitled to presumptive deference in future cases. Assuming that the original meaning of the First Amendment affords protection to false speech, might an originalist object to this conception of precedential scope?

The answer is certainly yes, though only for some originalists. Originalists who emphasize stability, constraint, and impersonality as crucial to the rule of law may be amenable to a broad definition of precedential scope even if it occasionally means tolerating a departure from the Constitution's original meaning. Likewise, consequentialist originalism is compatible with a relatively broad view of scope if the renunciation of a decision's rationale would create extraordinary costs. Yet other originalists undoubtedly would prefer a narrower conception of scope that limits the extent to which judicial pronouncements can displace the Constitution's original meaning as properly understood. If such originalists are nevertheless willing to adopt second-best stare decisis, it must be because they accept the general need for accommodation and compromise in seeking out common ground.

THINKING TRANSITIONALLY: STARE DECISIS FOR STARE DECISIS?

Stare decisis is, at base, a legal doctrine. It is an established set of factors that the justices commonly apply. The Supreme Court sometimes emphasizes different factors from case to case, but the core issues – factual accuracy, procedural workability, reliance interests, jurisprudential coherence, and so on – pop up again and again. When the justices refer to the Court's "precedent about precedent," this seems to be what they mean.[19]

Second-best stare decisis builds from the Court's existing doctrine. At the same time, it recognizes the need for some important revisions. They include the exclusion of familiar considerations such as whether a precedent's overruling would enhance jurisprudential coherence. They also include stringent limitations on the extent to which a precedent's substantive effects can enter the overruling calculus.

Proposing these changes creates a conceptual puzzle: Should the Court give presumptive deference to its precedent about precedent, such that any revisions to the doctrine of stare decisis must be supported by a special justification above and beyond disagreement with the doctrine on the merits? This issue would be of lesser interest if one favored a structural response via the introduction of a supermajority voting requirement, as discussed in Chapter 7. But to the extent we are talking about doctrinal revisions, the question is salient.

In discussing the scope of precedent, I argued that interpretive methodologies like originalism and living constitutionalism are not entitled to deference in future cases. The rules of precedent should be understood in the same way. Stare decisis is a doctrine in the sense that it consists of several oft-recited considerations designed to shed light on a particular issue. But like the rules of constitutional interpretation, the rules of precedent are wide-ranging. They apply to thousands of cases dealing with all manner of fact, law, and procedural posture. They often have only the slimmest connection to particular disputes, operating instead at high levels of generality. The rules of stare decisis are thus best understood as residing outside a precedent's scope of applicability in future disputes. A precedent might stand for the proposition that, for example, states lack the power to impose tax-collection obligations on out-of-state sellers. But the precedent should not be construed as standing for the further proposition that in all future cases – whether they deal with tax obligations, or freedom of speech, or police searches, or anything else – the justices must presumptively apply a specific protocol in assessing whether it is more important for the law to be settled or right.

This reasoning suggests that the Supreme Court need not feel bound to preserve its existing doctrine of stare decisis. Rather, it should adopt an approach to stare decisis that it believes to be desirable in its own right. I have tried to demonstrate that the second-best version of stare decisis is well suited to a

---

[19] See Harris v. Quinn, 134 S. Ct. 2618, 2651 (2014) (Kagan, J., dissenting); Alleyne v. United States, 133 S. Ct. 2151, 2173 (2013) (Alito, J., dissenting).

world of interpretive pluralism. If my arguments are unpersuasive, they ought to be rejected for that reason alone. Conversely, if the second-best approach – or any other version of stare decisis – is to find and retain support at the Court, it should be because it works well. This does not mean existing practice is unimportant. On the contrary, the establishment of a past practice might itself furnish a reason for preserving it according to some judicial philosophies. But that sort of analysis should be undertaken by each justice based on her own judicial philosophy. Notwithstanding the virtues of continuity and impersonality, denying the justices' discretion to make their own methodological choices would strike the wrong balance between individual and institution.

Conclusion

This book began by describing the law of precedent in both theory and practice. From there, it developed a set of suggestions for revising the prevailing approach to precedent at the US Supreme Court. My touchstone has been the role of precedent in promoting continuity and impersonality even as individual justices come and go.

Many aspects of my treatment should, I think, be uncontroversial. For example, I have emphasized that the *strength* of precedent must always be considered in tandem with the *scope* of precedent, because it is the interplay of those two factors that determines the impact of stare decisis. I have also defended the continued relevance of familiar considerations such as factual accuracy and reliance expectations to the overruling calculus.

At other points I have urged departures from current practice. Most significant is my claim that in the ordinary course, Supreme Court justices should set aside their individual perceptions of a precedent's substantive effects in deciding whether to overrule it. In suggesting this change, I have drawn from decades of Supreme Court pronouncements regarding the role of precedent in the constitutional order. My basic point has been that if those pronouncements are sound – which I think they are – there is good reason to revise the current doctrine of stare decisis to better reflect them. I have taken a similar approach to the scope of a precedent's applicability by developing a framework that revolves around compromise and common ground rather than contests between competing interpretive philosophies.

Ultimately, the vision of stare decisis that I have defended is one that prizes continuity. Of course, there are other ways to design a system of constitutional adjudication. Perhaps it would be better to embrace the notion that new presidents will be elected, new justices will be appointed, and constitutional law will ebb and flow in kind. When originalists hold sway, they should feel free not only to adopt originalist interpretations in cases of first impression, but also to rectify mistaken interpretations from prior years. When living constitutionalists hold sway, they should do the same. Both camps occasionally may see fit to stand by precedent. But those choices will reflect their respective interpretive methodologies, not a concession to other philosophies. There will be no attempt by originalists to forgive the deleterious effects of nonoriginalist precedents. Nor will there be any corresponding effort on the part of living constitutionalists in regard to originalist precedents.

Such an approach strikes me as entirely legitimate. It is unremarkable that the president should seek to appoint Supreme Court justices (and other federal judges) who see the world like she does. Nor is there anything untoward about the tendency of justices who adopt competing interpretive philosophies to approach thorny constitutional disputes in different ways. Yet there is a reason why justices across the methodological spectrum have united in describing stare decisis as fundamental to the integrity of constitutional law. For all its complexities, stare decisis can reduce the extent to which people must rethink and revise their behaviors to keep pace with an unsteady legal backdrop. The doctrine furnishes common ground among jurists who are inclined to see the world quite differently. Deference to prior decisions takes the abstract ideal of impersonal judging and transforms it into something concrete. Judges come and go, but the law remains the law. That is the promise of precedent.

Index

Aldisert, Ruggero, 82
Alexander, Larry, 40, 71, 146
Alito, Samuel, 1–2, 25, 172
Alleyne v. United States, 24, 117, 172
In re *American Express Merchants' Litigation*, 82
Arizona State Legislature v. Arizona Independent Redistricting Commission, 165
Arkansas Game & Fish Commission v. United States, 71
Ashcroft v. al-Kidd, 21

Balkin, Jack, 68–9, 169
Barnett, Randy, 54, 169
Barrett, Amy, 27, 52, 99
Baude, William, 55
Blackstone, William, 34, 42
Boggs, Danny, 81–2
Boys Markets, Inc. v. Retail Clerks Union, Local 770, 25
Brandeis, Louis, 9, 23–4, 33, 60
Breyer, Stephen, 25, 36, 40, 75–6, 88–9, 109, 117, 124
Brown v. Board of Education of Topeka, 2, 62, 102, 111
Bruhl, Aaron-Andrew, 20
Burke, Edmund, 38
Burnet v. Coronado Oil & Gas Co., 9, 23–4
Bush, George W., 1
Butterworth v. United States, 74–5

Calabresi, Steven, 32
Caminker, Evan, 20, 159
Cardozo, Benjamin, 37

Carey v. Musladin, 74
Central Virginia Community College v. Katz, 71
certiorari, 142
Chevron U.S.A. Inc. v. Natural Resources Defense Council, Inc., 76, 141, 152, 155–6, 159
Citizens United v. FEC, 5, 23–4, 36, 51, 60, 95, 102, 104, 114–9, 125, 135
Cohens v. Virginia, 35, 71
Colby, Thomas, 53
common law, 25–8, 34, 55–6
common law constitutionalism, 63–4, 67–8, 83–5, 100, 110, 120–2, 138, 156, 161–4
consequentialist originalism, 65–6, 86–90, 166, 170–1
Constitution, US
  Article III, 54–5, 58–9, 90–1, 147, 150, 165
  Article V, 125, 166
  First Amendment, 3, 5, 56, 72, 86, 95, 112, 115, 147–9, 154, 171
  Second Amendment, 76, 95, 154
  Fourth Amendment, 150
  Fourteenth Amendment, 75–8
construction, constitutional, 68–9, 168–9
County of Allegheny v. ACLU, 80
courts of appeals, 20, 37, 158

Devins, Neil, 82
Dickerson v. United States, 22–3, 27, 35, 51, 80, 109, 117, 124
dicta, 10, 16, 22, 70–94, 145–53
Direct Marketing Association v. Brohl, 113
DIRECTV, Inc. v. Imburgia, 19

distinguishing, 21, 44, 73, 149–51
district courts, 21, 23, 158
District of Columbia v. Heller, 76, 95, 154
Dorf, Michael, 42, 90, 150
Driver, Justin, 68
Duxbury, Neil, 33–4, 43–4, 50, 71, 142
Dworkin, Ronald, 22, 51

Easterbrook, Frank, 27, 79, 80
en banc review, 21, 158
Epstein, Lee, 26
Eskridge, William, 25–7, 37

Faheem-El v. Klincar, 79–80
Fallon, Richard, 30, 44–7, 54–5, 102, 121, 129, 137, 161–2
Farber, Daniel, 90, 105
FCC v. Fox Television Stations, Inc. (2009), 111–2
FCC v. Fox Television Stations, Inc. (2012), 112
FCC v. Pacifica Foundation, 111–3
federalism, 135, 159–60
Fisch, Jill, 120
Florida Department of Health and Rehabilitative Services v. Florida Nursing Home Association, 125
Friedman, Barry, 109

Garner, Bryan, 47, 87
General Motors Corp. v. Tracy, 88
The Genesee Chief v. Fitzhugh, 28
Gerhardt, Michael, 54–5, 114, 132, 144
Gersen, Jacob, 141
Ginsburg, Ruth Bader, 31, 112, 124
Gonzales v. United States, 31, 71
Griffin, Stephen, 96
Grutter v. Bollinger, 76, 82

Hamburger, Philip, 34, 155
Hamilton, Alexander, 34, 42, 58–9, 108
Harris v. Quinn, 24, 116–9, 172
Harris v. United States, 117
Harrison, John, 46, 55
Hart, Henry, 37
Hawking, Stephen, 143
Hellman, Deborah, 39, 57
Hilton v. South Carolina Public Railways Commission, 117

Hohn v. United States, 127
holdings, 10, 22, 70–94, 102–3, 145–53
horizontal precedent, 7, 20–1, 41
House of Lords, 33, 142
Hubbard v. United States, 47
Humphrey's Executor v. United States, 72

James v. City of Boise, 159
John R. Sand & Gravel Co. v. United States, 23, 124
Johnson v. Transportation Agency, 25–6
Johnson v. United States, 109

Kagan, Elena, 2, 24, 97, 116, 119, 172
Kaplow, Louis, 49
Kappos v. Hyatt, 74–6
Kasten v. Saint-Gobain Performance Plastics Corp., 30
Kennedy, Anthony, 33, 80, 113
Kimble v. Marvel Entertainment, LLC, 24–8, 50
Kirtsaeng v. John Wiley & Sons, 71, 89
Klein, David, 82

Landes, William, 26
Larsen, Allison, 111
Lash, Kurt, 66–7, 92–3, 170
Lawrence v. Texas, 4, 22, 36, 51, 93, 101, 115, 124
Lawson, Gary, 54, 62
Lee, Thomas, 26, 109
Leegin Creative Leather Products, Inc. v. PSKS, Inc., 26, 47, 109
Leval, Pierre, 80, 82, 152
Liptak, Adam, 26
liquidation, 108
living constitutionalism, 15–7, 50, 63–4, 68, 88, 107, 130, 134–5, 154, 161–4, 172
living originalism, 68–9
Local 28, Sheet Metal Workers' International Association v. EEOC, 80
Lochner v. New York, 111
Lund, Nelson, 159

Madison, James, 34, 108
Maltz, Earl, 106
Marks v. United States, 142
Marshall, John, 35, 71

Index

Marshall, Lawrence, 26
Marshall, Thurgood, 4, 27, 35, 124–6
McCutcheon v. FEC, 126
McDonald v. City of Chicago, 36, 77–8, 87
McGinnis, John, 55–6, 65, 86–7, 122, 166, 170
Merrill, Thomas, 45, 138
Michigan v. Bay Mills Indian Community, 40, 104, 116
Michigan v. Environmental Protection Agency, 155
Michigan v. Long, 159–60
Miranda v. Arizona, 3, 22, 27, 35, 51, 79–80, 93, 109, 117–8
Mitchell v. Helms, 124
Monaghan, Henry, 4, 6, 46, 116, 121
Montejo v. Louisiana, 48, 109, 119, 124
Moragne v. States Marine Lines, Inc., 41, 104

National Bellas Hess v. Department of Revenue, 12, 112–3
National Federation of Independent Business v. Sebelius, 31
National Labor Relations Board v. Noel Canning, 95
Nelson, Caleb, 51, 55, 108, 119
Norden, Lawrence, 5

Obama, Barack, 3
Obergefell v. Hodges, 95–6
O'Connor, Sandra Day, 1, 80
Ogden v. Saunders, 35
Oldfather, Chad, 154
Oliphant, Herman, 80
originalism, 17, 47, 62–9, 85–90, 94–5, 107, 119–22, 134, 138, 165–73

Parents Involved in Community Schools v. Seattle School District No. 1, 75–6, 89
Patterson v. McLean Credit Union, 126
Paulsen, Michael, 39, 49–50, 54, 62, 109
Payne v. Tennessee, 4, 24, 27–8, 35, 48–9, 104, 119, 124–6
Pearson v. Callahan, 126, 151
Pepper v. United States, 40
Perez v. Mortgage Bankers Association, 155
persuasive authority, 30–1
Peugh v. United States, 76

Pfander, James, 159
Planned Parenthood of Southeastern Pennsylvania v. Casey, 24, 27, 32, 35–6, 47, 49, 51, 56, 73, 78–9, 93, 104, 108–9, 111, 114–9, 124–5
Plessy v. Ferguson, 11, 93, 111
pluralism, 16–7, 97–106, 142–4, 161–73
popular sovereignty, 61, 66–9, 86, 92–4, 102, 122–3, 139, 167–70
positivism, 45
Postema, Gerald, 34
Powell, Lewis, 5
pragmatism, 1, 87–90, 119–20, 156

Quill Corp. v. North Dakota, 48, 93, 112–3, 116

Randall v. Sorrell, 36, 117
Rappaport, Michael, 55–6, 65, 86–7, 122, 166, 170
ratio decidendi, 71
Rawls, John, 46, 162
Re, Richard, 150–2
Red Lion Broadcasting Co. v. FCC, 112
Rehnquist, William, 1, 76
reliance, 3, 13, 29, 47–9, 88–9, 103–4, 112–3, 116–21, 124–9, 137, 149, 152, 156, 167, 170–1, 175
Roberts, John, 1–3, 23, 25, 58–60, 74, 97, 102, 104, 125, 165
Roe v. Wade, 2–3, 27, 35, 51, 73, 78–9, 93, 108–9, 111, 117, 125
rule of law, 5–6, 12, 15–6, 34, 41–2, 49, 52–3, 87–8, 90, 104–6, 130–1, 151, 171

Sachs, Stephen, 55
Sacks, Albert, 37
Scalia, Antonin, 4, 24–6, 30–1, 47, 71, 76–8, 87–8, 94–5, 109, 116, 124, 127, 138, 166, 170
Schauer, Frederick, 21, 27, 40, 44, 82, 99, 130, 133, 150
Seminole Tribe of Florida v. Florida, 81, 135, 147
separation of powers, 91
Shapiro, David, 46
Slaughter-House Cases, 77–8
Solum, Lawrence, 62, 90, 133, 168
Sotomayor, Sonia, 2, 24
South Carolina v. Gathers, 124

South Carolina v. North Carolina, 74
Specter, Arlen, 2
state courts, 158–60
State Farm Mutual Automobile Insurance Co. v. Campbell, 76
State Oil Co. v. Khan, 20
statutory precedent, 25–7, 126
Stevens, John Paul, 74, 125
Stone, Geoffrey, 41–2
Stop the Beach Renourishment, Inc. v. Florida Department of Environmental Protection, 29
Strauss, David, 38, 45, 56–7, 63, 67–8, 83–5, 129, 138, 161–2
Sunstein, Cass, 129, 142–3, 162–4
supermajority voting, 15–6, 141–2, 157, 172
Swann v. Charlotte-Mecklenburg Board of Education, 75–6
Swift & Co. v. Wickham, 109

Thayer, James, 136
Thomas, Clarence, 77, 111–2, 155

Union Pacific Railroad Co. v. Mason City & Fort Dodge Railroad Co., 152
United States v. Alvarez, 22, 72–3, 81, 149
United States v. Collins, 21
United States v. Elonis, 148
United States v. Lopez, 33
United States v. Stevens, 72–3, 81, 147–9

Vasquez v. Hillery, 27, 41, 104
Vermeule, Adrian, 41, 59, 98, 130–8, 141, 155
vertical precedent, 7–8, 19, 23, 37, 158–9
Virginia v. Black, 147–8

Waldron, Jeremy, 41–2, 52–3
Walton v. Arizona, 116
Wellness International Network, Ltd. v. Sharif, 59
West Coast Hotel Co. v. Parrish, 111
Whittington, Keith, 167–9
Wilkinson, J. Harvie, 97
workability, 3, 13, 103, 109–11, 115, 128–9, 140, 149, 163, 171